Thinking Linguistically

Thinking Linguistically

A Scientific Approach to Language

Maya Honda and Wayne O'Neil

Blackwell
Publishing

BLACKWELL PUBLISHING
350 Main Street, Malden, MA 02148-5020, USA
9600 Garsington Road, Oxford OX4 2DQ, UK
550 Swanston Street, Carlton, Victoria 3053, Australia

First published 2008 by Blackwell Publishing Ltd

1   2008

Library of Congress Cataloging-in-Publication Data

Honda, Maya.
    Thinking linguistically : a scientific approach to language / Maya Honda and Wayne O'Neil.
        p. cm.
    Includes bibliographical references and index.
    ISBN 978-1-4051-0831-7 (hardcover : alk. paper) — ISBN 978-1-4051-0832-4 (pbk. : alk. paper) 1. Linguistic analysis (Linguistics) I. O'Neil, Wayne A. II. Title.

    P126.H65 2008
    410—dc22

                                                                    2007022831

A catalogue record for this title is available from the British Library.

Set in 10/12.5pt Palatino
by Graphicraft Limited, Hong Kong
Printed and bound in Singapore
by Markono Print Media Pte Ltd

The publisher's policy is to use permanent paper from mills that operate a sustainable forestry policy, and which has been manufactured from pulp processed using acid-free and elementary chlorine-free practices. Furthermore, the publisher ensures that the text paper and cover board used have met acceptable environmental accreditation standards.

For further information on
Blackwell Publishing, visit our website at
www.blackwellpublishing.com

Contents

Preface

This is a work in progress. It has been in-progress, without our initially realizing that, for the last 20 years or so. The chapters and problem sets contained here are the product of our long collaboration, which began in the mid-1980s with the Nature of Science/Scientific Theory and Method Project at Harvard University's Educational Technology Center (ETC); it was there that we developed and first piloted several of the problem sets in this book. In the course of our work, we have come to believe that the study of mental grammar can help develop in students of all ages and of all languages an understanding of the nature of scientific inquiry, as well as an appreciation of the complexity and diversity of human languages. This book, a problem-set approach to doing linguistics and exploring language acquisition, is based in that belief, as well as in the knowledge that students enjoy the challenge of doing linguistics in this way, and take great pleasure in it.

In 1991, we began growing our early work into the substance of a course, Nature of Linguistic Knowledge, that we co-teach at Wheelock College in Boston, Massachusetts. Over the past decade and a half, as we have developed this book, we have benefited greatly from our work with Wheelock students, as well as with teachers and students in Australia, Brazil, China, Iceland, Japan, and Nicaragua, and with Native people at the American Indian Language Development Institute, a University of Arizona/Tucson summer program for Native educators, where we taught in June 2000, 2001, and 2002.

In its earliest form, our work was designed for an ETC secondary-school project (see Honda, 1994). In the ensuing years, the audience changed, overwhelmingly becoming teachers and future teachers. Then David Pippin, a Seattle schoolteacher, contacted us in 1999, and enabled us to bring the work back, in part, to its origins, with some of the problem sets, in a different format, becoming the basis for our continually developing work with him and with his students. Needless to say, our book has been enriched through this collaboration.

A book so long in gestation incurs a large number of intellectual debts, these requiring the naming of names. And insofar as we can recall their names, the following students, colleagues, and others have, knowingly or unknowingly, wittingly or unwittingly, contributed to the development and revision of our work. We leave it to them to decide which category they fall into: Virginia Beavert, Diane Bemis, Sylvain Bromberger, Ronald Brooks, Jane Rita Caetano da Silveiras, Jorge Campos, Susan Carey, Carol Chomsky, Noam Chomsky, Kristin Denham, Risa Evans, Nigel Fabb, Mary Greaves, Galio Gurdián, Ken Hale, Morris Halle, Daniel Harbour, Masami Honda, Höskuldur Þráinsson, Ana Ibaños, Dora Joiner, Albert Kitzhaber, Annabel Kitzhaber, Mr. Kobayashi, Richard Larson, Mary Laughren, Lucia Lobato, Anne Lobeck, Hope Lynn, Guillermo McLean, Jonathan Nissenbaum, Yukio Otsu, Steven Pinker, David Pippin, Danilo Salamanca, Filomena Sandolo, Judah Schwartz, Erwin Sice, Matthew Smith, Sandra Smith, Simonè N. Soultanian, Luciana Storto, Shirley Taylor, Al Weinstein, Walt Wolfram, Akira Yamamoto, Ofelia Zepeda, and three, maybe four, anonymous reviewers of all or part of earlier versions of the manuscript. We ask those whose names we have forgotten to list here to forgive our dual memory lapses.

We also want to thank all the Blackwell editors, past and present, who prodded us to make this book a reality. We particularly want to thank Anna Oxbury, our copyeditor, for her thoughtful attention and good humor throughout the production process.

For the students, instructors, and others who will read this book and use it, we suggest that this be done in the spirit that lay behind its creation: that the text and the problem sets be carefully worked through and that the working through be, as much as possible, a collective endeavor – as good science generally is. Students and instructors challenging one another while working together toward understanding a theoretical issue or a solution to a problem set are more likely to reach a better understanding of an issue and a more carefully articulated problem-set solution than a person working alone.

Finally, since we do really still think of this text as a work in progress, we would appreciate receiving comments on the material and our approach to it from any of the people named above as well as from anyone else who uses this book.

Maya Honda and Wayne O'Neil

Typographical Conventions

To help you use this book, we offer the following guide to the typographical conventions that we have adopted:

- *Italics* are used when citing a word in its spelled form; for example:

   Libro is a Spanish word.

- Single quotes are used to express the meaning of a word, phrase, or sentence and for the names of specific concepts; for example:

   Libro means 'book'.

   The concepts 'singular' and 'plural' are expressed in different ways in human languages.

- Slash marks are used to enclose phonemic or abstract representations of the sounds of a language; for example:

   While the plural ending of *cats* is /s/, of *dogs* is /z/, and of *buses* is /ɪz/, we assume there is one underlying form of the plural morpheme in English, /s/.

- Square brackets are used to enclose linguistic features and their values; for example:

   The Spanish word *canción* begins with /k/, which is [−voice], a phonological feature.

   A semantic feature distinguishes the nouns *bird* and *boy*: while both are [+animate], *bird* is [−human] and *boy* is [+human].

- Curly brackets are used to enclose names of morphemes; for example:

   In English, the plural morpheme for nouns is {plural}, its underlying form being phonologically /s/.

- An asterisk marks a word, phrase, or sentence that is not well-formed according to the rules of the language in question; for example:

  Who did Emma give the book?

  Mi prima está española.
  'My cousin is Spanish.'

- **Bold** type is used when introducing a technical term for the first time, or when it is reintroduced; for example:

  Our knowledge of the structure of language, quite generally referred to as **mental grammar**, appears to consist of four components, or **modules**.

- Double quotes are used for quoted material, but also for novel uses of words; an example of the latter:

  The morpheme {plural} has to find a "home" in a noun phrase.

- <u>Underlining</u> is used for emphasis; for example:

  Formulate a hypothesis that explains <u>all</u> of the data.

An Introduction to Thinking Linguistically

> Serious inquiry begins when we are willing to be surprised by simple phenomena of nature, such as the fact that an apple falls from a tree, or a phrase means what it does.
>
> Chomsky, 1993, p. 25

Language is a very rich and complex human endowment. Thus, the study of language can be approached from many different directions, all of them valid. Historical linguists seek to explain how and why languages change through time, while sociolinguists explore the role of language in society and the relationship between language and culture. Other linguists examine the literary forms and uses of language. There are no sharp boundaries between these and other ways of looking at language. However, they do have this in common: They all depend on the work of linguists who examine the <u>structure</u> of language.

In the chapters and problem sets that follow, we will investigate our knowledge of the structure of language, the surprises of which are many. Without being conscious of it, we know what phrases mean in the language or languages that we know, and also – among many other things – how plural nouns are formed and how to ask and answer questions. For example, as speakers of English, we know that the following question is ambiguous; that is, it has two meanings:

(1) *Who do you want to visit?*

Neither the words themselves nor the pronunciation of the question reveal this ambiguity: that *who* can be either the visitor or the visited, but not both. Yet we know the question is ambiguous. This is curious. How do we know this? In fact, how did we come to know this?

Linguistics is in part the attempt to make knowledge of language conscious and to <u>explain</u> the simple phenomena of language, their structure and acquisition. By thinking linguistically, we will examine the nature of this knowledge and on what basis it is acquired.

Knowledge of Language: Mental Grammar

In examining the structure of language, linguists focus their attention on what is quite generally referred to as **mental grammar**, that is, knowledge of language that a person has when we say that she or he knows a particular language.

'Grammar' and its meanings

Before we begin our investigation of mental grammar, we need to clarify our use of the word *grammar* in order to acknowledge that there is an important distinction to be made among different senses of the word. **Grammar**, with the meaning 'mental grammar' that we assume in this book, is a technical term in linguistics that refers both to what is in the mind/brain of a person who knows a language <u>and</u> to the linguist's theory about what is in the mind/brain.

In another of its senses, the word *grammar* is used to refer to **prescriptive grammar**: rules about how to use language that are taught in school in an attempt to make students conform to the norms imposed by the dominant society. Prescriptive grammarians are judgmental and attempt to <u>change</u> linguistic behavior of a particular sort and in a particular direction. Linguists – or mental grammarians, on the other hand, seek to <u>explain</u> the knowledge of language that guides people's everyday use of language irrespective of their schooling.

To clarify this distinction, return to (1), the ambiguous question, which is repeated below:

(1)   *Who do you want to visit?*

Prescriptive grammarians would find fault with this sentence on at least two counts:

- the use of *who* rather than the prescribed *whom*;
- the use of an ambiguous sentence at all.

Furthermore, they would not be at all amused by our demonstrating that the ambiguity of (1) disappears when we contract *want to* to *wanna*, as in (2):

(2)   *Who do you wanna visit?*

Instead, prescriptive grammarians would try to modify the behavior of people (most often, children and students) who utter such questions, directing them away from the use of *who* and *wanna* in everyday speech (and certainly in writing) and bringing them into conformity with dominant conventions of language use.

In contrast, linguists would want to figure out what the questions in (1) and (2) tell us about an English speaker's knowledge of language. For example, they would want to know:

- How does *who* fit into the system of question words?
- What allows the question in (1) to be ambiguous?
- Why does the ambiguity disappear when *want to* is contracted to *wanna*?
- When and how does an English speaker acquire this knowledge?

And on the basis of what they discover, linguists would begin to construct a description and an explanation of the speaker's mental grammar and its development. About *whom*, historical linguists would want to understand what led to its virtual disappearance from spoken English, while sociolinguists would want to investigate the socioeconomic class structure that distinguishes users of *whom* from users of *who*. A similar sociolinguistic investigation could be made of *wanna*.

In contrast, nearly all of what one hears about language in the media and in ordinary conversation deals with either prescriptive grammar or the propriety of language use: Is a particular word or expression offensive or not? Is "proper" grammar being followed or ignored? A word or expression can, of course, be taken as offensive because it violates some prescriptive norm or because it crosses a social boundary sensitive to class, race, or gender, for instance. It is often difficult to disentangle one kind of offense from another. Moreover, it is also possible to offend by obeying prescriptive grammarians – if, for example, having been schooled away from it, you return to a world in which *whom* is never used.

Too literal attention to the rules of prescriptive grammar can also result in what we will refer to as subjective misunderstanding. For example, consider double negatives in English. Say that a person says to someone, "He don't want none," which clearly means 'he really doesn't want any'. The listener might allow the use of a double negative to subjectively, even willfully, impede communication, by rejecting the speaker's grammar and claiming not to understand even though she or he gets the intended meaning.

Compare this to not knowing the words and structures of a language that someone is speaking, or to being misled by *faux amis* 'false friends', as when an English speaker mistakenly assumes that the French word *enfant* means 'infant' rather than 'child'. These are examples where communication is objectively impeded; the lack of understanding is real.

Modules of mental grammar

Let us return now to knowledge of language – mental grammar, the topic that we will begin telling a connected story about in what follows.

For all languages, signed and spoken, mental grammar consists of four components or **modules** in combination with a **lexicon**, or mental dictionary – the words of a language, roughly speaking:

- **phonology**: the structure of the sounds of spoken language (spoken languages being the focus of this book), or the structure of handshapes in signed language;
- **morphology**: the structure of the words and forms of language;
- **syntax**: the structure of the phrases and sentences of language;
- **semantics**: the structural contribution to the meaning of the phrases and sentences of language.

Thus, knowledge of language is modular, having these discrete components. As we will see, there is a good deal of interaction between and among the modules of grammar. Interaction between morphology and phonology, for example, is nicely illustrated by the formation of plural nouns in Armenian, to which we now turn our attention – as a way of beginning to do linguistic inquiry.

Problem Set 1: Plural Noun Formation in Armenian

From *Ethnologue: Languages of the World* (2005), we learn that Armenian is an Indo-European language spoken by people of all ages in Armenia and also by Armenians in 29 other countries, including Azerbaijan, Bulgaria, Canada, Cyprus, Egypt, Estonia, France, Georgia, Greece, Honduras, Hungary, India, Iran, Iraq, Israel, Jordan, Kazakhstan, Kyrgyzstan, Lebanon, Palestinian West Bank and Gaza, Romania, Russia, Syria, Tajikistan, Turkey, Turkmenistan, Ukraine, the United States, and Uzbekistan. Speakers refer to the language as Haieren.

The estimated number of native speakers of this language is 3,399,903 in Armenia (according to Johnstone and Mandryk, 2001 in *Ethnologue: Languages of the World*, 2005), while the estimated number of speakers in all countries totals 6,723,840.

Investigating Armenian Noun Pluralization

The data that follow illustrate singular nouns and their plural forms in Armenian.[1] The words are transliterated from Armenian orthography; that is, each letter of the Armenian alphabet is given its corresponding representation in the Latin alphabet.

For all of the data in this problem set, note that the following linguistic conventions are used:

- a period (.) marks syllable boundaries, breaking the word up into its syllables;

---

[1]   This problem set is based on one developed by Simonè N. Soultanian in fall 2001 for a linguistics class at Wheelock College. Note that the nouns are given in their nominative/accusative singular and plural forms, i.e., the subject and object forms. Soultanian's data have been augmented by and verified from Gulian (1977) and Vaux (2003).

- a hyphen (-) marks the boundary of a **suffix**, or ending – which may not necessarily coincide with a syllable boundary.

	singular		plural	
(1)	ga.dou	'cat'	ga.dou.-ner	'cats'
(2)	tas	'lesson'	ta.s-er	'lessons'
(3)	kirk	'book'	kir.k-er	'books'
(4)	shov.ga	'market'	shov.ga.-ner	'markets'

A   From the data in (1–4), we see that a plural is formed by adding a plural suffix (-ner or -er) to the singular form of the noun. On the basis of these data, formulate and state a **hypothesis**, or possible explanation, about the different conditions under which the plural suffixes -ner and -er are used to form plural nouns. Then discuss specific examples (from 1–4) that convincingly demonstrate how your hypothesis explains the data.

B   It is always necessary to test a hypothesis to see how well it explains a phenomenon and to see what predictions it makes. One way of testing a hypothesis is by searching for counterexamples. **Counterexamples** are data that disconfirm or falsify a hypothesis. But in order to recognize a counterexample when you come across one, it is useful to have figured out beforehand what kinds of data would disconfirm your hypothesis.

So, given the hypothesis that you formulated in A, identify and state the forms an Armenian plural noun would have to take in order to be a counterexample to your hypothesis. That is, what characteristics would the data have to have or what conditions would the data have to meet in order to be a counterexample?

Before you move on to C, be sure to think through and construct reasoned answers to A and B.

C   Now consider the following data. Note that by linguistic convention, a form that fluent speakers would judge to be ill-formed is marked with an asterisk (*):

	singular		plural		
(5)	ha.koost	'dress'	ha.koost.-ner	'dresses'	
(6)	au.to.nav	'airplane'	au.to.nav.-ner	'airplanes'	
(7)	doon	'house'	doo.n-er	'houses'	
(8)	du.gha	'boy'	du.gha.-ner	'boys'	
(9)	looys	'light'	looy.s-er	'lights'	but not
			*looys.-ner		
(10)	ba.doo.han	'window'	ba.doo.han.-ner	'windows'	but not
			*ba.doo.ha.n-er		

Does your hypothesis account for these additional data? If it does, then discuss how it does this for (5–10).

If these data are counterexamples, that is, if your hypothesis is disconfirmed by these data, then reformulate your hypothesis so that it explains all of the data given in (1–10). Demonstrate how your reformulated hypothesis explains the data, discussing specific examples.

Before you move on in this chapter, be sure to think through and construct a reasoned, convincing answer to C.

Working Through Problem Set 1

Let us now evaluate two of the many possible hypotheses in explanation of noun pluralization in Armenian. On the basis of patterns that we observe in the first set of data (1–4), we are led to formulate one or another of these competing hypotheses, or both of them:

> *Hypothesis I:*
> *-er* is suffixed to a one-syllable (a monosyllabic) singular noun and *-ner* is suffixed to a noun that has two or more syllables – a polysyllabic noun.

> *Hypothesis II:*
> *-er* is suffixed to a singular noun that ends with a consonant and *-ner* is suffixed to a noun that ends with a vowel.

Before we can decide between these two hypotheses, we need to test them against further evidence from speakers of Armenian to determine which is the crucial factor: the number of syllables that a singular noun has, or the final sound of the singular noun. And for this we need counterexamples to one or another of the hypotheses.

The forms of counterexamples

Counterexamples are data that disconfirm or falsify a hypothesis. We can identify the kinds of data that would constitute a counterexample to a hypothesis by thinking through what characteristics the data would have to have or what conditions the data would have to meet in order to disconfirm the hypothesis.

Let us first consider Hypothesis I. An Armenian plural noun would be a counterexample to Hypothesis I if it took one of two forms: *-er* suffixed to a <u>polysyllabic</u> singular noun like *ga.dou* 'cat', or *-ner* suffixed to a <u>monosyllabic</u> noun like *tas* 'lesson'. If plural nouns exist that meet either of these conditions, then Hypothesis I would be disconfirmed.

Counterexamples to Hypothesis II would take the form of *-er* suffixed to a singular noun like *ga.dou* that <u>ends with a vowel</u>, or *-ner* suffixed to a noun like *tas* that <u>ends with a consonant</u>. If plural nouns exist that take either of these forms, then Hypothesis II would be disconfirmed.

In the second set of data (5–10), we find counterexamples that disconfirm Hypothesis II while providing strong support for Hypothesis I; for in the well-formed plural nouns in (5–8), *-ner* is suffixed only to nouns with two or more syllables and *-er* is suffixed only to monosyllabic nouns. Thus, we are forced to reject Hypothesis II in favor of Hypothesis I.

The predictive power of a hypothesis

Notice that if we had stated Hypothesis I in a more restricted way, so that it distinguished only between monosyllabic and disyllabic (two-syllable) nouns, it would make <u>no</u> prediction about the plural nouns in (6) and (10). However, being wrong in such a clear way is a good result since it would lead us to revise Hypothesis I in order to account for the plurals of all polysyllabic nouns. Thus, we see that a hypothesis has predictive power and that further data test its predictions and may prompt its reformulation if necessary.

Parsimony: Economy of mind and explanation

Hypothesis I and Hypothesis II provide possible explanations for what a speaker of Armenian knows about noun pluralization, and both make an important claim: that the mind of the Armenian speaker efficiently stores <u>rules</u> about noun pluralization, not long lists of nouns and their plural forms. The hypothesized rules pick out some defining feature of the singular noun. In support of Hypothesis I, the data reveal that the number of syllables that a singular noun contains, appears to be the crucial feature.

Assuming that the mind is indeed efficient in the way it stores knowledge and information, we might try to go a step further, toward an even more parsimonious explanation of Armenian noun pluralization. The idea that **parsimony** is central to an explanation has a long history, going back at least to the medieval English philosopher William of Occam (1285–1349), who repeatedly insisted in Latin, as was required at the time: "Pluralitas non est ponenda sine necessitate," loosely translated as "What is done with fewer assumptions is done in vain with more" (Clancy, 2005, p. 159). The principle of parsimony, referred to as **Occam's razor** – since it requires us to cut away everything that is unnecessary to an explanation, is at the basis of all scientific hypothesis formation and theory building. In principle, it is possible to formulate an infinite set of hypotheses over any given set of data since the data do not directly determine the form that a theory or hypothesis can take. The principle of parsimony (Occam's razor) provides a way of choosing among the set of possibilities: Make it simple.

For the formation of the Armenian plural, for example, the linguist would make it simpler by hypothesizing a simple interaction between the components of morphology and phonology. The linguist would choose <u>one</u> of the two suffixes, -*ner* or -*er*, as <u>the</u> plural **morpheme** that is stored in the morphology of a speaker's mental grammar. The term morpheme is used to refer to the smallest units of meaning in language: a word, a prefix such as English *un-*, or a suffix such as Armenian -*ner/-er*. To introduce another linguistic convention, we enclose the name of the plural (and every) morpheme in curly brackets: {plural}.

Given the principle of parsimony, storing one basic **underlying form** of the morpheme {plural} in mental grammar is more efficient that storing two plural suffixes. To form an Armenian plural noun, the {plural} is first added to the singular noun by a rule of morphology, and a rule of phonology that is sensitive to the number of syllables of the singular noun then generates the **surface** (or pronounced) plural form, -*er* or -*ner*. Is there then a basis for choosing -*er* or -*ner* as <u>the</u> underlying {plural}?

Notice that *-er* and *-ner* are quite similar in form, differing by a single **phoneme** or sound. By yet another linguistic convention, we enclose this (and every) phoneme in slant marks: /n/. How we account for the presence of /n/ in *-ner* or its absence in *-er* may well determine which of the two suffixes we would choose to be the underlying {plural}.

From one perspective, it seems that *-ner* is the better choice, since the /n/ of *-ner* could then simply be deleted when {plural} is suffixed to a monosyllabic noun. From another perspective, *-er* is the better choice, since it is shorter and requires less computational space in the mind of the speaker. On this second view, /n/ would then be inserted between *-er* and a preceding polysyllabic noun. However, we would have to explain why /n/ (and no other arbitrary consonant) is inserted. One possibility is that /n/ is the default consonant in Armenian.

Clearly, we would have to look much further into the language in order to decide which is the truly parsimonious explanation.

Looking Ahead

This investigation of one simple phenomenon in Armenian demonstrates a scientific way of thinking about linguistic structure: identifying patterns in data, formulating hypotheses in explanation of those patterns, testing hypotheses by considering counterexamples, reformulating a hypothesis to account for counterexamples, and so on. By approaching language in this way, we can construct explanations of what someone knows when she or he knows a language.

Among the many interesting things that people can do with their unconscious knowledge of a language is to talk about more than one of something and to ask and answer questions. Thus, in the chapters and problem sets that follow, we will focus on two universal phenomena in language: plural formation and question formation, examining them in detail in a variety of languages. We will also explore how understanding plural formation and question formation extends to other seemingly unrelated linguistic phenomena. Our primary goals for doing this – and for this book – are three:

- to introduce a partial answer to the question: What is knowledge of language?
- to introduce some parts of an answer to the question: On what basis does knowledge of language develop in infants, and in children and adults acquiring a second language?
- to promote and to engage you in critical, scientific thinking through the close examination of language.[2]

---

[2]   The rationale for this educational use of linguistics is discussed in great detail in Honda (1994); for less detail, see Honda and O'Neil (1993).

Terms and Linguistic Conventions

mental grammar	suffix
grammar	hypothesis
prescriptive grammar	counterexample
module	parsimony
lexicon	Occam's razor
phonology	underlying form
morphology	morpheme
syntax	surface form
semantics	phoneme

-	A hyphen marks the boundary of a suffix.
.	A period marks a syllable boundary.
*	An asterisk indicates that a form is ill-formed.
{ }	Curly brackets enclose the name of a morpheme.
/ /	Slant marks enclose a phoneme.

Further Reading

The approach to language that we take in this book – that language is a system of knowledge internal to the mind/brain – was first introduced in 1957 by Chomsky in his book, *Syntactic Structures*. For more recent discussions of this approach, see *Language and Problems of Knowledge: The Managua Lectures* (Chomsky, 1988), *The Generative Enterprise Revisited* (Chomsky, 2004), and Baker's (2001) *The Atoms of Language: The Mind's Hidden Rules of Grammar*.

Prescriptive grammar – an approach that we do not pursue – is the focus of a lively chapter on "The language mavins" in Pinker's (1994) book, *The Language Instinct*. For a critical examination of the role and effects of prescriptive grammar in schooling, see O'Neil's foreword to Cattell's (1969) *The New English Grammar*.

Part I

Noun Pluralization, or How to Talk About More Than Two Dogs in Kiowa

Chapter 1

Noun Pluralization: An Introduction

It is fundamental to using language that a person be able to talk about more than one of something, whether the somethings be mad cows, red onions, or bold ideas. In Part I of this book, we expand on the discussion of Armenian noun pluralization by exploring several ways in which **noun phrases** (or **NPs**) are pluralized in language. This will require that we examine the phonological and morphological components of mental grammar in some detail, and – to some extent – its syntax.

Let us begin by looking at the structure of NP plurality in the way introduced long ago by Chomsky (1957, pp. 29, 111). On this view, noun phrases come in two varieties: singular NPs and plural NPs, and it is at this <u>phrasal</u> level that the concepts 'singular' and 'plural' are semantically interpreted. In English, although the plural suffix generally shows up only on the noun – as it does in Armenian, it is the <u>whole</u> NP that is interpreted as plural. When we say, for example:

(1) *I saw the books on the table.*

the entire NP, *the books on the table*, is understood as plural; we must be referring to a particular set of books on a particular table, and not to just any set of books regardless of its location.

Although the concepts 'singular' and 'plural' are <u>always</u> represented in mental grammar, the **morphemes** {singular} and {plural} may or may not be overtly realized within an NP as a suffix or a prefix; that is, they may or may not be pronounced. Whenever the morpheme {singular} or {plural} is realized in speech, it has to find a "home" or "homes" – and often does so in the NP. In English, for example, the morpheme {singular} has **zero phonological form**, that is, there is no spoken form. But the morpheme {plural} generally does have phonological form in English. Looking back to sentence (1), we see that the morpheme {plural} finds a "home" on *book*, the head N of the plural NP.

In structural terms, we represent this way of thinking about plural NPs by diagramming the plural NP in sentence (1) as follows:

(2)   a

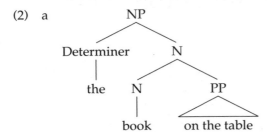

A plural NP is then constructed by the merger of the NP of (2a) with {plural}, giving us the representation shown in (2b):

(2)   b

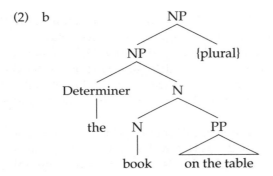

The diagram in (2b) represents the fact that the morpheme {plural} **merges** with the entire NP (2a) – and not just with the **head** N (*book*) of that NP, the head being the noun that the phrase is organized around. That is, {plural} affects the whole NP and is interpreted in our minds at this phrasal level. However, phonologically, {plural} finds its way home in English only to the head N of the NP, as the plural suffix /s/.

In these diagrams, **Determiner** is a general term for the words and groups of words that may quantify a noun with respect to singularity or plurality. This term includes the articles (*a, the*, etc.), possessors (*his, her, our*, etc.), and words like *some, many, several, these, those*, etc. (Determiners are discussed in further detail in Chapters 5 and 15. The branching structure of the diagrams is the topic of Chapter 8 Merge.)

In some languages, the morpheme {plural} finds multiple "homes" in an NP. For example, consider the following Spanish NPs:

(3)   a   *el   libro   interesante*
          the book interesting
          'the interesting book'

b   *los libros interesantes*
the books interesting
'the interesting books'

c   *un libro interesante*
a   book interesting
'an interesting book'

d   *unos libros interesantes*
some books interesting
'some interesting books'

Comparing (3a) and (3b), we see that {plural} makes itself at home on the determiner (*el* 'the' becoming *los*), on the N (*libro* 'book' becoming *libros*), and on the adjective modifying the N (*interesante* 'interesting' becoming *interesantes*). A parallel analysis can be made of (3c) and (3d). Thus, in Spanish, every word in a plural NP that can be pluralized is pluralized overtly.

English is much more restrictive than Spanish in this respect. The morpheme {plural} usually finds only one "home": on the head N of a plural NP, as in (1) above. To only a very limited extent does {plural} find more than one "home" in an NP, as the following contrasts reveal:

(4)   a   *this interesting book*
      b   *these interesting books*
      c   *that interesting book*
      d   *those interesting books*

Given the plural NPs in (4), we see that in English the morpheme {plural} finds its way phonologically to the N (*book* becomes *books*) and to the demonstratives (*this* becomes *these*; *that* becomes *those*), but not to the adjective (*interesting*).

In some languages of the world, including some varieties of English, the morpheme {plural} has zero phonological form, that is, {plural} results in no observable pronunciation. A highway sign in Missouri provides an illustration: "Joplin, Seven Mile From Here" (Cassidy & Hall, 1996, p. 592). In this variety of English, {plural} can be "satisfied" in a different way: not by a plural suffix on the N, but by the presence of an inherently plural word in the NP, the cardinal number *seven*.

To summarize: All languages have plural NPs. The concept 'plural' is semantically interpreted at the NP level, as a result of the NP and the morpheme {plural} merging. However, the phonological form of the morpheme {plural} can be found on the head N of the NP, on the adjectives modifying the N, on the determiners, or on all of the above. Or on none of the above; that is, the morpheme {plural} does not have to be realized phonologically at all within the NP.

Looking Ahead

Examining further the ways that {plural} manifests itself in a plural NP is the focus of Part I of this book. For any given language, the question we want to answer is this: What phonological effects, if any, does the morpheme {plural} have on the head N of the NP? We represent this question in the following stripped-down NP structure, in which an NP and the morpheme {plural} **merge** to form a higher NP:

(5)

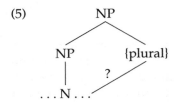

The question mark at the end of the diagonal line in (5) that runs from {plural} to N asks us to consider whether the morpheme {plural} shows up as a prefix to the N, a suffix to the N, or not on the N at all but somewhere else in the structure of a sentence – to mention some of the questions that will be answered as we move through Part I. It is important to note at the outset of this investigation that we will find that there is only a narrow range of alternative ways of pluralizing NPs among languages of the world. Not everything is possible.

We continue our examination of plural NPs by next analyzing the phonology of English noun pluralization.

Problem Set 2: Plural Noun Formation in English

Suppose a linguist is doing research on the phonology of English plural nouns. By listening carefully to fluent English speakers' pronunciation of some plural nouns, she notices that the plural endings sound like the last sound in the word *buzz*. For example, say the following sentences aloud. Concentrate on the sound of the plural endings of the underlined words:

There are _bugs_ on this plant.
The _pears_ are rotten.
There are two _birds_ in the sky.

Even though the plurals are not spelled this way, fluent English speakers pronounce these plural nouns as if they end with /z/. On the basis of these data, the linguist formulates the following hypothesis to explain how English plural nouns are formed in speech:

/z/ is suffixed to the singular form of a noun to make it plural.

A   Does this hypothesis explain how the plurals of the words below are pronounced? Why or why not? Explain why you answer as you do, giving specific examples from the data.

pig   robot   judge
rock   lunch   cloud
shape   star   kiss

Before you move on in the problem set, be sure to think through A and construct a reasoned answer.

B   The linguist investigates further. By listening to someone say the sentences shown below, she notices some differences in the way the plural suffixes of the underlined words sound. Say the sentences aloud. Concentrate on how the plural suffixes of the underlined words sound.

   All of the _spoons_ and _cups_ and _dishes_ are on the table.
   There are _goats_ and _horses_ and _cows_ on the farm.

   Some of the plural suffixes sound the same. Which of the underlined words have plural suffixes that sound the same?
      Put the underlined words into groups according to the pronunciation of their plural suffixes, leaving off the suffixes. Then, using the linguistic convention of enclosing phonemes in slant marks (/ /), label the groups according to the sound of the plural suffixes.

C   Look again at the list of nouns from A, repeated below. Say the plurals of these words aloud, and then assign them to the groups that you made in B.

pig   robot   judge
rock   lunch   cloud
shape   star   kiss

D   Consider your answers to A, B, and C. Think about what your work shows about how English speakers form plural nouns in speech. Formulate a hypothesis that explains how speakers of English form plural nouns in speech.

E   Does your hypothesis explain the pronunciation of all the plural nouns of English? Why or why not? Demonstrate how your hypothesis does (or does not) explain the data, discussing specific examples.

F   Fluent speakers of English and people who know English quite well have no trouble forming the correct plurals of nouns like those in this problem set. Their knowledge of English enables them to produce, perceive, and comprehend the correct plural forms without hesitation.

   Suppose we ask the following question: How do speakers of English do this? In other words, in what way do speakers of English internalize their knowledge of plural noun formation? A related question is: How does an infant/child growing up in an English-speaking family come to know how to form plural nouns in English? Consider these four possibilities:[1]

   Hypothesis I:
   Speakers of English memorize the plural form for every noun they come across.

----
[1]   This part of the problem set is paraphrased from Halle and Clements (1983, p. 69).

Hypothesis II:
Speakers of English learn the plural forms on the basis of spelling. For example, they learn that nouns that end with the letter *b* are pluralized by suffixing /z/.

Hypothesis III:
Speakers of English know that the final sound (not the letter) of the singular noun determines the pronunciation of the plural suffix.

Hypothesis IV:
Speakers of English know that some feature or characteristic of the final sound of the singular noun determines the pronunciation of the plural suffix.

Why should Hypothesis I and Hypothesis II be eliminated from consideration?
G   Hypothesis III and Hypothesis IV are similar, but they differ in an important way. Why does Hypothesis IV present a more efficient way in which the mind might work?

Before you move on to Chapter 2, be sure to think through and construct reasoned, convincing answers to B through G.

Terms

noun phrase, NP
morpheme
zero phonological form
merge
head
determiner

Chapter 2

Noun Pluralization: The Role of Phonology

A word is represented in the mind as a collection of characteristics, or features. The linguistic features of a word come in three different flavors:

- Some features represent the semantics of the word, or some aspects of its meaning. For example, the **semantic features** [human] and [animate] play a role in distinguishing among the nouns of a language and what can be said of them: People and animals, which are [+animate], sleep and show fear, but rocks, which are [−animate], don't − except perhaps in poetry.
- Some features represent the **grammatical categories** that the word belongs to. For example, is a word a noun, a verb, a preposition, or a determiner?
- Some features of a word represent its **phonology** − the way it is pronounced and perceived. For example, a phonological feature of the first sound of *visit* is [+voice]; that of its final sound is [−voice]: In the pronunciation of /v/, the vocal cords vibrate; in /t/, they do not.

In this chapter, we focus on phonology, examining a number of phonological features and considering the role they play in the structure of English. In subsequent chapters, we consider the role of phonological features in other languages.

Building Sounds Up from Their Distinctive Features

Although we perceive a word as being made up of sequences of sounds and syllables, the individual sounds are themselves collections of phonological features. These are referred to as **distinctive features** because they serve to distinguish sounds from one another within a language as well as among the languages of the world. Each sound is represented in the mind as a set of distinctive features, many of which are binary, or two-valued: + (yes) or − (no).

By linguistic convention, we enclose these features and, if necessary, their values in square brackets, for example: [+voice] or [−voice]. These features are the mental instructions to the hearing and speaking neural systems, and thus are the fundamental building blocks of the sounds of language.

Depending on whether they form a syllable or not, the sounds of language fall into two broad categories: consonants and vowels. Oversimplifying somewhat, we can say that vowels form syllables, and that consonants do not. The distinction between consonants and vowels depends on whether there is constriction or closure in the oral cavity [+consonantal], or not [−consonantal]. In pronouncing the vowel /a/ of *pa*, for example, air flows freely from the lungs out through the mouth unimpeded. In the pronunciation of the consonant /p/ of *pa*, the lips prevent air from leaving the mouth until the speech organs move on to the vowel of the word.

The feature **[consonantal]** is just one of a number of distinctive features. Other features are necessary to differentiate the individual consonants and vowels of language.

We will now take a phonological journey through the human vocal tract, a journey which you can follow in the diagram of the vocal tract in Figure 1. As we take this journey, we will establish the set of distinctive features necessary for categorizing and distinguishing the sounds of English and of languages in general. Distinctive features will be crucial for our understanding of how languages are structured phonologically and, more narrowly, for an explanation of English noun pluralization and other language phenomena.

A Phonological Journey: Articulator-Bound Features

The distinctive features result from the gestures made by six speech articulators in the vocal tract: the lips, the tongue blade, the tongue body, the tongue root, the soft palate, and the larynx.[1] Each sound of a language has one of these articulators as its **primary articulator**.

As we will see on our phonological journey, some articulators have only one feature associated with them while other articulators have more than one associated feature. All such features are articulator-bound. Other features, which we take up later in this chapter, are articulator-free; that is, they are not bound to a particular articulator.

---

[1]   Much of what follows in this and the next section is based on Halle (2003). At the suggestion of Halle, we have, where possible, labeled the articulators with Old English-based terms rather than Latin-based terms: tongue body, not dorsal; tongue blade, not coronal; lips, not labial. Tongue root is already widely used in the literature.

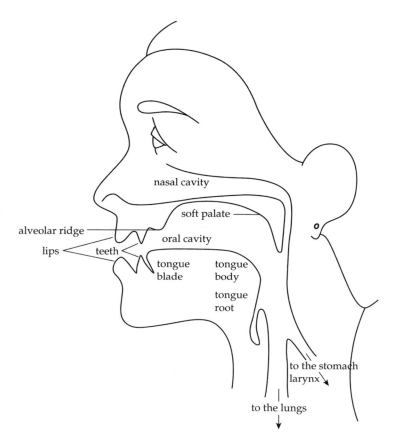

nasal cavity

soft palate

alveolar ridge

oral cavity

lips   teeth

tongue   tongue
blade   body

tongue
root

to the stomach
larynx

to the lungs

Figure 1   Articulators in the vocal tract

The larynx and the feature [voice]

Let us start at the far, lower end of the vocal tract with the larynx (or voice-box). In English, the distinctive feature associated with the larynx is [voice], a binary feature. The vocal folds (or cords) of the larynx can be stiffened and thus made to vibrate – resulting in a [+voice] or voiced sound. Or the vocal folds can be relaxed – resulting in a [–voice] or unvoiced sound. This is the distinction, for example, between /z/ and /s/. To demonstrate this voicing contrast for yourself, place your finger on your Adam's apple and pronounce /z/ in a drawn out manner; you will feel the vibration of the vocal folds. You will feel no vibration in the pronunciation of /s/, the [–voice] counterpart to /z/.

The same voicing difference exists between /v/ and /f/ and between /ð/ and /θ/ (the last pair of symbols representing the initial consonants of *this* and *thin*, respectively). For each of these pairs, the first member is [+voice]; the second is [−voice].

In English, the larynx is the primary articulator for only one sound, the [−voice] glide /h/, the initial sound of *hat*.

The soft palate and the feature [nasal]

Further up the vocal tract from the larynx, we come to the soft palate. This articulator is aptly named, as you can discover by running the tip of your tongue straight back beyond the bony hard palate at the roof of your mouth.

The distinctive feature associated with the soft palate is [nasal]. The soft palate can either be left in its relaxed, open position, allowing air to flow through the nasal cavity as well as through the oral cavity, producing a [+nasal] sound, or it can be moved to close off the nasal cavity, forcing air to escape only through the mouth in the production of a [−nasal] sound. Sounds are thus either [+nasal] like /m/, /n/ and /ŋ/ (the final sound of *sing*), or [−nasal] like /b/, /d/, and /g/. Nearly all their other distinctive features except nasality are held constant in the production of these pairs of sounds: /m/ and /b/, /n/ and /d/, and /ŋ/ and /g/.

There are no sounds in English for which the soft palate is the primary articulator.

The tongue root and the feature [ATR]

Continuing our journey from the larynx toward the outside world, we arrive next at the tongue, at its root first. The tongue root can either be advanced, that is moved forward in the mouth [+ATR], or not [−ATR] (where [ATR] = Advanced Tongue Root). This feature marks the distinction between tense [+ATR] vowels and lax [−ATR] vowels. The tenseness of [+ATR] vowels can be felt in the root of the tongue as opposed to the laxness of [−ATR] vowels. The contrast is illustrated by alternating between the pronunciation of the vowels in the following word pairs:

- the /i/ of *beet* is [+ATR] while the /ɪ/ of *bit* is [−ATR];
- the /e/ of *bait* is [+ATR] while the /ɛ/ of *bet* is [−ATR].

While in other languages, [ATR] is a distinctive feature for consonants as well as for vowels, in English, it is a distinctive feature only of vowels. Moreover, the tongue root is not a primary articulator in English phonology.

The tongue body and the features [high], [low], [back]

Next we move to the tongue body: In the production of the consonants /g/, /k/, and /ŋ/, the body of the tongue, the primary articulator for these sounds, makes contact with the roof of the mouth.

The tongue body can be either [high] or [low] or [back]. Although these features are active in the production of consonants in many languages, this is not the case for English.

For English vowels, however, the features associated with the tongue body are crucial; for the tongue body plays the role of primary articulator for English vowels. The body of the tongue can be raised to a position above its neutral resting position [+high], or moved to a point lower than that position [+low], or left in its neutral position [–high, –low]. These three tongue-body positions are illustrated by the vowels in the following words:

- *bit*: /ɪ/, which is [+high];
- *bat*: /æ/, which is [+low]; and
- *bet*: /ɛ/, which is [–high, –low].

Notice that for a vowel to be [+high, +low] would constitute a contradiction. Thus the possible combination of values for these two features allows for only three vowel heights: [+high], [+low], and mid, that is, [–high, –low].

The body of the tongue can also be retracted toward the rear wall of the oral cavity [+back] or not [–back], as in the vowels in the following words:

- *boat*: /o/, which is [+back];
- *beet*: /i/, which is [–back].

The tongue blade and the feature [anterior]

The tongue blade (including the tip of the tongue) can create a constriction at or near the alveolar ridge (which is located immediately behind the teeth) or along the roof of the mouth. The tongue blade is the primary articulator for a number of coronal consonants in English. Depending on where the tongue blade makes contact in the mouth, it divides the oral cavity into sounds made – speaking nautically – fore [+anterior] or aft [–anterior]. The feature [anterior] is bound to the tongue blade and distinguishes between sounds articulated at points along the roof of the mouth from the teeth to the soft palate – the initial sounds of the following words, for example:

- *seat*: /s/, which is [+anterior];
- *sheet*: /š/, which is [–anterior].

The lips and the feature [round]

The lips are the sixth, and last, of the articulators. Labial consonants are articulated at the lips; /p/ and /f/ are examples of sounds whose primary articulator is the lips.

Although in other languages the feature [round] – bound to the lips – plays a role in the production of consonants, this is not the case for English. However, the lips are either rounded or not in the production of the vowels of English. In the pronunciation of the vowel of *oats*, for example, the lips are rounded [+round] while in the pronunciation of the vowel of *ate*, the lips are spread [−round].

A Phonological Journey, Continued: Articulator-Free Features

The articulator-free feature **[consonantal]** was introduced at the beginning of the discussion of phonological distinctive features. As noted earlier, its value primarily serves to mark the distinction between consonants and vowels: For consonants, which are [+consonantal], there is constriction in the oral cavity; for vowels, which are [−consonantal], there is no constriction: air flows freely from the lungs in the production of vowels.

The remaining articulator-free features are these: [sonorant], [continuant], [strident], and [lateral] − all of them binary features.

The feature **[sonorant]**

[sonorant] distinguishes **obstruent** consonants or [−sonorant] sounds, such as /b/, /d/, and /g/, from the [+sonorant] sounds: the vowels, the **glides** /w/, /y/, and /h/, the nasals /m/, /n/, and /ŋ/, and the **liquids** /l/ and /r/. Sounds that are [+sonorant] are produced without any buildup of pressure inside the vocal tract. In the production of the [+nasal] sounds, for example, pressure is released through the nasal cavity and not through the vocal tract.

The feature **[continuant]**

[+continuant] sounds (/f/, /s/, /š/, for example) are produced without interruption of airflow through the oral cavity; their pronunciation can be continued on a single breath till that breath runs out. [−continuant] sounds (or stops: /p/, /t/, /k/, for example) are produced with interruption somewhere in the oral cavity. Vowels are by definition [+continuant].

The feature **[strident]**

[+strident] sounds are produced with a maximum amount of turbulence; [−strident] sounds are produced with minimum turbulence. For example, the initial consonant of *zen* /z/ is [+strident] while the initial consonant of *then* /ð/ is [−strident]. Vowels are by definition [−strident].

With respect to the features [continuant] and [strident], /č/ and /j/ (the initial and final consonants of *church* and *judge*, respectively) are of interest. In their production, /č/ and /j/ begin more or less like the stops /t/ and /d/: [−continuant, +anterior, −strident]. But then they "explode" and have the noisy turbulence of the [+continuant, −anterior, +strident] sounds /š/ and /ž/

(the final consonant of *dish* and *rouge*, respectively). We capture these facts about /č/ and /j/ with the distinctive feature specification [–continuant, +strident].

The feature [lateral]

[+lateral] sounds are produced by lowering one or both sides of the tongue allowing air to flow around the tongue in their production; [–lateral] sounds are produced without lowering. The /l/ in *let*, for example, is [+lateral]; this contrasts with [–lateral] /d/ in *debt*. Although the feature [lateral] is distinctive in English only for /l/ (as opposed to /r/), it can do further work and does in other languages of the world.

Representing Language Sounds: Distinctive Feature Matrices

The following pages provide distinctive feature matrices representing the consonants, liquids, vowels, and glides of English as columns of distinctive features and distinctive feature values.[2] Liquids and glides are presented as separate phonemic categories since under certain phonological conditions they can be either vowel-like or consonant-like while under other conditions they will be what they are: liquids and glides.

For each **phoneme** given in the distinctive feature matrices, the first articulator listed, shown in bold, is that phoneme's **primary articulator**. Other articulators as well as articulator-bound features and articulator-free features for that phoneme then follow. Consider, for example, the entry for the phoneme /p/, which is the initial consonant of *pat*:

	Example:	*pat*
Primary articulator:	**Lips**	/p/
Secondary articulator:	Soft palate	
Bound feature:	[nasal]	–
Secondary articulator:	Larynx	
Bound feature:	[voice]	–
Articulator-free features:	[consonantal]	+
	[sonorant]	–
	[continuant]	–
	[strident]	–

---

[2] For the most part, the symbols used here to represent the sounds of English (and later, other languages) are the ones commonly used in North America; they differ from the International Phonetic Alphabet (IPA) in only a few ways. For the four consonants here represented as /č j š ž/, the final sound of *church, judge, push,* and *rouge*, respectively, the IPA uses /tʃ dʒ ʃ ʒ/. For the glide represented here as /y/, the initial sound of *yet*, the IPA uses /j/.

Table 2.1 Distinctive feature matrix for CONSONANTS

(a)

Example	pat	bat	mat	fat	vat
Lips	/p/	/b/	/m/	/f/	/v/
Soft Palate					
[nasal]	−	−	+	−	−
Larynx					
[voice]	−	+	+	−	+
[consonantal]	+	+	+	+	+
[sonorant]	−	−	+	−	−
[continuant]	−	−	−	+	+
[strident]	−	−	−	+	+

(b)

Example	tie	die	nigh	thigh	thy	sigh	zit	chai	gin	shin	azure
Tongue blade	/t/	/d/	/n/	/θ/	/ð/	/s/	/z/	/č/	/j/	/š/	/ž/
[anterior]	+	+	+	+	+	+	+	−	−	−	−
Soft palate											
[nasal]	−	−	+	−	−	−	−	−	−	−	−
Larynx											
[voice]	−	+	+	−	+	−	+	−	+	−	+
[consonantal]	+	+	+	+	+	+	+	+	+	+	+
[sonorant]	−	−	+	−	−	−	−	−	−	−	−
[continuant]	−	−	−	+	+	+	+	−	−	+	+
[strident]	−	−	−	−	−	+	+	+	+	+	+

(c)

Example	cane	gain	rang
Tongue body	/k/	/g/	/ŋ/
Soft palate			
[nasal]	−	−	+
Larynx			
[voice]	−	+	+
[consonantal]	+	+	+
[sonorant]	−	−	+
[continuant]	−	−	−
[strident]	−	−	−

Table 2.2 Distinctive feature matrix for LIQUIDS

Example	right	light
Tongue blade	/r/	/l/
[anterior]	−	+
Larynx		
[voice]	+	+
[consonantal]	+	+
[sonorant]	+	+
[continuant]	+	+
[lateral]	−	+

Table 2.3   Distinctive feature matrix for VOWELS

Example	beet	kit	Kate	get	gas	coop	put	vote	dog	ma	but
Tongue body	/i/	/ɪ/	/e/	/ɛ/	/æ/	/u/	/ʊ/	/o/	/ɔ/	/a/	/ʌ/
[high]	+	+	−	−	−	+	+	−	−	−	−
[low]	−	−	−	−	+	−	−	−	+	+	−
[back]	−	−	−	−	−	+	+	+	+	+	+
Tongue root											
[ATR]	+	−	+	−	−	+	−	+	−	−	−
Lips											
[round]	−	−	−	−	−	+	+	+	+	−	−
Soft palate											
[nasal]	−	−	−	−	−	−	−	−	−	−	−
Larynx											
[voice]	+	+	+	+	+	+	+	+	+	+	+
[consonantal]	−	−	−	−	−	−	−	−	−	−	−
[sonorant]	+	+	+	+	+	+	+	+	+	+	+
[continuant]	+	+	+	+	+	+	+	+	+	+	+

Table 2.4   Distinctive feature matrix for GLIDES

Example	wet		yet		hit
Lips	/w/	**Tongue blade**	/y/		/h/
[round]	+	[anterior]	+		
Larynx				**Larynx**	
[voice]	+		+		−
[consonantal]	−		−		−
[sonorant]	+		+		+
[continuant]	+		+		+

English has two additional vowel sounds, [ə] (schwa) and [ɨ] (barred *i*). These are the vowels that other vowels collapse onto when their stress, loudness, or length is lost. Compare, for example, the sound of the second *i* of *civil* with that of *civility*; the *a* of *moral* with that of *morality*; etc. In the simple words *civil* and *moral*, the second vowel is [ə] or [ɨ]; in *civility* and *morality*, the second vowel is [ɪ] or [æ], respectively. The difference between the vowels of these pairs of words follows from the differences in stress.

While the **glides** of English have different primary articulators, they share the same values for the articulator-free features: [−consonantal], [+sonorant], and [+continuant]. These feature values are among those which are character-istic of vowels. But glides are not true vowels, for they do not form syllables on their own. However, glides play a role in **diphthongs**; we can say that diph-thongs "glide" off onto a glide. The diphthongs of *write*, *brown*, and *broil*, for example, consist of a vowel followed by a glide: /ay/ in *write*; /aw/ or /æw/ in *brown*; and /ɔy/ in *broil*. Moreover – like consonants, glides can introduce a syllable, as in *yet*, *wet*, and *hat*.

Looking Ahead

Beyond the distinctive features that are active in English (and which many languages share), the larger **universal set** of distinctive features makes it possible to cross-classify and distinguish all the sounds of all languages. This cross-classification also allows us to identify the natural subsets of sounds by simply referring to the distinctive feature or features that pick them out of the matrix. For example, we can refer to the subset of [+voice, −continuant] sounds – the voiced stops; to the subset of [+nasal] sounds; to the subset of [+strident] sounds; the subset of tongue body consonants, and so on by focusing on the unique characteristic or characteristics of a subset.

As we shall see, the phonological rules of languages pay attention to such subsets of sounds.

In addition to the features being analytical tools, the symbols given at the head of each column in the distinctive feature matrices are representational tools: These symbols provide us with a way of consistently representing the individual sounds of a word, thus avoiding the ambiguities of English spelling. Consider, for example, two of the example words from the feature matrix for vowels, *beet* and *coop*. Compare the single phonological representation of the vowel sound in *beet* and *coop*, respectively, with their various spelled forms in different words:

/i/:   b<u>ee</u>t, k<u>ey</u>, s<u>ea</u>t, bab<u>y</u>, cook<u>ie</u>s
/u/:   c<u>oo</u>p, thr<u>ough</u>, sh<u>oe</u>, s<u>ui</u>t

Similarly, consider the example word *sigh* from the feature matrix for consonants. Compare the single phonological representation of the consonant sound in *sigh* with its various spelled forms in different words:

/s/:   <u>s</u>igh, <u>p</u><u>s</u>ychology, ki<u>ss</u>, <u>sc</u>ien<u>c</u>e

Thus, with the symbols from the distinctive feature matrices, we are able to unambiguously transcribe the sounds of words. This is illustrated in the transcriptions of the example words given below and enclosed in slash marks (/ /):

beet: /bit/
coop: /kup/
sigh: /say/

In the chapters and problem sets that follow, there are a number of such phonological representations, for English as well as for the other languages that are analyzed.

We return now to noun pluralization in English to consider the role that distinctive features can play in explaining this phenomenon.

The Phonology of English Plural Noun Formation

The goal of Problem Set 2 (in Chapter 1) on English noun pluralization is to try to explain the knowledge that English speakers have which allows them to freely form the plurals of nouns and to correctly interpret the plural forms that they hear. With this goal in mind, let us work through the sections of the problem set toward a possible explanation.

The initial hypothesis – /z/ is suffixed to the singular form of a noun to make it plural – only accounts for some of the plurals. We can see this by strictly applying this hypothesis for noun pluralization to the following set of words, an asterisk (*) indicating that the word is not well-formed:

pig/z/	**robot/z/*	**judge/z/*
*rock/z/	**lunch/z/*	*cloud/z/*
*shape/z/	*star/z/*	**rat/z/*

Note, however, that it was not a bad strategy to begin with this simple hypothesis since in general, it is much easier to broaden a hypothesis than it is to narrow one. This is because when a narrow hypothesis is shown to be wrong, you can often see how to reformulate it; but how to narrow a hypothesis is often a much more difficult matter.

Given the following sentences repeated from Problem Set 2:

All of the <u>spoons</u> and <u>cups</u> and <u>dishes</u> are on the table.
There are <u>goats</u> and <u>horses</u> and <u>cows</u> on the farm.

each of the following pairs of words has the same plural suffix:

dishes, horses	/ɪz/
cups, goats	/s/
spoons, cows	/z/

Notice that the plural forms *dishes* and *horses* differ from those of the other words in an important way: Their plural forms are one syllable longer than their singular forms. This is not true of *cups, goats, spoons, cows*, or for many other nouns that we could think of. For them, the singular and plural forms have the same number of syllables.

Thus there appear to be three groups, or categories, of nouns: those that take an /ɪz/ plural suffix, those that take a /s/ plural suffix, and those that take a /z/ plural suffix, as in the following examples:

/ɪz/:   *wish*/ɪz/, *lunch*/ɪz/, *kiss*/ɪz/, and so on
/s/:   *graph*/s/, *myth*/s/, *rock*/s/, and so on
/z/:   *rib*/z/, *room*/z/, *star*/z/, *tree*/z/, and so on

At first, it might seem that there are only two groups: Those that take /ɪz/ in the plural, increasing the number of syllables in a word by one, and those for which the plural does not result in an additional syllable, simply adding /s/ or /z/. Another way to view the data is to separate those words that have a final /s/ in the plural from those that have a final /z/ in the plural – when /z/ or /ɪz/ are added. These two ways of looking at the data are valid <u>in part</u>, but neither one gives us a complete picture of the full range of regular plural endings.

Hypotheses I–IV offer different explanations of an English speaker's unconscious knowledge of language or **mental grammar**. Thus, they make different predictions about how an English speaker forms plural nouns.

Hypothesis I:
Speakers of English memorize the plural form for every noun they come across.

Hypothesis I makes the claim that a speaker of English cannot form the plural of a noun that she or he has learned only in its singular form. Since it is easy to demonstrate that a speaker of English can readily form plurals of unfamiliar or even nonsense words, Hypothesis I is an inadequate hypothesis.

Hypothesis II:
Speakers of English learn the plural forms on the basis of spelling. For example, they learn that nouns that end with the letter *b* are pluralized by suffixing /z/.

Hypothesis II makes the claim that people who are illiterate in English, including young children, would be unable to form the plurals of English nouns, another demonstrably incorrect claim.

Hypothesis III:
Speakers of English know that the final sound (not the letter) of the singular noun determines the pronunciation of the plural suffix.

Hypothesis III makes a more serious claim, but a questionable one: that a speaker of English knows the list of speech sounds to which the plural suffix /s/ is added; the list of speech sounds to which the plural suffix /z/ is added; and the list of speech sounds to which the plural suffix /ɪz/ is added. What makes this claim questionable is that such lists are not a parsimonious characterization of our linguistic knowledge. We could well be driven to accepting

Hypothesis III as an adequate hypothesis if we were unable to find any distinctive feature or features that define the lists. This brings us to the claim of:

Hypothesis IV:
Speakers of English know that some feature or characteristic of the final sound of the singular noun determines the pronunciation of the plural suffix.

Let us now explore Hypothesis IV more carefully.

Problem Set 2, Revisited: Plural Noun Formation in English

We now shift the nature of this problem conceptually by considering Occam's razor, or the principle of parsimony. Recall how we attempted to apply Occam's razor to the explanation of Armenian noun pluralization (Problem Set 1) in the introductory chapter: hypothesizing that one of the two suffixes, *-ner* or *-er*, is the underlying form of the plural morpheme, or {plural}, from which the other form can be derived.

Let us take a similar approach to English noun pluralization. Is there a basis for choosing /ız/, /s/, or /z/, three very similar suffixes, as the underlying {plural}? From the perspective that a shorter suffix requires less computational space in the mind of the speaker, we would want to choose either /s/ or /z/ as the form of {plural}. At this point in our investigation, we have no basis for choosing between these two forms, so let us make the following assumption and examine its consequences: /s/ is the <u>single</u> underlying form of {plural} from which its other surface forms are derived by phonological rules.

On this assumption, we hypothesize that the first step in forming a plural noun in English is this:

Add /s/, the underlying form of {plural}, to the singular form of the noun; for example, *cat/s/, dog/s/, dish/s/.*

A   What rules need to be added to this explanation in order to account for the different forms that {plural} /s/ assumes at the surface, in speech, as in *cat/s/, dog/z/, dish/ız/*? To answer this question, you need to elaborate the concept 'some feature(s) or characteristic(s)' of the final sound of the singular noun given in Hypothesis IV. Use the distinctive feature matrices in this chapter to sharpen and extend this hypothesis for plural noun formation in English.

Before you move on to Chapter 3, be sure you think through A and construct a reasoned answer.

Terms and Linguistic Conventions

semantic feature	sonorant
grammatical category	obstruent
phonology	glide
distinctive feature	liquid
consonantal	continuant
primary articulator	strident
voice	lateral
nasal	anterior
ATR	phoneme
high	universal set
low	diphthong
back	mental grammar
round	

[ ]   Square brackets enclose a feature and, where relevant, its value.

Further Reading

The analysis of distinctive features that we present here is more fully explicated in Halle (2003).

The distinctive feature analysis is an important tool for investigating and understanding language learners' speech perception and speech production. For a brief survey of research on infants' perceptual sensitivity to the sounds and distinctive features of language and the development of phonological knowledge, see Werker (1995). For more extensive surveys of this work, see Jusczyk's (1997) *The Discovery of Spoken Language,* and Boysson-Bardies' (1999) *How Language Comes to Children: From Birth to Two Years.*

Chapter 3

Noun Pluralization: Morphology Meets Phonology

Recall that the goal of our examination of English noun pluralization is to explain the knowledge that English speakers have that allows them to freely form the plurals of nouns and to correctly interpret the plural forms that they hear. In Chapter 2, we saw that Hypothesis IV makes a strong and interesting claim about English speakers' unconscious knowledge of how plural nouns are formed:

Hypothesis IV:
Speakers of English know that some feature or characteristic of the final sound of the singular noun determines the pronunciation of the plural suffix.

We now attempt to show that Hypothesis IV points us in the right direction and forms the basis for explaining one small part of an English speaker's mental grammar.

The Phonology of English Plural Noun Formation

We have seen that one way of explaining the data is to hypothesize that there are three different forms of the plural ending in English and that our knowledge of English plural formation involves always picking the <u>right</u> ending: /ɪz/, /s/, or /z/. According to Hypothesis IV, picking the "right" ending means picking the one that somehow fits the feature(s) or characteristic(s) of the sound with which the singular word ends.

By analyzing the final sounds of the singular nouns according to their **distinctive features**, we could then further hypothesize that there are three different rules for attaching the plural forms:

- add /ɪz/ to words ending in [Tongue blade, +strident] sounds;
- add /s/ to words ending in [−voice] sounds; and
- add /z/ elsewhere, that is, to words ending in [+voice] sounds.

Importantly, on this view, the mind of the English speaker stores rules about noun pluralization, not lists of nouns and their plural forms. Rules of this sort pick out some defining feature(s) of the final sound of the singular noun.

Applied in a certain way, then, this is an adequate explanation only if we are unable to find a more parsimonious or economical explanation.

Hypothesizing an underlying morpheme

A more parsimonious hypothesis might, for example, replace the three plural suffixes with a <u>single</u> **underlying form** of the morpheme {plural} plus some rules of phonology to generate the three slightly different pronounced or **surface forms**.

Here then is a more parsimonious hypothesis – a possible explanation of the data:

A   First, assume that the unconscious mind is as efficient as possible in the way in which it stores knowledge and information. Assume further that noun pluralization can be broken down into a step-by-step, rule-governed process. Under the first assumption, a native speaker of English will have a single form of the {plural} stored in her or his brain, call it /s/. Under the second assumption there is the following **morphological rule** for English: To form the plural of a given regular noun, add the {plural} /s/ to the end of the singular form of the noun.

B   Under the second assumption, there are two **phonological** generalizations about English, presented here as <u>ordered</u> rules:

1   If the singular noun ends in one of the [Tongue blade, +strident] sounds, which we will refer to informally as **sibilants**, then insert the vowel /ɪ/ between the final sibilant and the plural /s/ (itself a sibilant) by a process known as **epenthesis**.

2   If the sound preceding the plural /s/ is [+voice], then voice the plural /s/ to /z/ by a process known as **assimilation**.

Applying the rules, in the order given, we derive the following correct results:

	bus	rat	dog
	bʌs	ræt	dɔg
Morphological rule:			
A add {plural} /s/:	bʌs+s	ræt+s	dɔg+s
Phonological rules:			
B1 insert /ɪ/ between sibilants:	bʌsɪs	ræts	dɔgs
B2 voice /s/ after a voiced sound:	bʌsɪz	ræts	dɔgz

The phonological rules of epenthesis (B1) and assimilation (B2) work this way for two quite natural reasons: In English, since the plural /s/ (which is itself a sibilant) cannot blend with a sibilant, the sequences /ss/, /zs/, /js/, etc. are broken up by the epenthetic vowel /ɪ/. The plural /s/ then assimilates to the voicing characteristic of the sound immediately preceding it. The plural ending becomes /z/ (a voiced sound) if the sound preceding it is [+voice]; and remains /s/ (a voiceless sound) if the sound preceding it is [−voice]. Since the vocal folds are always vibrated in the production of vowels, vowels are by definition [+voice]. So having rule (B1) (which inserts /ɪ/ before the plural ending /s/) precede rule (B2) ensures the correct result for plural forms like *bu*/sɪz/.

Testing the hypothesis

We can test this set of rules by running the two parts of the phonological rule in the opposite order, and then noting that this derivation does not yield a good result:

	bus	*rat*	*dog*
	bʌs	ræt	dɔg
Morphological rule:			
A add {plural} /s/:	bʌs+s	ræt+s	dɔg+s
Phonological rules:			
B2 voice /s/ after a voiced sound:	bʌss	ræts	dɔgz
B1 insert /ɪ/ between sibilants:	*bʌsɪs	ræts	dɔgz

Thus we conclude that the order B1 followed by B2 is the correct one for English noun pluralization.

To test this hypothesis further, consider words whose final sounds do not appear in the examples given so far: the words *lathe* and *garage*, for example. *Lathe* ends in /ð/, the voiced counterpart to the sound with which *myth* ends: /θ/. *Garage* (in the pronunciation of some English speakers) ends in the sibilant /ž/, the voiced counterpart to the sound /š/ with which *bush* ends. What does the rule predict for the plural forms for these words, and are these predictions correct?

Since /ž/ is a sibilant and /ð/ is voiced but not a sibilant, application of the rules will yield:

	lathe	*garage*
	leð	gəraž
Morphological rule:		
A add {plural} /s/:	leð+s	gəraž+s
Phonological rules:		
B1 insert /ɪ/ between sibilants:	leðs	gəražɪs
B2 voice /s/ after a voiced sound:	leðz	gəražɪz

These are the right results, further evidence that explaining English noun pluralization with this ordered set of rules is on the right track.

Looking Back, Looking Ahead

From our initial investigations of noun pluralization, first in Armenian (in the introductory chapter) and now in English, we have learned quite a bit. We have seen that in both languages, the morpheme {plural} is realized phonologically on the noun as a suffix: in Armenian, there are two spoken or surface forms, *-ner* and *-er*, while in English there are three (all of them familiar by now). We have come to understand that parsimony, that is, economy of mind and explanation, is achieved by hypothesizing that, for each language, a speaker stores a <u>single</u> underlying form of {plural} from which the surface forms are derived by phonological rules. These hypothesized rules pick out some crucial aspect of the phonology of the singular noun: in Armenian, it is the number of syllables, while in English, it is the distinctive phonological feature(s) of the final sound of the singular noun. The interaction between morphology and phonology exemplified by pluralization in Armenian and English is referred to as **morphophonology**.

As we will see when we turn to Spanish and Brazilian Portuguese later in this chapter, there are other ways to form plural nouns in the languages of the world. But first, before making a brief detour to look at the morphophonology of English past tense formation, we examine what appears to be an interesting set of counterexamples to our hypothesis about English plural nouns.

Problem Set 3: Regular-Irregular Noun Plurals in English

Let us return to a question asked in Problem Set 2: Does your hypothesis explain the pronunciation of all the plural nouns of English? Why or why not?

Clearly, the answer is "No," for there are clear and absolute exceptions which lie outside the general rules for plural noun formation in English: the plural forms of these nouns are simply memorized as an infant or adult develops knowledge of the language; or perhaps we should say that there is a distinctive rule for each of these words or groups of words. The irregular plurals *feet*, *deer*, *children*, *oxen*, and so on are examples of absolute exceptions.

There are also partial exceptions to the rules for the formation of noun plurals. Let us call them the **regular-irregulars**. As this term suggests, there is something about plural formation for these nouns that is irregular, but also something that follows the general rules. Here are some examples of nouns of this type, given in their singular form followed by their plural suffix:

singular	plural suffix
elf, knife, leaf, loaf, shelf, wife, wolf	/z/
bath, mouth, wreath, path	/z/
house	/ɪz/

Note that for some English speakers, one or another of these words may no longer belong to the set of regular-irregulars.

Nevertheless, assume – for the purposes of this problem set – that the data are valid as given here, and answer questions A, B, and C below.

A   What special phonological rule needs to be added to the regular plural noun forma-
    tion rules to account for the irregularity of the plural forms of these nouns? Formulate
    the additional rule and determine its ordering with respect to the regular plural noun
    formation rules. Then demonstrate how your hypothesized rule and its ordering
    explain the data by showing how the plurals of specific examples are derived.
B   In what way are the regular-irregular plural forms regular?
C   Given the assumption that the minds of language learners are as efficient as possible,
    why might the set of regular-irregulars lose members over the course of the English
    language's history?

Before you move on to Problem Set 4, be sure to think through and construct reasoned, convincing answers to A–C.

Problem Set 4: Past Tense Formation in English

And now for something completely different – or maybe not that different, we turn to English past tense formation.

The simple past tense is generally used when we talk about something that has already happened. For example:

Last night, he <u>cried</u> and <u>stomped</u> his feet, and <u>sounded</u> awfully upset.
Yesterday, she <u>jumped</u> up, <u>climbed</u> a tree, and <u>waited</u> at the top.

A   Say these sentences to yourself. Concentrate on how the past tense endings of the
    underlined words sound. Put the underlined words into groups according to the pro-
    nunciation of their past tense suffixes, leaving off the suffixes. Then, using the lin-
    guistic convention of enclosing phonemes in slant marks (/ /), label the groups according
    to the <u>sound</u> of the suffixes.
        The following is a list of some more English verbs:

   walk, rob, kiss, treat, laugh, play, raid, buzz, shove, knead, drag, shout, flip

    Next, form the simple past tense of these verbs and then assign them to the groups
    that you have already made.
B   Fluent speakers of English have no trouble forming the correct past tense of verbs
    like those above. Their knowledge of English enables them to produce, perceive, and
    comprehend the correct past tense forms without hesitation. Suppose we ask the
    following question (paralleling the one that we asked about plural noun formation
    in English): How do speakers of English do this? In other words, in what form do
    speakers of English internalize their knowledge of past tense formation? Consider these
    four (familiar) possibilities:

    Hypothesis I:
    Speakers of English memorize the past tense form for every verb they come across.

    Hypothesis II:
    They learn the past tense on the basis of spelling. For example, they learn that
    verbs that end with the letter *k* form the past tense by suffixing /t/.

Hypothesis III:
They know that the sound with which a verb ends determines the pronunciation of the past tense suffix.

Hypothesis IV:
They know that the distinctive feature(s) of the sound with which a verb ends determines the pronunciation of the past tense suffix.

Explain why Hypotheses I, II, and III should be eliminated from consideration.

C   Formulate the set of rules represented by Hypothesis IV, including the morphological rule that identifies a single underlying form of the morpheme {past}, as well as the phonological rules needed to get from the underlying morpheme to the full set of surface (or spoken) forms.

D   Demonstrate how your hypothesized set of rules for past tense formation explains the data by showing and discussing how specific examples are derived.

E   What forms would counterexamples to your hypothesis have to take? Can you think of other types of counterexamples to your hypothesis?

F   In what way(s) are the rules for forming the simple past tense like the rules for forming plural nouns in English? In what way(s) are they different?

Before you move on to Problem Set 5, be sure to think through and construct reasoned, convincing answers to A–F.

Problem Set 5: Plural Noun Formation in Spanish

Spanish belongs to the Romance group of Indo-European languages. From *Ethnologue: Languages of the World* (2005), we learn that Spanish is spoken in central and southern Spain and the Canary Islands (which is an autonomous community of Spain), as well as in many other places around the world, including: Andorra, Argentina, Aruba, Australia, Belgium, Belize, Bolivia, Canada, Cayman Islands, Chile, Colombia, Costa Rica, Cuba, Dominican Republic, Ecuador, El Salvador, Equatorial Guinea, Finland, France, Germany, Gibraltar, Guatemala, Honduras, Israel, Jamaica, Mexico, Morocco, Netherlands Antilles, Nicaragua, Norway, Panama, Paraguay, Peru, Philippines, Puerto Rico, Sweden, Switzerland, Trinidad and Tobago, US Virgin Islands, Uruguay, the United States, and Venezuela. The language is also referred to as Español, Castellano, and Castilian.

From *Ethnologue: Languages of the World* (2005), we also learn that in 1986 there were 28,173,600 speakers of Spanish in Spain, while the estimated number of speakers in all countries totaled 322,299,171. Another interesting fact is this: Spanish is a second language for 60,000,000 people in the world.

Investigating Spanish Noun Pluralization

Consider Spanish, its general Latin American variety, from the point of view of an English-speaking adult learning Spanish as a second language. This is a thought experiment, in which we want to see if we can predict the problems an English-speaking adult will run into in forming plural nouns in Spanish, assuming interference between the Spanish and the English rule systems.

But first we have to work out the rule (or rules) for forming plural nouns in Spanish. So below, in phonological transcription, are the data sufficient for figuring that out. For these data, note that:

- an acute accent (´) over a vowel indicates that the syllable containing that vowel bears **stress**; that is, the syllable is louder or longer or in some way more prominent than the other syllables in the word;
- Spanish /β/ is a continuant English /b/: [Lips, +voice, +continuant, etc.];
- Spanish /x/ is like an English /k/ made strident and continuant: [Tongue body, –voice, +continuant, +strident, etc.];
- all other symbols used are those given in the distinctive feature matrices in Chapter 2.

It is important to note that <u>none</u> of the given forms is irregular; in other words, <u>all forms are regular</u>.

		singular		plural	
(1)	libro	/líβro/	'book'	/líβros/	'books'
(2)	clase	/kláse/	'class'	/kláses/	'classes'
(3)	mesa	/mésa/	'table'	/mésas/	'tables'
(4)	cebolla	/seβóya/	'onion'	/seβóyas/	'onions'
(5)	mujer	/muxér/	'woman'	/muxéres/	'women'
(6)	papel	/papél/	'paper'	/papéles/	'papers'
(7)	canción	/kansyón/	'song'	/kansyónes/	'songs'
(8)	joven	/xóβen/	'young person'	/xóβenes/	'young people'
(9)	vez	/vés/	'occasion'	/véses/	'occasions'
(10)	interés	/interés/	'interest'	/interéses/	'interests'
(11)	paraguas	/parágwas/	'umbrella'	/parágwas/	'umbrellas'
(12)	tesis	/tésis/	'thesis, theory'	/tésis/	'theses, theories'

A First, identify the surface (or spoken) forms of the morpheme {plural} in Spanish.

B Next, formulate a hypothesis that identifies a <u>single</u> underlying form of the {plural} in Spanish, as well as the phonological rules required to get from the underlying morpheme to the surface forms. Demonstrate how your hypothesized set of rules works by showing and discussing how specific examples are derived.

C Compare and contrast English and Spanish plural noun formation rules. In what ways are the two sets of rules alike? And in what ways do they differ?

D What are the expected consequences of the differences as well as the overlap between the two systems for an English-speaking adult acquiring just this bit of Spanish morphophonology? How might her or his plurals of each of the nouns in the word list be pronounced? (Ignore any problems that might arise for the non-English sounds /x/ and /β/.)

E Now turn the question around: What are the expected consequences of the differences and the overlap between the two systems for a Spanish-speaking adult acquiring the plural noun formation rules of English? How might she or he pronounce the plural forms of typical regular English nouns?

F Would the predicted pronunciation errors objectively impede communication; that is, would speakers of Spanish or English understand second language speakers of their languages? Would the errors subjectively impede communication?

Before you move on to Problem Set 6, be sure to think through and construct reasoned, convincing answers to A–F.

Problem Set 6: Plural Noun Formation in Brazilian Portuguese

Portuguese belongs to the Romance group of the Indo-European family of languages. According to *Ethnologue: Languages of the World* (2005), Portuguese is spoken by slightly more than 177 million people: in Angola, Cape Verde, East Timor, France, Mozambique, Portugal, São Tomé e Principe, and in more than two dozen other countries. But Portuguese is primarily spoken in its Brazilian variety; for over 90 percent (more than 163 million) of its speakers are located in Brazil.

Investigating Brazilian Portuguese Pluralization

Let us now analyze how nouns are pluralized in Brazilian Portuguese.[1] In the following data:

- a tilde (˜) over a vowel indicates that the vowel is [+nasal];
- an acute accent mark (´) over a vowel indicates that the syllable containing that vowel bears stress, and a period (.) divides the words into their syllables;
- all other symbols used are those given in the distinctive feature matrices in Chapter 2.

Note that <u>all forms are regular</u>.

		singular		plural	
(1)	*casa*	/ká.za/	'house'	/ká.zas/	'houses'
(2)	*nó*	/nɔ́/	'knot'	/nɔ́s/	'knots'
(3)	*bebé*	/be.bé/	'baby'	/be.bés/	'babies'
(4)	*mesa*	/mé.za/	'table'	/mé.zas/	'tables'
(5)	*mes*	/més/	'month'	/mé.zis/	'months'
(6)	*acelerador*	/a.se.le.ra.dór/	'accelerator'	/a.se.le.ra.dó.ris/	'accelerators'
(7)	*dólar*	/dó.lar/	'dollar'	/dó.la.ris/	'dollars'
(8)	*país*	/pa.ís/	'country'	/pa.í.zis/	'countries'
(9)	*lus*	/lús/	'light'	/lú.zis/	'lights'
(10)	*lapis*	/lá.pis/	'pencil'	/lá.pis/	'pencils'
(11)	*onibus*	/ó.ni.bus/	'bus'	/ó.ni.bus/	'buses'

A On the basis of patterns that you observe in the data (1–11), formulate a hypothesis that explains plural noun formation in this language. Identify the underlying form of the morpheme {plural} and then formulate the ordered rules required to get from the underlying form of the morpheme to the surface or spoken forms shown above. If you notice any other difference between the singular and plural forms of these nouns, incorporate the rule that explains this difference into your hypothesis.

---

[1] This problem set is based on one that we developed with Filomena Sandolo, a professor at the Universidade de Estadual de Campinas, Brazil, for a course on Linguistics and the Teaching of Science at the 3rd International Linguistics Conference at the Pontífica Universidade Católica do Rio Grande do Sul, Porto Alegre, Brazil, August 19–23, 1996.

The data in section B of the problem set are taken or projected from Scherre (2001) and Cristófaro-Silva, Gomes, Guimarães, and Huback (2005).

Show and discuss the derivation of specific examples to demonstrate how your hypothesized set of ordered rules works.

B   Now let us examine the role of determiners in Brazilian Portuguese NPs (noun phrases). The definite and indefinite determiners in Brazilian Portuguese are these:

	singular				plural			
	masculine		feminine		masculine		feminine	
definite	o	/o/	a	/a/	os	/os/	a	/as/
		'the'		'the'		'the'		'the'
indefinite	ũ	/ũ/	uma	/uma/	ũs	/ũs/	umas	/umas/
		'a, an'		'a, an'		'some'		'some'

For each singular NP in (12–17), the first two plural NPs given are well-formed for many Brazilian Portuguese speakers. The third is not grammatical (as indicated by an asterisk, *).

		singular			plural	
(12)	o aluno	/o aluno/	'the student'		/os alunos/	'the students'
					/os aluno/	'the students'
					/*o alunos/	
(13)	a pimenta	/a pimenta/	'the pepper'		/as pimentas/	'the peppers'
					/as pimenta/	'the peppers'
					/*a pimentas/	
(14)	ũ livro	/ũ livro/	'a book'		/ũs livros/	'some books'
					/ũs livro/	'some books'
					/*ũ livros/	
(15)	uma estrada	/uma estrada/	'a road'		/umas estradas/	'some roads'
					/umas estrada/	'some roads'
					/*uma estradas/	
(16)	a porta aberta	/a porta aberta/	'the open door'		/as portas abertas/	'the open doors'
	the door open					
					/as porta aberta/	'the open doors'
					/*a portas abertas/	
(17)	ũ dia chuvoso	/ũ dia šuvozo/	'a rainy day'		/ũs dias šuvozos/	'some rainy days'
	a day rainy					
					/ũs dia šuvozo/	'some rainy days'
					/*ũ dias šuvozos/	

So here is the question for part B: What principle explains the difference between the grammatical plural NPs given in (12–17) and the ungrammatical ones? What is necessarily present in a plural NP for it to be grammatical in Brazilian Portuguese?

C   Taking into consideration your hypothesis in part A <u>and</u> the conclusions you reached in part B, what problems do you predict for a Brazilian Portuguese-speaking person acquiring English NP pluralization?

Before you move on to Chapter 4, be sure to think through and construct reasoned, convincing answers to A–C.

Terms

distinctive features
underlying form
surface form
morphological rule
phonological rule
sibilants
epenthesis
assimilation
morphophonology
regular-irregulars
stress

Chapter 4

The Acquisition of Morphophonology

As we have seen, a parsimonious explanation of how regular plural nouns are formed in English assumes one underlying form of the the morpheme {plural}, call it /s/, that is attached to the singular noun by a rule of morphology, and two ordered rules of phonology that get us from this underlying morpheme to the full range of plural suffixes that are realized at the surface in speech: /ɪz/, /z/, and /s/.

We continue this discussion of English **morphophonology** – the interaction of morphology and phonology – by first examining the regular-irregular plural nouns of English and then turning to past tense formation in English, which is strikingly parallel to plural noun formation. We then move on to a discussion of first and second language acquisition of English plural noun and past tense morphophonology, as well as to their differential loss in people suffering from Alzheimer's and Parkinson's diseases and two types of aphasia.

Irregular Plural Nouns in English

As long as we pay attention only to the regular plural nouns, the hypothesis formulated in Chapter 3 and the set of rules associated with it will nicely explain plural noun formation. Yet eventually, the hypothesis will appear to fail because there are clear **counterexamples** and exceptions to it – what we might think of either as noise in the system or as linguistic fossils left behind from what English used to be.

Exceptions are of two kinds: absolute and partial. Absolute exceptions lie outside the scope of the hypothesis for regular plural nouns and must simply be memorized by the person developing knowledge of the language. The irregular plurals *children*, *deer*, and *oxen* are examples of absolute exceptions, because they do not follow the general rules of plural formation. Each exception is a rule to itself, with some exceptions (such as *foot : feet*; *goose : geese*;

tooth : teeth) clustering together in groups with a rule that bears no obvious relation to regular noun plural formation.

Then there are partial exceptions – the **regular-irregulars** examined in Problem Set 3: a small set of nouns in which the final /f/, /s/, or /θ/ of the singular is voiced in tandem with adding the morpheme {plural}. A noun's belonging to this set must also be memorized. Note, however, that following the change in voicing, the phonological rules for regular plurals apply. The plurals of *leaf*, *house*, and *bath* are examples of these partial exceptions.[1] We hypothesize that they are to be explained in the following way:

	leaf	*house*	*bath*
	lif	haws	bæθ
Morphological rules:			
A1 add {plural} /s/:	lif+s	haws+s	bæθ+s
A2 voice final sound of singular	liv+s	hawz+s	bæð+s
Phonological rules:			
B1 insert /ɪ/ between sibilants:	livs	hawzɪs	bæðs
B2 voice /s/ after a voiced sound:	livz	hawzɪz	bæðz

In this set of nouns, then, there is double plurality, for the plural is marked not only by the usual suffix, but also by the voicing of the final consonant of the singular form.

The Morphophonology of English Past Tense Formation

The hypothesis for English plural noun formation in Chapter 3 depends on the systematic categorization of the sounds of English, and of language in general. The noun pluralization hypothesis focuses on three categories of sounds: the set of [Tongue blade, +strident] sounds – the sibilants, and the sets of [+voice] and [–voice] sounds that are not themselves sibilants. The hypothesis provides a model for the explanation of the English past tense formation, the focus of Problem Set 4, including the phonological processes in play.

At first glance at the data, we might assume that the pronunciation and form of the regular past tense morpheme is captured by its most common spelling, *-ed*, or /ɪd/ phonemically. But, as with English noun pluralization, the facts are more complicated than this. We can represent this complication as follows: there are three suffixes, /ɪd/, /t/, and /d/, parallel to plural noun formation

---

[1]   Note that in some varieties of English the plural of these words has been fully regularized: the plural of *house* (the only one of its type) being *hou*/sɪz/, with no voicing shift. Note also that the same voicing shift occurs in some of the verbs derived from this set of nouns: the verbs *live*, *house*, and *bathe*, for example.

in English. This gives us the following representations for the past tense forms of some English verbs:

/ɪd/: *sound*/ɪd/, *wait*/ɪd/, *knead*/ɪd/, *shout*/ɪd/, *treat*/ɪd/, *raid*/ɪd/
/t/: *stomp*/t/, *jump*/t/, *kiss*/t/, *flip*/t/, *laugh*/t/
/d/: *crie*/d/, *climb*/d/, *rob*/d/, *buzz*/d/, *shove*/d/

Following the lead of the hypothesis for regular plural nouns, we can now try to formulate a similarly parsimonious hypothesis, one that replaces the list of three past tense suffixes with <u>one</u> underlying morpheme and that reduces the number of rules to a minimum while still explaining all the data.

A parsimonious hypothesis for past tense formation

Assume, as before, that the mind is as efficient as possible in the way in which it stores knowledge and information – Occam's razor at work unconsciously. And adopt the assumption made about plural noun formation that word formation can be broken down into step-by-step, rule-governed processes. Under the first assumption, we hypothesize that a speaker of English will have a <u>single</u> form of the morpheme {past} stored in her or his brain, call it /t/. Under the second assumption, past tense formation has these rules in the following order:

A There is first a rule of English morphology: The {past} /t/ is attached to the end of the simple form of a verb as the first step in forming its past tense form.

B The three forms that the {past} /t/ takes in speech are then explained by two ordered rules of English phonology:

1 If the verb ends in /d/ or /t/, sounds that share the distinctive features [Tongue blade, +anterior, –continuant], then insert /ɪ/ between the final /t/ or /d/ of the verb and {past} /t/ (which is itself [Tongue blade, +anterior, –continuant]).

2 If the sound preceding the {past} /t/ is voiced, voice the /t/ to /d/.

Applying the rules, in the order given, to the three different types of verbs, we derive the following past tense forms:

	treat	*flip*	*rob*
	trit	flɪp	rab
Morphological rule:			
A add {past} /t/:	trit+t	flɪp+t	rab+t
Phonological rules:			
B1 insert /ɪ/ between /t/ or /d/ and /t/:	tritɪt	flɪpt	rabt
B2 voice /t/ after a voiced sound:	tritɪd	flɪpt	rabd

The phonological rules work this way for the same quite natural reasons given for the plural nouns. In some cases in English, a sequence of two sounds that are too much alike has to be broken up by a vowel inserted through **epenthesis**. By the phrase "too much alike," we refer to the fact that the sets of sounds in question belong to the same narrowly defined category. Since in English the {past} /t/ cannot blend with a sound just like itself or a sound belonging to the same category, /t/ and /d/ respectively, the sequences /dt/ and /tt/ are separated by an epenthetic vowel.

The {past} /t/ then assumes, by **assimilation**, the voicing value (+ or −) of the sound immediately preceding it. We say that the voicing of the last sound of the verb spreads to the past tense suffix: the suffix will be /d/ (a voiced sound) if the sound preceding it is voiced, as in *rob*/d/; and it will remain /t/ (a voiceless sound) if the sound preceding it is voiceless, as in *flip*/t/.

Note that since vowels (including the epenthetic vowel /ɪ/ that is inserted between the sequences /dt/ and /tt/) are voiced, the fact that rule B1 precedes rule B2 ensures the correct result for past tense forms like *treat*/ɪd/, *knead*/ɪd/, and so on. Indeed, the hypothesis <u>requires</u> that these rules come in the order given, for note the effect of applying the rules in the opposite order:

	treat	*flip*	*rob*
	trit	flɪp	rab
Morphological rule:			
A add {past} /t/:	trit+t	flɪp+t	rab+t
Phonological rules:			
B2 voice /t/ after a voiced sound:	tritt	flɪpt	rabd
B1 insert /ɪ/ between /t/ or /d/ and /t/:	*tritɪt	flɪpt	rabd

Counterexamples and exceptions

Counterexamples to the hypothesized rules of English past tense formation would have at least one of the following structures:

- verbs ending in /t/ or /d/ that take /t/ or /d/ as their past tense suffixes;
- verbs ending in [+voice] sounds other than /d/ that take /t/ as the past tense suffix;
- verbs ending in [−voice] sounds other than /t/ that take /d/ as their past tense suffix.

Consider the following nonsense words: *mot, flod, spow,* and *rick*. Any one of them would be counterexamples to the rules of past tense formation if their past tense forms were, for example: **mot*/d/, **flod*/d/, **spow*/t/, **rick*/ɪd/, and so on. However, even for these nonsense words, the past tense will be formed according to the rules given above.

Although clarifying the forms that counterexamples to a hypothesis would take is always a good intellectual exercise, the search for them in this case would be futile.

There are, however, absolute exceptions to the hypothesis, which is to say that there are past tense forms in English that lie outside the hypothesis. Absolute exceptions of several types come easily to mind: *sing : sang* (in which there is a vowel change between the simple verb and its past tense form within a fixed consonant framework – /s . . . ŋ/, in this case), and *go : went* (in which the simple verb and its past tense form are entirely unrelated phonologically). A speaker of English commits to memory the fact that these verbs are irregular, along with the idiosyncratic rules for forming their past tense and other irregular forms, such as the participial forms *sung* and *gone*.

As we found for plural formation, there are also partial exceptions, represented by *sleep : slept*, for example. In verbs of this type, the past tense suffix comes out as /t/, as we would expect given that the final sound of *sleep* /p/ is [–voice], but there is also the difference between the vowel of the simple form of the verb and that of the past tense form. Thus, the exceptional nature of this type of partial exception lies in the modification of the vowel and not in the past tense suffix itself. This set of verbs and the special rule that accounts for its irregularity also have to be committed to memory.

A fourth type of irregular verb (*hit : hit*; *put : put*; and so on) represents another way of dealing with the illegal sequence /tt/: by the simplification or reduction of /tt/ to /t/. We return to this type of exception below in the discussion of the acquisition of past tense morphophonology.

The Universality of Voicing Assimilation and Vowel Epenthesis

It must be emphasized that these hypotheses about plural noun and past tense formation in English have to be evaluated both in the context of universal phonology and as part of an overall understanding of a particular language, in this case English.

Thus, we would be pleased to learn that the hypotheses about English plurals and past tense say something about how language works in general. And they do, since one piece of each of the hypothesized sets of rules, **voicing assimilation**, is a very general phonological process in the languages of the world.

Consider, for example, Japanese noun compounds from the *sushi* menu. *Sushi* is the generic name for many types of vinegared-rice dishes, but when this word is compounded with another noun to denote a specific kind of vinegared-rice dish, *sushi* becomes *zushi*, by a process referred to in Japanese as *rendaku* 'sequential voicing'. For example:

(1) *maki + sushi*   becomes   *makizushi*   'vinegared rice and vegetables rolled in seaweed'

(2) *maze + sushi*   becomes   *mazezushi*   'vinegared rice mixed with vegetables and seafood'

Since the first member of each of these compounds ends in a vowel, which is [+voice] by definition, we might assume – correctly – that the /s/ of *sushi* voices to /z/ when immediately preceded by a voiced sound, a clear example of voicing assimilation in Japanese. (For further details – of which there are many, see O'Neil & Honda, 1996.)

Another example of voicing assimilation is found in Brazilian Portuguese noun pluralization. Returning to Problem Set 6, we find these data:

	singular			plural	
(3)	*mes*	/més/	'month'	/mé.zis/	'months'
(4)	*país*	/pa.ís/	'country'	/pa.í.zis/	'countries'
(5)	*lus*	/lús/	'light'	/lú.zis/	'lights'

In cases like these, where the morpheme {plural} is realized phonologically at the surface, the word-final /s/ of the singular noun is separated from the {plural} /s/ by the epenthetic vowel /i/. The word-final /s/ is then surrounded by voiced sounds (in this case vowels) and thus we find that the /s/ voices to /z/.

We would also be pleased to learn that the phonological rules of voicing assimilation and **vowel epenthesis** hypothesized for English plural noun and past tense formation have generality in English. And indeed, they do. Notice, for example, the pronunciation of:

- the possessive morpheme {poss} in English, as in:

  horse's, dog's, and cat's tails – /ɪz/, /z/, and /s/, respectively;

- the 3rd person singular present tense morpheme for regular verbs, as in:

  He fusses, frets, and worries. – /ɪz/, /s/, and /z/, respectively;

- the contraction of *is* /ɪz/ and *has* /hæz/, as in:

  The horse's fast; the horse's won. – /ɪz/
  The dog's angry; the dog's been chased. – /z/
  The cat's furry; the cat's been fed. – /s/;

- the contractions of *did, would,* and *had,* as in:

  What'd he do? – /ɪd/
  Jack'd've done it if we'd asked him to. – /t/, and /d/, respectively.

A detailed consideration of these and other constructions in English would reveal that the phonological rules B1 (insert /ɪ/ between sounds that are "too much alike") and B2 (voicing assimilation) affect a wide variety of word-final, underlying /s/-morphemes and /t/-morphemes in English – perhaps all of them.

Vowel epenthesis, a process whereby sequences of like sounds are broken up by the insertion of a vowel, is also a universal phonological process as well as an English-specific one, occurring quite generally cross-linguistically. Languages will, however, differ with respect to which sounds are considered too much alike. For example, in plural noun formation in Spanish and Brazilian Portuguese, the notion 'too much alike' is defined much more broadly than the sibilants of English pluralization, for vowel epenthesis is required in order to break up any sequence of consonants.

Acquisition and Loss of English Morphophonology

First language acquisition: Plural noun formation

A good deal of research has been done on the child's acquisition of English plural noun and past tense formation, beginning with the classic study by Berko (1958; but also see Pinker, 1995, 1999). Berko developed a relatively straight-forward **elicited production task** for determining whether a child knows the rules of English noun pluralization. She simply showed her subjects (pre-schoolers, aged 4 to 5 years; and first-graders, aged 5;6 to 7 years) a picture of an object and said, "This is a wug." Then she pointed to a picture of a pair of these same objects and elicited the plural by saying:

(6)   "Now, there's another one. There are two of them. There are two —?"

Berko hypothesized that children who knew the rules for plural formation would respond with *wug*/z/. Table 4.1 lists the nonsense words she used and shows some of her results, given as percentages of correct responses. As you

Table 4.1   (percentage correct)

Plural suffix	Word	Preschoolers	First-graders
/s/	*heaf*	79	80
/z/	*wug*	76	97
	lun	68	92
	tor	73	90
	cra	58	86
/ɪz/	*tass*	28	39
	gutch	28	38
	kazh	25	36
	nizz	14	33

can see from this table, children do quite well except in their use of the syllabic plural suffix /ɪz/: children up to the age of seven do not even get close to half of these forms right. What does it mean for them to get the syllabic form of the plural wrong?

Notice, first of all, that it is not immediately obvious that the children are making <u>phonological</u> errors. Indeed, a close examination of Berko's data reveals that almost all of their errors result from using the unchanged forms *tass*, *gutch*, and so on for the plural. That is, they tend not to mark the plural form with a suffix at all. Why might this be so?

Recall the explanation of the syllabic suffix in Chapter 3: by epenthesis, /ɪ/ is inserted between a word-final sibilant and the {plural} /s/, which itself is a sibilant. The insertion of /ɪ/, a vowel, creates the syllabic plural suffix, which following voicing assimilation becomes /ɪz/. If we look further afield in the world's languages – beyond standard English, we find that one widely used way to resolve the sibilant + /s/ sequence is by simplifying the sequence of sibilants. This is done by simply deleting the /s/. This may be what the children in Berko's experiment are doing in their pronunciation. That is, it could be that they are sometimes deleting the {plural} /s/ when it follows a sibilant at the end of a word (*tass*, *gutch*, etc.). Given the structure of Berko's interview, a form without a plural suffix offers no objective interpretive difficulty since the probe (or interview question) for plural forms is always preceded by a cardinal number (like *two*) that indicates plurality. In this respect, it is interesting to note that Berko found that nearly all errors for the nonsyllabic plurals also involved omitting the plural suffix /s/ or /z/. This fact supports our view that omitting the suffix is due to the pluralizing presence of cardinal numbers in the probe.

Nevertheless, because of the high percentage of correct responses for non-syllabic plurals, we assume that the children know that the plural morpheme is /s/, which is then realized phonologically in different ways according to the final sound of the singular noun. Furthermore, in some varieties of English (as we shall see), plural suffixes are used as a last resort. Indeed, many languages of the world work this way. Since this is another way languages of the world mark (or do not mark) noun plurality, we assume that this is an option within **Universal Grammar** (UG). Children acquiring English – like children everywhere – have a range of UG-compatible options available to them that they narrow on the basis of the positive evidence they get from their linguistic environment.

In conducting this research in the late 1950s, Berko worked within the then prevailing language development framework, in which it was assumed that what children say reveals the full extent of their knowledge of language. What we have since learned about language acquisition highlights the <u>difference</u> between children's ability to produce their native language and their ability to perceive and comprehend it. Thus, in evaluating Berko's research findings, we now question her conclusion that the children's responses reveal <u>everything</u>

they know about English plural formation. We wonder whether the results are due instead to the limitations of the elicited production task.

To test this idea, run through the following thought experiment: Imagine a situation in which there are a number of dishes sitting on a table, some of which are blue. Then say to one of Berko's subjects, "Give me the blue dish." Our intuition is that the child, even one who produces *gutch* as the plural of *gutch*, would respond with something like, "Which one?" On the other hand, if you had said, "Give me the blue dishes," our hunch is that the child would respond appropriately by gathering up all the blue dishes for you. If our intuitions were borne out, then we would have to reconcile this evidence about how the child responds in a comprehension task with what the child says in Berko's production task.

Finally, we should ask a more general question about the percentages of correct responses given in Table 4.1: What does it mean for a child (or a set of children) to get something partly right, partly wrong? And what are we to compare these child percentages to?

Assuming that a person with full knowledge of English (an adult, say) would be near perfect on this task, the fact that the child does not match adult perfection can mean only one of two things: either that the child does not know how to form plurals in English, or that Berko's experiment is not designed to reveal fully what the child knows. We strongly believe that the latter is the case.

First language acquisition: Past tense formation

As part of her experiment to determine whether a child knows certain rules of English morphology, Berko also investigated some verbal forms in children's speech, past tense forms among them. This part of her work is subject to the same criticism given in the previous section.

In the experiment, Berko showed her subjects (the same preschoolers, aged 4–5 years, and first-graders, aged 5;6 to 7 years) a picture of some activity or event, and then attempted to elicit a past tense form by reading aloud the text printed below the picture:

(7) Picture: Man with a steaming pitcher on his head.
    Probe: "This is a man who knows how to spow. He is spowing. He did the same thing yesterday. What did he do yesterday? Yesterday he —."

And so on for the other nonsense words *rick*, *bing*, *gling*, *mot*, and *bod*, and for the real word *ring*. However, for *melt*, the other real word that was probed, the text was quite different:

(8) Picture: An ice cube, then a puddle of water.
    Probe: "This is an ice cube. Ice melts. It is melting. Now it is all gone. What happened to it? It —."

Table 4.2   (percentage correct)

Past tense suffix	Word	Preschoolers	First-graders
/t/	*rick*	73	73
/d/	*spow*	36	59
	bing	60	85
	gling	63	80
/ɪd/	*melt*	72	74
	mot	32	33
	bod	14	31
/ɪ/ → /æ/	*ring*	0	25

Berko hypothesized that children who knew the rules for past tense formation would respond with *spow*/d/, *rick*/t/, *melt*/ɪd/, and so on.

Table 4.2 shows her results, given as percentages of correct responses. As you can see from this table, children do quite well on the past tense suffixes /t/ and /d/ and on the syllabic /ɪd/ for the real verb *melt*. Their performance is worst for the syllabic suffix /ɪd/ with nonsense words and for the irregular *rang* for which they used either *ring* or *ring*/d/. Thus, from the point of view of the adult grammar, children up to the age of seven are correctly producing only a third or less of the forms for *mot*, *bod*, and *ring*.[2]

Again we can ask what it means for the children to get forms of the past tense wrong. Other than their often using past-progressive forms like *was spowing*, for example, nearly all of the children's errors were due to their answering the questions with the simple forms *rick*, *spow*, *bing*, *gling*, *melt*, *mot*, *bod*, and *ring*. That is, often they simply did not mark the past tense forms with a suffix at all. Remember, as noted above in our discussion of exceptions to the past tense rules, that for verbs whose last sound is /d/ or /t/, there is another way in English to resolve the sequence word-final /t/ or /d/ + {past} /t/: simplify the sequence, as in *hit* (/hɪtt/ → /hɪt/), *put* (/pʊtt/ → /pʊt/), and so on. This may be what the children in Berko's experiment did, most often deleting the {past} /t/ when it followed a /t/ or /d/ at the end of a nonsense word.

Given the structure of Berko's interview, using forms without a past tense suffix causes no difficulty for interpretation since the probe (or interview question) for past tense forms is – except for *melt* – always preceded by the adverbial *yesterday*, which in itself indicates pastness.

Because of the high percentage of correct responses for nonsyllabic past tense forms, we assume that the children know that the morpheme {past} is

---

[2]   Notice that the percentages correct for *spow* are much lower than for the other words that end in a [+voice] sound. In addition to the correct *spow*/d/, the children answered with the following: *spow*/zd/ (retaining the present tense suffix /z/ followed by past tense suffix /d/); *was spowing* (the past-progressive form); or simply *spow*. "No child supplied a /-t/", however (Berko, 1958, p. 165).

abstractly /t/ and that there is a rule that voices /t/ to /d/ when the {past} is attached to a verb ending in a [+voice] sound. Interestingly, Berko found that nearly all errors for the nonsyllabic past tense forms involved omitting the suffix /t/ or /d/. We believe that this is also due to the presence of the word *yesterday* in the interview, which allows for this optional omission of the past tense suffix.

How to explain the children's quite different performance on the real word *melt*? The point that Berko would like to make about their performance on this item (as good as that for *rick*) is that the children's knowledge of the correct adult form *melted* had not yet generalized to the formation of new words. But the fact that she changed the question asked of the children for this one word, leaving out the word *yesterday*, opens up the possibility that children will form the past tense correctly when indication of the pastness of a sentence is not clearly contained in the probe sentence. That is, they may vary between *melt* and *melted*, using *melted* when the sentence contains no other indication of its intended pastness.

It is interesting to note that in many varieties of English, past tense forms are used only if pastness is not indicated in some other way in the expression. Speakers of these varieties of English would thus say and not say, when referring to a past event:

(9)   *Yesterday I call my sister.*
(10) **Yesterday I called my sister.*
(11) *I called my sister.*

Indeed, many languages of the world work this way. Since this is another way languages mark (or do not mark) pastness, we assume that this is among the options in Universal Grammar (UG). Children acquiring English might initially choose this UG-compatible option and later reject it on the basis of the positive evidence that they get from the linguistic environment.

To repeat a point we made earlier, in conducting this research in the late 1950s, Berko worked within the then dominant language-development framework which assumed that what children say reveals the full extent of their knowledge of language. What we have since learned about first language acquisition highlights the <u>difference</u> between children's ability to produce forms and their ability to perceive and comprehend them. This is clearly illustrated by examining children's errors of **overgeneralization** (where a rule is incorrectly generalized to other, often irregular, forms), and their understanding of the corresponding correct forms. For example, preschool children spontaneously produce past tense forms such as those in the following sentences:

(12) *Mommy go/d/ to work.*
      We come/d/ home.
      It [the block] fall/d/ down.

Here the past tense rule has been generalized to irregular verbs. Yet children who produce such errors clearly comprehend the correct, adult forms. For example, in a well-known conversation repeatedly reported in the child language literature, Berko tried and failed to correct a four-year-old girl who said, "My teacher hold/id/ the baby rabbits and we patted them."

(13)   JB: *Did you say your teacher held the baby rabbits?*
       Girl: *Yes.*
       JB: *What did you say she did?*
       Girl: *She hold/ɪd/ the baby rabbits and we patted them.*
       JB: *Did you say she held them tightly?*
       Girl: *No, she hold/ɪd/ them loosely.*

Clearly, this child understood and responded to the meaning (though not the intention) of Berko's questions. This case highlights an important point about development: If we were to focus solely on the child's productive linguistic ability, we would underestimate her or his actual knowledge of English.

Although there is much more to say about this matter and about the apparent distinction between what the child knows and what the child produces, we leave this topic for now.

Second language acquisition: Plural noun formation

Consider the following: Having come to a hypothesis about plural formation in English, we might want to see if it (or something similar) is at work in other languages. With this in mind, let's look at Spanish, the focus of Problem Set 5 – its general Latin American variety, examining it from the point of view of an English-speaking adult learning Spanish as a second language – another thought experiment. Can we predict the problems an adult is likely to run into in trying to form plural nouns in Spanish if she or he follows the English rules?

But first the relevant facts about the Spanish sound system and noun pluralization:

- Spanish does not have the phoneme /z/; there is no distinctive /s/ : /z/ voicing contrast.
- In Spanish, plurals are formed by adding /s/ to nouns that end in a vowel.[3]
- /es/ is added elsewhere – that is, if the noun ends in a consonant (except for words whose final /s/ ends an unstressed syllable: for example, the plural of *paraguas* 'umbrella' is *paraguas*).

---

[3]   In many varieties of Latin American Spanish, final /s/ is realized as /h/.

We explain these facts about Spanish noun pluralization by hypothesizing that there is one form of the morpheme {plural} stored in the Spanish speaker's mind, call it /s/, and that there are the following rules that get from this underlying form to the full range of regular plural forms in speech:

A   There is first a rule of Spanish morphology: The {plural} /s/ is attached to the end of the singular form of a noun as the first step in the formation of the plural form.
B   The three phonological forms that the plural morpheme take (/s/, /es/, /Ø/) are then explained by two ordered rules of Spanish phonology:

   1   If the singular noun ends in /s/ and the final syllable of the singular does not bear stress, simplify /ss/ to /s/.
   2   If the sound preceding the {plural} /s/ is [+consonantal], epenthesize /e/ between that sound and /s/ (which is itself [+consonantal]).

   Applying the rules, in the order given, to the four different types of nouns, we get:

		mesa	*papel*	*tesis*	*interés*
		mésa	papél	tésis	interés
Morphological rule:					
A	add /s/:	mésa+s	papél+s	tésis+s	interés+s
Phonological rules:					
B1	if final syllable is unstressed, simplify /ss/ to /s/:	mésas	papéls	tésis	interéss
B2	insert /e/ between [+consonantal] sounds:	mésas	papéles	tésis	interéses

   Given this information about Spanish pluralization, we would likely conclude that English-speaking adults learning Spanish would form plurals like those illustrated below:

/*líβroz/	instead of	/líβros/	for the plural of	*libro*	'book'
/*seβóyaz/	instead of	/seβóyas/	for the plural of	*cebolla*	'onion'
/*muxérz/	instead of	/muxéres/	for the plural of	*mujer*	'woman'
/*vésɪz/	instead of	/véses/	for the plural of	*vez*	'occasion'

These ungrammatical forms wouldn't be too far off, because only errors of the type /*muxérz/ would be wide of the mark to a native speaker of Spanish. Moreover, this type of error is one that the language learner would probably quickly correct on the basis of further evidence, and for a quite simple reason. In Spanish, the suffix /es/ is added to nearly all words that end in a consonant sound; in English, the suffix /ɪz/ is added only to words that end in consonant sounds belonging to the category we informally call sibilants. Thus, the condition under which Spanish nouns are pluralized by adding the syllable /es/ is a rather simple extension of the condition under which English nouns are pluralized by adding the syllable /ɪz/. It is not a big step, nor a difficult one, to get from the restricted English rule B1 (insert /ɪ/ between sibilants) to the more general Spanish rule B2 (insert /e/ between consonants).

Moreover, using /s/ instead of /z/ to mark the plural is only minimally different from what goes on in English; for as we have seen, the difference between /s/ and /z/ is itself a minimal one, involving only the feature [voice]. Thus, although an English speaker developing knowledge of Spanish as a second language may continue to make an inappropriate /s/ – /z/ distinction in her or his Spanish pronunciation, it has to be admitted that this is a trivial error. In fact, this error is characteristic of the pronunciation of nonnative speakers who come to Spanish from English.

Still – as with the evidence from Berko (1958), we want to know what this production error tells us about English speakers' knowledge of Spanish. Are English speakers of Spanish as a second language able to correctly perceive the plural suffix of *clases* and *mesas*, say, as /s/ even though they do not produce /s/ in forms like these? Interestingly, nonnative speakers of a language often know that the pronunciation of their second language is imperfect, so they may know perceptually the very things that from their actions (their speech production) they appear not to know.

Now, consider the question from the opposite point of view: What difficulties will native speakers of Spanish have when they are developing knowledge of English noun plural formation? What do you predict their pronunciations of English plural forms will be? Why, as is widely observed, might they use the syllabic plural /ɪz/ too generally?

And looking beyond Spanish, consider what you have learned from Problem Set 6 about noun phrase (NP) pluralization in Brazilian Portuguese. What difficulties do you predict native speakers of Brazilian Portuguese will have acquiring English NP pluralization?

Second language acquisition: Past tense formation

The cross-linguistic analysis of noun pluralization in English, Spanish, and Brazilian Portuguese has allowed us to think through the challenges of forming plural nouns for second language learners moving from one language to the other. There are many other points of difference between languages that may interfere with the acquisition and production of a second language.

Let us turn to English past tense formation and its acquisition by second language learners. The way in which the regular past tense is formed in English could be quite a challenge for second language learners, depending on their first language. For example, the fact that Spanish does not allow more than one consonant at the end of a syllable has clear consequences for Spanish speakers acquiring this piece of English morphophonology. Consider why this is so.

Assume the following universal structure for the syllable:

(14)

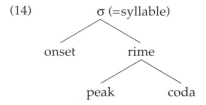

Syllable **peaks** are generally vowels, while **onsets** and **codas** are generally consonants. The only requirement of a syllable is that its **rime** have a peak. Onsets and codas are optional; for example, the lone vowel /a/ of the English word /a.lɪv/ *olive* is a syllable.

Languages differ in how this universal syllable structure is filled out. In Japanese, for example, there can only be a single consonant in the onset of the syllable and only a nasal consonant in the coda; the family name *Honda* /hɔn.da/ illustrates this. In contrast, both onsets and codas in English can be quite complex, as we see in a word like *strengths*, with its three-consonant onset, single-vowel peak, and three-consonant coda: /strɛŋθs/!

In Spanish, we find more syllable complexity than in Japanese but not as much as in English. Thus, beside null and single-consonant onsets, Spanish allows **consonant clusters** of a very restricted sort: two-segment onsets consisting of a consonant followed by the glides /y/ or /w/, or a consonant followed by the liquids /r/ or /l/. These two-segment onsets appear at the beginning of the words given below. (Recall that by linguistic convention, a period marks a syllable boundary.)

/b/ + liquids or
    + /w/ glide: *blanco* /blan.ko/ *bravo*   /bra.vo/   *bueno* /bwe.no/
/k/ + liquids or
    + /w/ glide: *claro*   /kla.ro/   *cruz*   /krus/   *cuerpo* /kwer.po/
/f/ + liquids or
    + /w/ glide: *flor*   /flor/   *frijol*   /fri.xol/   *fuerte* /fwer.te/
/p/ + liquids or
    + /w/ glide: *plato*   /pla.to/   *pronto*   /pron.to/ *puerta* /pwer.ta/
/m/ + /w/ or
    /y/ glide: *muerte* /mwer.te/ *miércoles* /myer.ko.les/

A Spanish syllable need not contain a coda, as we see from the data above. Consider, for example, the structure of the first syllables of *claro* and *frijol* and the last syllable of *cuerpo*: /kla./, /fri./, and /.po/, respectively:

(15)

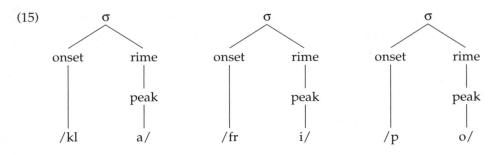

Or the coda of a Spanish syllable may consist of a single consonant, as illustrated below by the structure of the first syllables of *blanco* and *cuerpo* and the last syllable of *frijoles*: /blan./, /kwer./, and /.les/, respectively:

(16)

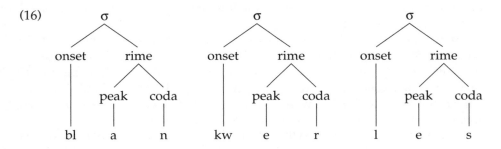

Given these facts about Spanish syllable structure, we might expect that native speakers of Spanish would have difficulty with English past tense forms whose codas consisted of two consonants, *dragged* /drægd/ and *flipped* /flɪpt/ – for example. And, in fact, they do: The ill-formed **drag*/ɪd/ and **flip*/ɪd/ are found alongside the well-formed *wait*/ɪd/ and *sound*/ɪd/ in their speech. In fact, for Spanish-speaking adults who are quite fluent in English, the use of the syllabic form of the past tense morpheme following <u>all</u> consonant-final verbs generally stabilizes.

The past tense complexities of English are quite daunting in another way. For example, there is a complexity of tense formation in English noted above that we have ignored until now. This is the fact that there is an alternative way of indicating tense in English that uses the forms of *do* in negating, questioning, or strongly affirming a statement, for example:[4]

---

[4]   It is also possible to tie tense entirely to the forms of *do* – *do* or *does* for the present tense; *did* for the past tense. Present and past tense are then expressed as follows, with no emphasis on *does* or *did*:

(i)   *Emma does work late every evening.*
(ii)   *Emma did work late last night.*

In Caribbean English, this is the form that present and past tense take.

(17) *Emma doesn't admire Alex.*   but not
      *Emma not admires Alex.

(18) *Who did Emma admire?*   but not
      *Who Emma admired?

(19) *Emma <u>does</u> admire Alex!*   as well as
      Emma <u>admires</u> Alex!

In the face of this added complexity of English past tense formation, people acquiring English as a second language will often use the simpler progressive forms to express tense, or ignore the construction altogether, letting the adverbs carry the weight of tense, for example:

(20) **Emma is/was knowing the answer.*
(21) **Emma work late yesterday.*

Finally, difficulties will arise for people acquiring the regular past tense in English when they come from languages in which tense is not marked morphologically, that is, by adding a morpheme to a verb. This is the case for Chinese, for example:

(22) *ta   kàn yìben shu   le*
      she/he read one   book now
      'She/he is reading a book now.'

(23) *zuótian   ta   tiào   zài chuáng shang*
      yesterday she/he jump at bed   on
      'Yesterday she/he jumped into bed.'

Thus, we expect that Chinese speakers acquiring English would have difficulty – at least initially – with marking tense morphologically.

First language loss of past tense formation

Support for distinguishing between regular, rule-governed past tense forms and irregular, memorized past tense forms comes from research on the nature of language impairment brought about by brain lesions and by familiar diseases. Research by Ullman et al. (1997) seems to demonstrate quite striking differences between the effect of different neurological diseases. Thus, **Alzheimer's disease**, which is associated with word-finding deficits, results in loss of <u>irregular</u> past tense forms. A person suffering from Alzheimer's will, for example, have great difficulty retrieving *sang*, the irregular past tense form of *sing*, from memory, but will exhibit little difficulty following the rule that leads to *walk*/t/, the regular past tense form of *walk*.

On the other hand, **Parkinson's disease**, which is associated with the degeneration of a variety of procedural skills, results in difficulty accessing the rules that account for <u>regular</u> forms. For people afflicted with Parkinson's disease, memory is not impaired, but rule-following is. Thus a person with Parkinson's will have no difficulty retrieving the irregular past tense form *sang* from memory, but will be unable to follow the rule that leads to the regular past tense form *walk*/t/. Presumably, the same difficulties would emerge for Ullman et al.'s subjects were they to be tested for their ability to form the plurals of regular and irregular nouns.

Next consider aphasia. **Aphasia** is a term used to refer to a family of symptoms involving language impairment that results from damage to the brain. Research on two forms of aphasia – **agrammatic** and **anomic** – yields findings quite similar to those for Alzheimer's and Parkinson's diseases (further work by Ullman et al. – summarized in Pinker, 1999, pp. 248–259). Anomics have trouble with word retrieval, while agrammatics find it difficult to produce well-formed words. Thus, anomics have the same difficulty as people with Alzheimer's; they are able to follow the rules to produce regular forms, but unable to retrieve the irregular past tense forms. Agrammatics, in contrast, have the same difficulty forming words as people with Parkinson's disease; that is, agrammatics can generally call up from memory an irregular past tense form, but have difficulty forming the regular ones.

Another thought experiment: What would be the likely result of running Ullman et al.'s subjects through Berko's *wug* and *spow* production tasks?

Modeling Language Acquisition

An infant is surrounded by language at least from birth, though there is strong evidence that significant experience with **prosody**, the rhythmic nature of the ambient language, begins *in utero* (for discussion of the evidence, see Jusczyk, 1997). Experience with the language in its environment quickly gives rise to the infant's knowledge of that language, with its motor control of the organs of speech developing a good deal later than its conceptual and perceptual control of language. The world over, infants pass through universal stages of language development and they acquire mature knowledge that is surprisingly uniform within a language community, despite variations in their experience with the language. We assume that the universality and uniformity of language development must be due to an innate human capacity. On this view, we model the growth of the infant's developing knowledge of language as follows, where **UG** stands for **Universal Grammar**, the capacity to acquire language, and **PG** for **Particular Grammar**:

Experience in a language → UG → PG of that language

That is, on the basis of the interaction between UG and the **positive evidence** about the language (or languages) in its experience, knowledge of the PG of that language (or those languages) <u>grows</u> in the infant – without caregivers paying much attention except at the very earliest stages. The infant will develop mature knowledge of the structure of that language by the age of four or five years: an amazing feat.

The infant's knowledge develops very early on in its existence in a UG-consistent way, but this knowledge is only imperfectly reflected in the infant's speech – a fact that we infer from Berko's work and that of others. Thus, in order to truly understand what an infant knows, it is necessary to carry out noninvasive experiments of the sort done by Werker (1995), for example, on phonetic perception. As we see in current research on child language acquisition, if one is clever enough in devising such experiments, infants seem to know all there is to know about their native languages as early as it is reasonable to experiment with them. Moreover, they get their knowledge on the basis of little or no experience from their linguistic environment. Indeed, Werker and her colleagues have shown that infants are born "universal listeners," sensitive not only to phonetic differences in the language they are exposed to, but also to phonetic differences in languages they have <u>never</u> been exposed to.

When we turn to a consideration of the development of second languages by people older than about five or six years of age, we must immediately acknowledge that both children and adults (as distinct from infants) already know a language;[5] that is, they have knowledge of a particular grammar (PG). Beyond this important similarity, the chief differences between a child getting a second language and an adult are perhaps these: The child's brain exhibits more plasticity and the child has more time for the task. Other than these matters, which may be big "others," children and adults are more or less equals; <u>both</u> have Universal Grammar (UG). Logically, UG is available to them if only because they have a UG-compatible PG.

The question, then, is how to model second language development. On the view just stated, we could say that there is no difference between a child or an adult getting a second language and an infant getting its native language:

Model 1:
Experience with L2 → UG → PG2

Model 1 predicts that the grammar of the second language would be acquired perfectly.

Alternatively, we could factor the language learner's first language knowledge into the model:

---

[5]   Note that we are making a two-way distinction here: between infants and children/ adults.

Model 2:
Experience with L2 → UG - PG1 → PG2

In the case of Model 2, we would have to determine to what extent PG1, or knowledge of the first language, interferes with the course of acquisition and thereby influences the PG2 that is acquired. The idea here is that PG1 may subtract from UG, making some aspects of UG unavailable for the acquisition of a second language. If this were true, then the grammar of the second language would likely be imperfectly acquired.

Another suggestion is that <u>only</u> knowledge of the first language is available for getting a second language: UG itself – having been "spent" getting a first language – is no longer directly available:

Model 3:
Experience with L2 → PG1 → PG2

Model 3 predicts that the language learner would overlay her or his PG1 on the L2 experience and that PG2 would be imperfect in every way: syntactically, morphologically, and phonologically.

In addition to the **interference** of PG1 suggested by Model 2 and Model 3, another source of interference that is often invoked in discussions of L2 acquisition is that of a **critical period** for language acquisition: There is a window of opportunity for the perfect acquisition of a first language and the closing of that first language window prevents the perfect acquisition of a second language. This view is compatible with Model 2 and Model 3, both of which predict imperfect acquisition of PG2. Moreover, given that language is modular, there could be different critical periods within phonology, morphology, and syntax that influence the subtractive effect of PG1 on UG in Model 2.

Finally, still another possible model suggests that second languages are acquired, at least by adults, in an entirely different way: through general problem-solving strategies, which we will simply signify by *X*:

Model 4:
Experience with L2 → X → XG

Model 4 predicts that L2 knowledge develops without the constraints of UG or of PG1 (itself constrained by UG). This could lead to an L2 grammar, XG, that is not a possible human language. There is little evidence to support Model 4. There is, moreover, no substance to the notion 'general problem-solving strategies'; for human beings like other organisms in the natural world are designed to be particular problem solvers, and not general problem solvers.

Looking Ahead

In our discussion of second language acquisition of English plural and past tense forms, we have seen that the acquisition of L2 phonology is not perfect – at least not on the pronunciation side of phonology. There seems always to be L1 interference.

However, in order to complete the picture it would be necessary to know more about the child or adult language learner's phonological <u>perception</u> of the L2. Research on very fine-graded phonological differences between languages in Spanish-Catalan bilingual communities in Spain (Pallier et al., 1997) reveals that fluent bilinguals do not have the perceptions in their L2 that L1 speakers of the languages have. For example, in Catalan, /o/ and /e/ are distinguished from /ɔ/ and /ɛ/ by the phonological feature [ATR]; the former pair being [+ATR], the latter [–ATR]. In Spanish, [ATR] is not used to distinguish between vowels; Spanish has only /o/ and /e/. As a consequence of this difference between the two languages, Spanish-Catalan bilingual adults whose L1 is Spanish and who began acquiring Catalan at about five years of age are <u>not</u> able to perceive the difference between /o/ and /ɔ/ or between /e/ and /ɛ/. Thus, they cannot reliably distinguish between the Catalan words /te/ 'take' and /tɛ/ 'tea', and between /pera/ 'Peter' and /pɛra/ 'pear', treating each pair instead as homophones. Apparently, the UG available to these L2 acquirers of Catalan has been diminished by the loss of [ATR] as a distinctive feature because [ATR] is not active in Spanish, their L1. This L2 imperfection follows directly from Model 2.

However, if we were to look at less subtle differences between an L1 and an L2, would there always be a little voice inside the mind of L2 speakers of a language telling them that what they are saying is not exactly right? And how does the little voice know <u>that</u>?

We return to a more detailed discussion of these matters in Chapters 12 and 14.

Terms

morphophonology
counterexamples
regular-irregulars
epenthesis
assimilation
voicing assimilation
vowel epenthesis
elicited production task
Universal Grammar, UG
overgeneralization
syllable, σ

coda
rime
consonant cluster
Alzheimer's disease
Parkinson's disease
aphasia
agrammatic
anomic
prosody
particular grammar, PG
positive evidence

peak   interference
onset   critical period

Further Reading

A good deal of research has been done to investigate the role of a language learner's PG1 (or native language knowledge) in acquiring a second language (L2). Much of this research – which tests models of L2 acquisition – has focused on phonology. For an in-depth discussion of studies of L2 acquisition of phonological stress and what is called the Rhythm Rule in English, see O'Neil (1998b). In this paper, O'Neil analyzes what the results of a variety of studies show about the interaction between UG and PG1 in L2 acquisition. For a discussion of the role of distinctive features in the acquisition of L2 phonology, see Brown (2000).

For an overview of L1 and L2 acquisition in the context of the movement to revitalize dying languages, see Honda and O'Neil (2004).

For an excellent and accessible discussion of L1 acquisition, see Yang's (2006) *The Infinite Gift*. For a detailed summary of L1 acquisition of phonology and further references, see chapter 2 of Guasti's (2002) *Language Acquisition: The Growth of Grammar*.

Pinker's (1999) *Words and Rules: The Ingredients of Language* is a lively exploration of regular and irregular verbs.

Chapter 5

Noun Pluralization: Morphology Meets Syntax and Meaning

Our analyses of noun pluralization have thus far revealed the interaction between two modules of mental grammar: morphology and phonology. The morpheme {plural} can be realized phonologically on the noun as a suffix, as in Armenian and English, and it can be realized phonologically on other elements of the noun phrase (NP), as in Spanish and Brazilian Portuguese. In each of these languages, there is more than one spoken or surface form of {plural}. With parsimony, or economy of mind and explanation, as our goal, we hypothesize then that for each of these languages there is an underlying phonological form of the morpheme {plural} from which the surface forms are derived by phonological rules. The phonological rules pick out a particular aspect of the phonology of the singular noun: the number of syllables, the position of stress, or the distinctive features of the word-final sound. On this view, a speaker of one of these languages efficiently (though unconsciously) stores in her or his mind morphophonological rules for forming plural nouns, not lists of nouns and their plural forms. Importantly, the rules of mental grammar are productive; they enable the speaker to pluralize newly acquired or newly created nouns.

In this chapter, we explore further the variety of ways that nouns are pluralized – in varieties of English.

Noun Pluralization in Varieties of English

English is a member of the Germanic group of the Indo-European language family. Worldwide, nearly 400 million people speak English as a first language and about 200 million others speak it as a second language (*Ethnologue: Languages of the World*, 2005).

In *Ethnologue: Languages of the World* (2005), English is listed first of all as "A language of the United Kingdom," which in one form or another is also spoken in the following countries and territories: "American Samoa, Andorra, Anguilla, Antigua and Barbuda, Aruba, Australia, Bahamas, Barbados, Belize, Bermuda, Botswana, British Indian Ocean Territory, British Virgin Islands, Brunei, Cambodia, Cameroon, Canada, Cayman Islands, China, Cook Islands, Denmark, Dominica, Dominican Republic, Ecuador, Eritrea, Ethiopia, Falkland Islands, Fiji, Finland, Gambia, Germany, Ghana, Gibraltar, Greece, Grenada, Guadeloupe, Guam, Guyana, Honduras, India, Ireland, Israel, Italy, Jamaica, Japan, Kenya, Kiribati, South Korea, Lebanon, Lesotho, Liberia, Malawi, Malaysia (Peninsular), Malta, Marshall Islands, Mauritius, Mexico, Micronesia, Montserrat, Namibia, Nauru, Netherlands Antilles, New Zealand, Nigeria, Niue, Norfolk Island, Northern Mariana Islands, Norway, Pakistan, Palau, Papua New Guinea, Philippines, Pitcairn, Puerto Rico, Rwanda, Saint Helena, Saint Kitts and Nevis, Saint Lucia, Saint Pierre and Miquelon, Saint Vincent and the Grenadines, Samoa, Saudi Arabia, Seychelles, Sierra Leone, Singapore, Solomon Islands, Somalia, South Africa, Sri Lanka, Suriname, Swaziland, Switzerland, Tanzania, Tokelau, Tonga, Trinidad and Tobago, Turks and Caicos Islands, U.S. Virgin Islands, Uganda, United Arab Emirates, USA, Vanuatu, Venezuela, Zambia, Zimbabwe."

The varieties of English spoken throughout the world have a great deal in common, but there are also quite striking differences. It is these differences among Englishes that most often intrigue us rather than the many properties they have in common.

Consider, for example, one way in which plural nouns may be differently formed in different varieties of English: A number of years ago, we were in San Diego driving along with a family friend, Mr. Kobayashi. We came to an intersection where we would have turned right in order to get from where we were to where we wanted to be, but Mr. Kobayashi turned left instead. When we asked whether the other way wasn't shorter, Mr. Kobayashi said it was, but that there was "too much stoplight that way."

What explains Mr. Kobayashi's phrase "too much stoplight"? Here are two hypotheses:

Hypothesis I:
In this variety of English, the set of stoplights is expressed as a **mass noun**, like milk or money, for example: "There is too much milk in my glass, but never too much money in my bank account, and far too much stoplight that way."

Hypothesis II:
In this variety of English, the concepts 'many' for **countable nouns** and 'much' for mass nouns are expressed with the single word *much*, a UG-compatible possibility in human languages (as exemplified by Mandarin Chinese *duo* 'much, many'). The word *much* is interpreted as 'many' when it is used with countable nouns; as 'much' when it is used with mass nouns. Since the word *much* labels the plural concept 'many' for countable nouns, there is no need

to mark the noun itself with the plural ending. The label *much*, meaning 'many', is sufficient to indicate plurality.

In order to decide between these competing hypotheses, or to come up with a different hypothesis, we would have to carry out a much more extensive investigation than this one example allows. The little investigation that we have done suggests that Hypothesis II is on the right track.

More interesting than Mr. Kobayashi's "too much stoplight," since the data are more readily available and since there is an apparent solution to the problem, is noun pluralization in another variety of English, Nicaraguan English (Honda and O'Neil, 1987; O'Neil, 1993). We now turn our attention to investigating noun pluralization in this variety of English.

Problem Set 7: Plural Noun Formation in Nicaraguan English

Nicaraguan English is spoken by the thirty thousand or so descendants of the Afro-Caribbeans who – in the eighteenth century – were enslaved on the Caribbean coast of Central America when it formed the westernmost edge of the British Caribbean empire, and by the indigenous Rama Indians and the transported Carib peoples, who have largely lost their languages in favor of Nicaraguan English. The language, alternatively called Miskito Coast Creole English (Holm, 1978), is also widely spoken among the indigenous Miskitu Indians in the urban areas on the Caribbean side of Nicaragua.

Investigating Nicaraguan English Noun Pluralization

In Nicaraguan English – which is similar to the Englishes spoken widely in the Caribbean area, plurality for nouns can be marked in pronunciation by the suffix *-dem* /dɛm/, a suffix historically related to and derived from the 3rd person plural pronoun *them*.[1] Note the following examples:

(1) a *The boat-dem de   in the river.*
              'are'
           'The boats are in the river.'

     b *I did see Ronald book-dem.*
           'I saw Ronald's books.'

     c *The boy-dem want food.*
           'The boys want food.'

     d *Manuel baby-dem happy.*
           'Manuel's babies are happy.'

---

[1]   This problem set is based on data in Holm (1978) and on the authors' field and educational work in Bluefields, Nicaragua (1986–1991). In the Nicaraguan English data, we depart from ordinary spelling only when it is necessary to represent a word or form that is not part of standard English.

Since we find such one-to-one matches as the following:

(2) <u>Nicaraguan English</u>   <u>standard English</u>
     the boat-dem   *the boats*
     Ronald book-dem   *Ronald's books*
     the boy-dem   *the boys*
     Manuel baby-dem   *Manuel's babies*

it seems reasonable to make this initial hypothesis about plural noun formation in Nicaraguan English:

> *Hypothesis:*
> Add {plural} *-dem* to the singular noun to form its plural.

However, a fuller set of data reveals a more complicated picture. Let us now explore the nature of this complication, a piece of it at a time, assuming, nevertheless, that the initial hypothesis is more or less correct.

A popular Nicaraguan musical group, Dimensión Costeña (Coast Dimension), has recorded a number of traditional British Christmas songs, including "The Twelve Days of Christmas," in an album entitled *Navidad con Dimensión Costeña*. Their idiosyncratic Nicaraguan English version of the song consists entirely of this verse, twice repeated:

(3) *On the first day of Christmas, my true love send to me two turtledove, four calling-bird, five golden ring, four callingbird, three Frenchhen and a partridge in a pear tree.*

As indicated by an asterisk (*), the relevant noun phrases (NPs) would be ill-formed in this variety of English if the lyrics took this form:

(4) *On the first day of Christmas my true love send to me *two turtledove-dem, *four callingbird-dem, *five golden ring-dem, *four callingbird-dem, *three Frenchhen-dem, and a partridge in a pear tree.*

A   On the basis of the additional data in (3) and (4), how should you revise the hypothesis, "Add {plural} *-dem* to the singular noun to form its plural"?

Before you move on to B, be sure to think through and construct a reasoned, convincing answer to A.

B   Next, consider the following data:

    (5) *Some dog did bark loud.*   'Some dogs barked loud.'
        Some dog-dem did bark loud.

    (6) *Is*   *many dog in Bluefields.*   'There are many dogs in Bluefields.'
        'there are'
        Is   *many dog-dem in Bluefields.*

On the basis of the data in (5) and (6), how should you further reformulate the hypothesis to account for the *-dem*-less plural forms found in the NPs? Your reformulated hypothesis should also explain, for example, the ungrammaticality of (7) and the grammaticality of (8):

(7)   *Several dog-dem did bark last night.   'Several dogs barked last night.'

(8)   *These dog de* in the street.   'These dogs are in the street.'
        'are'

C A final detail of Nicaraguan noun pluralization: Note the grammaticality judgments for the following types of constructions in (9–15):

(9)   *He want seven case of beer.*   'He wants seven cases of beer.'

(10) *He want only one case of beer.*   'He wants only one case of beer.'

(11) *He did see the case of beer-dem.*   'He saw the cases of beer.'
       *He did see *the case-dem of beer.*

(12) *She did buy the bunch of banana-dem.* 'She bought the bunches of bananas.'
       *She did buy *the bunch-dem of banana.*

(13) *She did buy the bunch of banana.*   'She bought the bunch of bananas.'

(14) *She like the boy-dem in her class.*   'She likes the boys in her class.'
       *She like *the boy in her class-dem.*

(15) *She like the boy in her class-dem.*   'She likes the boy in her classes.'

Given these data, how can you reformulate your hypothesis to explain:

- the grammaticality judgments for (9–15); and
- the difference between the position of -*dem* in the grammatical NPs of sentences (11) and (12) as opposed to its position in the grammatical NPs of sentence (14) and (15)?

Do not forget the plural NPs in the sentences of (1a) through (1d) at the beginning of this problem set. Your final hypothesis must be able to explain <u>why</u> the suffix -*dem* is <u>required</u> in those plural NPs.

Finally, remember too to strive for parsimony in your explanation.

Before you move on in this chapter, be sure to think through and construct reasoned, convincing answers to B and C.

Noun Pluralization in Nicaraguan English: Its Syntax

Solving Problem Set 7 requires looking beyond the structure of the noun and instead paying deeper attention to the structure of the plural NP (noun phrase). Recall from Chapter 1 that a plural NP is the result of an NP merging with the morpheme {plural}:

(1)

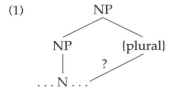

Recall also that the question mark at the end of the diagonal line in this tree asks us to consider whether the morpheme {plural} is realized in speech as a prefix to the N (noun), a suffix to the N, or elsewhere in the structure of the sentence.

In Nicaraguan English, the {plural} suffix *-dem* merges with an NP, yielding the following underlying structure:

(2)

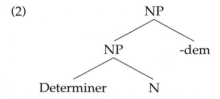

Determiner is where words and groups of words that may quantify a noun with respect to singularity or plurality are located. Thus, Determiner will include the articles (*a, the,* etc.), possessors (*his, her, our,* etc.), and words like *some, many, several, these, those,* etc., which can by themselves **satisfy** plurality – as we shall see. Tree (2) above represents all the grammatical NPs given in examples (1–8) of Problem Set 7. For example, here is the underlying tree for the NP in sentence (5), repeated below as (4):

(3)   a

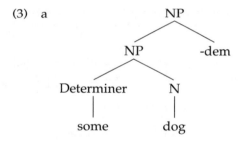

Since the determiner *some*, when merged with a countable noun, is inherently plural, the plurality of the NP in sentence (4) is **satisfied** in this language; thus {plural} *-dem* is deleted and does not surface in speech suffixed to *dog*, as shown in tree (3b):

(3)   b

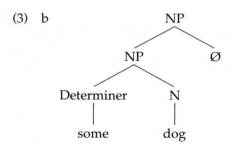

(4)   *Some dog did bark loud.*   'Some dogs barked loud.'

However, the determiner *the* is not inherently plural in either form or meaning. Thus, the suffix *-dem* must remain in sentence (1a), repeated below as (6), in order to satisfy the plurality of the NP because something <u>must</u> satisfy NP plurality. The underlying structure of the NP *the boat-dem* in sentence (6) is shown in tree (5a); the surface structure of this NP is shown in tree (5b) in which *-dem* has been moved to a lower position in the tree and attached to *boat*:

(5)   a

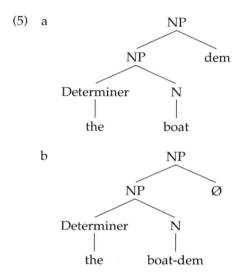

b

(6)   *The boat-dem de in the river.*   'The boats are in the river.'

Turn now to examples like (11) and (12), and (14) and (15), repeated below as (7–10) to which we now add (11):

(7)   *He did see the case of beer-dem.*   'He saw the cases of beer.'
       He did see *the case-dem of beer.

(8)   *She did buy the bunch of banana-dem.*   'She bought the bunches of
       She did buy *the bunch-dem of banana.   bananas.'

(9)   *She like the boy-dem in her class.*   'She likes the boys in her class.'
       She like *the boy in her *class-dem.

(10) *She like the boy in her class-dem.*   'She likes the boy in her classes.'

(11) *She like the boy-dem in her class-dem.*   'She likes the boys in her classes.'

The correct intuition here is to take the pluralizable units to be *the case of beer* and *the bunch of banana* in (7) and (8) and *the boy* and *her class* in (9–11). But how are we to "tree" that intuition? Again a first approach is to interpret *the case* and *the bunch* as determiners. This means that the tree for the plural NP of (7) would be:

(12)

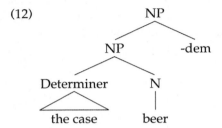

(13)   *He did see the case of beer-dem.*   'He saw the cases of beer.'

The suffix *-dem* is then copied to the N *beer* giving us *beer-dem*. The final surface structure will then look like this, with the preposition *of* inserted to make the structure grammatical:

(14)

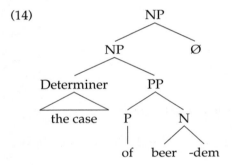

Sentences (9), (10), and (11) are different from sentences (7) and (8); the world is not measured out or quantified in terms of *boys*. Thus in the case of the plural *the boy-dem in her class*, we have something much like tree (3b) except that there is an adjoined **locative** PP (a prepositional phrase denoting place) in the construction that has to be pulled in:

(15)

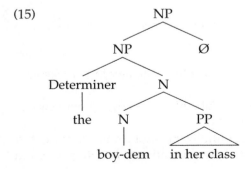

A solution to Problem Set 7 must take the notion NP (or at least 'phrase') into account and then deal with the difference between *the case* and *the bunch* as determiners containing measure words and *the boy* and *her class* as straight-forward noun phrases.

As a final remark, note that words like *bunch* confer plurality on the head noun of their NPs by the fact that a bunch requires more than one of some-thing. Thus, we interpret Nicaraguan English *the bunch of banana* to mean 'the bunch of bananas'. In this respect *bunch* is like *many*, *some*, and so on: an inher-ently plural word.

Terms

mass noun
countable noun
Determiner
satisfy, satisfied
locative

Further Reading

Nicaraguan English is the subject of Holm's lengthy, largely sociolinguistic dissertation *The Creole English of Nicaragua's Miskito Coast* (1978) and is also dealt with briefly in his *Pidgins and Creoles, Volume II* (1988). Honda and O'Neil (1987) and O'Neil (1993), based on their work in Nicaragua and on data in Holm's work, analyze the language from the linguistic perspective that guides this book.

Chapter 6

Noun Pluralization: The Interaction of Linguistic Features

As we have seen, the concepts 'singular' and 'plural' are expressed in different ways in human languages. Some languages always mark their nouns with a plural morpheme that has phonological content at the surface in speech, as in standard English *cow : cow*/z/. But in other languages, the expression of the concept 'plural' with a morpheme that is realized phonologically is subject to certain conditions, as we have seen in Nicaraguan English:

> *the three cow*, or
> *the cow-dem*, but not
> **the three cow-dem.*

Despite these cross-linguistic differences in how the concept 'plural' is realized in speech, we recall Chomsky's view, introduced in Chapter 1, that the concept 'plural' is interpreted in human languages at the <u>phrasal</u> level – a point made quite clear from our analysis of Nicaraguan English.

Moreover, we note that it is <u>not</u> necessary that a language express the concept 'plural' morphologically in speech at all. Thus, it is important to pay attention to the complicated relationships that exist between meaning and form in our discussion of phonology or morphology, or of any component of language. In the discussion and problem sets that follow, the focus is not only on the phonological and morphological forms that plural nouns take in Mandarin Chinese and in Cherokee, but also on the semantic features relevant to the formation of plural nouns in these languages.

Problem Set 8: Plural Noun Formation in Mandarin Chinese

According to *Ethnologue: Languages of the World* (2005), Chinese is a Sino-Tibetan language with 13 major varieties. The variety of Chinese called Mandarin Chinese in the English-speaking world is referred to as *Putonghua* ('common language') in the People's Republic of China, and as *Guoyu* ('national language') in the Chinese province of Taiwan.

From *Ethnologue: Languages of the World* (2005), we also learn the following: In addition to the People's Republic of China and Taiwan, Mandarin Chinese is spoken in Brunei, Cambodia, Indonesia, Laos, Malaysia, Mauritius, Mongolia, the Philippines, Russia, Singapore,Thailand, the United Kingdom, the United States, and Viet Nam. As of 1999, there were nearly 900 million speakers of Mandarin Chinese as a first language world-wide, with a total of over a billion speakers if second language speakers are included.

Investigating Mandarin Chinese Noun Pluralization

In Mandarin Chinese, plural noun formation is marked sometimes by an overt (pronounced) suffix, sometimes not.[1] The goal of this problem set is for you to formulate a hypothesis that accounts for the patterns exhibited in the following sets of data.

The data that follow are given in *pinyin*, the phonetic alphabet adopted in China and adopted for use at the United Nations in 1979.[2] Note that the following by-now-familiar linguistic conventions are used in this problem set:

- a period (.) marks syllable boundaries, breaking the word up into its syllables;
- an asterisk (*) before a word indicates that it is not well-formed or acceptable in Mandarin Chinese – for the meaning indicated in single quotes.

It is important to note that <u>none</u> of the given forms is irregular; this means that <u>all forms are regular</u>.

		singular		plural	
(1)	/hai.zi/	'child'	/hai.zi.men/	'children'	or
			/hai.zi/	'children'	
(2)	/jie/	'elder sister'	/jie/	'elder sisters'	but not
			/*jie.men/	'elder sisters'	
(3)	/xue.sheng/	'student'	/xue.sheng.men/	'students'	or
			/xue.sheng/	'students'	
(4)	/shu/	'book'	/shu/	'books'	but not
			/*shu.men/	'books'	
(5)	/xiong.di/	'brother'	/xiong.di.men/	'brothers'	or
			/xiong.di/	'brothers'	
(6)	/peng.you/	'friend'	/peng.you.men/	'friends'	or
			/peng.you/	'friends'	

[1]   The analysis and the data are from Li and Thompson (1981), or projected from this source.

[2]   In China, Mandarin Chinese is seldom written alphabetically and then only decoratively, although the rise of "internet" Chinese may change that. Instead, each morpheme is represented by a character that is unrelated to its pronunciation, or related to it in only in a charade-like way. For example, /-men/ the plural morpheme, is represented by the character: 们

The first piece of this compound character 亻 represents the semantic area that the morpheme belongs to; the second part 门 indicates that the morpheme rhymes with or sounds like (in this case, exactly like – except for the rising tone): /mén/ 'gate'.

(7)	/jing.yu/	'whale'	/jing.yu/ /*jing.yu.men/	'whales' 'whales'	but not
(8)	/gou/	'dog'	/gou/ /*gou.men/	'dogs' 'dogs'	but not
(9)	/nian.tou/	'idea'	/nian.tou/ /*nian.tou.men/	'ideas' 'ideas'	but not
(10)	/guan/	'official'	/guan/ /*guan.men/	'officials' 'officials'	but not
(11)	/bing/	'soldier'	/bing/ /*bing.men/	'soldiers' 'soldiers'	but not

A   On the basis of the data in (1–11), formulate a hypothesis that explains how Mandarin Chinese plurals are formed. Your hypothesis should identify the underlying form of the morpheme {plural} and explain how the surface (or spoken) forms are derived.

    Hint: Pay attention to both the syllable structure of the words and a **semantic feature** of the words. Note also that although you might be tempted on the basis of your own cultural knowledge to read ideas of authority and social hierarchy into a solution to this problem set, you do not have such information about Chinese culture; therefore, you should <u>not</u> yield to this temptation.

B   Strictly applying the hypothesis that you formulated in A, explain why a fluent speaker of Mandarin Chinese would make the following grammaticality judgments. That is, explain how your hypothesis accounts for each case, (12–18):

	singular		plural	
(12)	/tong.bao/	'countryman'	/tong.bao.men/	'countrymen'
(13)	/kuai.zi/	'chopstick'	/*kuai.zi.men/	'chopsticks'
(14)	/xiong/	'elder brother'	/xiong/	'elder brothers'
(15)	/ji/	'chicken'	/*ji.men/	'chickens'
(16)	/ya.zi/	'duck'	/*ya.zi.men/	'ducks'
(17)	/mei/	'younger sister'	/*mei.men/	'younger sisters'
(18)	/ke.ren/	'guest'	/ke.ren/	'guests'

C   Does your hypothesis account for the following pronoun forms in (19) and (20)? If not, reformulate your hypothesis so as to account for <u>all</u> of the data, (1–20).

(19)	/wo/	'I, me'	/wo.men/ /*wo/	'we, us' 'we, us'
(20)	/ni/	'you – singular'	/ni.men/ /*ni/	'plural you' 'plural you'

D   According to your reformulated hypothesis, which one of the following plural words, (21) or (22), is well-formed, and which one is ill-formed? Explain each case.

(21)	/ta/	'they = plural she/he' 'them = plural her/him'	(formed from /ta/ 'she/he, her/him')
(22)	/ta.men/	'they = plural she/he' 'them = plural her/him'	(formed from /ta/ 'she/he, her/him')

E   What, if anything, does your hypothesis predict about the well-formedness of (23) and (24)? What would you like it to predict? Specify and explain your prediction for each case.

(23) /ta.men/   'they = plural it'   (formed from /ta/ 'it')
                         'them = plural it'
(24) /wu.li.xue.jia.men/ 'physicists'   (formed from /wu.li.xue.jia/ 'physicist')

F   On the basis of what you have learned from examining plural noun formation in other languages, why would (25) be judged ungrammatical by speakers of Mandarin Chinese?

(25) /*san.ge lao.shi.men/   'three teachers'   (formed from /san.ge/ 'three', /lao.shi/ 'teacher')

G   Do you think that Mandarin Chinese speakers are often confused about whether they or the people they are talking to are using singular or plural noun phrases? Why or why not?

H   Given what you now know about both languages, what difficulties do you predict speakers of Mandarin Chinese will have in acquiring English noun pluralization?

Before you move on to Problem Set 9, be sure to think through and construct reasoned, convincing answers to A–H.

Problem Set 9: Plural Noun Formation in Cherokee

Cherokee is one of the indigenous Native American languages of North America. It belongs to the Iroquoian language family and is spoken in eastern and northeastern Oklahoma and on the Cherokee Reservation there, in the Great Smoky Mountains, and in western North Carolina. The language is called *Tsalagi* by its speakers.

According to *Ethnologue: Languages of the World* (2005), there are from 15,000 to 22,500 Cherokee speakers, including 14,000 speakers out of the 70,000 people on the Oklahoma rolls of the Cherokee Nation (reported in by Durbin Feeling in 1986). There are 130 monolingual speakers of the language.

Early in the nineteenth century, Chief Sequoyah, the great Cherokee leader, developed a syllabary as a systematic way of writing Cherokee. In a **syllabary**, each syllable – rather than each sound – of a language is represented by a distinct symbol. The course of Cherokee literacy as it relates to the history of the Cherokee people and their language is an instructive one, as we learn from the following account by Walker in an undated essay written in the late 1960s:

> Cherokee society has a long tradition of literacy. It has been estimated that the Cherokee were 90 percent literate in their native language in the 1830's. By the 1880's the Western Cherokee had a higher English literacy level than the white populations of either Texas or Arkansas . . . (Walker, n.d., p. 3)

Since the federal government took over the Cherokee school system in 1898, Cherokees have viewed the school as a white man's institution which Cherokee children are bound by law to attend, but over which their parents have no control. Most Cherokee speakers drop out of school as soon as this is legally possible. While in school, they learn relatively little due to the language barrier and also due to this . . . accurate definition of the school as a white man's institution. As a further complication, Cherokee parents are well aware that educated children tend to leave the community, either geographically or socially. To them the school threatens the

break-up of the family and the division of the community, precisely those consequences which no genuinely tribal society can tolerate . . . (p. 4)

It seems clear that the startling decline [since the federal takeover of schools] of
both English and Cherokee literacy in the Cherokee tribe is chiefly the result of the
scarcity of reading materials in Cherokee, and the fact that learning to read has
become associated with coercive instruction, particularly in the context of an alien
and threatening school presided over by English speaking teachers and controlled
by English speaking superintendents and PTA's which conceive of Cherokee as a
"dying" language and Cherokee school children as "culturally impoverished" candidates for rapid and "inevitable" social assimilation . . . (p. 8)

Whether the Cherokee people can ever fully recover from this period of external control over their educational systems, maintain their language, and revive Cherokee literacy
are open questions. The Cherokee did recover from the destruction of their printing presses
in the 1830s, destroyed by the United States government because they were used to organ-
ize opposition to the forced exile of the Cherokee from their lands east of the Mississippi
to Oklahoma, then officially Indian Territory. But that recovery took place in a less complicated world.

Investigating Cherokee Noun Pluralization

Cherokee has more than one way to pluralize a singular noun and pays attention to the
phonological structure and a **semantic feature** of nouns.[3] The most common ways of pluralizing Cherokee nouns are illustrated in the following set of data.
    The data are represented in a phonologically-based Cherokee orthography that was devel-
oped by Durbin Feeling (1975), one that is very different from Chief Sequoyah's syllabary.
Note the following special conventions of this orthography:

- /v/ represents a slightly nasalized vowel (like the *u* of English *fun*);
- /y/ and /w/ are glides and together with the liquid /l/ should be grouped among the
  Cherokee consonants for purposes of analysis;
- /?/ is [+consonantal]: a glottal stop (like the *ttl* of *little* in some varieties of English).

Note that none of the given forms is irregular; in other words, all forms are regular.

	singular		plural
(1)	/achuja/	'boy'	/anichuja/
(2)	/agehuja/	'girl'	/anigehuja/
(3)	/yvgi/	'fork'	/diyvgi/
(4)	/gakohdi/	'plant'	/digakohdi/
(5)	/taluja/	'basket'	/ditaluja/
(6)	/asgaya/	'man'	/anisgaya/

[3]   This problem set is closely based on one developed by Matthew Smith, a member of the
    Workshop in Linguistics at the 21st Annual American Indian Language Development
    Institute, University of Arizona, Tucson, June 5–30, 2000. The Cherokee orthography is
    that of Feeling (1975), which was also used to verify Smith's data.

(7)	/a?da/	'young animal'	/ani?da/
(8)	/gasaleni/	'coat'	/digasaleni/
(9)	/ageya/	'woman'	/anigeya/
(10)	/ayvwi/	'person'	/aniyvwi/
(11)	/atelido/	'plate'	/ditelido/
(12)	/aditohdi/	'spoon'	/diditohdi/
(13)	/uguku/	'hoot owl'	/uniguku/
(14)	/kanesa?i/	'box'	/dikanesa?i/
(15)	/ujiya/	'worm'	/unijiya/

A What are the surface (or spoken) forms of the morpheme {plural} in Cherokee?

B What semantic feature divides the nouns in (1–15) into two groups?

C Using these data, formulate a hypothesis about Cherokee noun pluralization. Carefully consider the phonological structure and semantic features of the singular nouns. What rules are needed to form a plural noun in Cherokee? Demonstrate how your rules work by showing how specific examples are derived.

Before you move on to D, be sure to think through and construct reasoned, convincing answers to A–C.

D Now consider these additional Cherokee data. Do these regular plural forms fit into either of the groups that you identified in B? If not, reformulate the hypothesis you constructed in C in order to explain these data (16–23) as well as the previous set of data (1–15).

	singular		plural
(16)	/ugidahli/	'feather'	/jugidahli/
(17)	/uweji/	'egg'	/juweji/
(18)	/ulvsa?di/	'drinking glass'	/julvsa?di/
(19)	/ugaloga/	'leaf'	/jugaloga/
(20)	/ulogili/	'cloud'	/julogili/
(21)	/uhalvni/	'bell'	/juhalvni/
(22)	/unegvha?i/	'blanket'	/junegvha?i/
(23)	/unadadesvda/	'chain'	/junadadesvda/

E Now consider the similarities and differences in the distinctive features of the initial sound of the plural prefix in (16–23) and the initial sound of the plural prefix and **infix** in (1–15), consulting the distinctive feature matrices in Chapter 2. There are certainly differences in the distinctive features of these initial sounds, but there are clear similarities that should lead you to think that they are all related at some level of analysis.

With parsimony, or economy of mind and explanation, as your goal, assume then that there is a single underlying form of the morpheme {plural} from which the other forms are derived. Assume further that the underlying morpheme is prefixed onto a singular noun to form its plural.

What is the best choice for the underlying morpheme and what rules are necessary in order to get from this prefixed form of {plural} to the variety of surface or pronounced forms exhibited in the plural nouns (1–23)? Formulate a hypothesis and demonstrate how your hypothesized set of rules works by showing how specific examples are derived.

F Finally, what are we to make of the following data?

	singular		plural
(24)	/usdi/	'baby'	/junisdi/
(25)	/ayohli/	'child'	/diniyohli/

Before you move on in this chapter, be sure to think through and construct reasoned, convincing answers to D–F.

Linguistic Features in Mandarin Chinese Noun Pluralization

Constructing an explanation of Mandarin Chinese noun pluralization (Problem Set 8) requires that we look into the nouns of this language at their features – something that we will do shortly. An explanation of Cherokee noun pluralization (Problem Set 9) makes a similar requirement, but for its solution, for now at least, you are more or less on your own.

Recall that a word – a singular noun, for example – is represented in the mind as a collection of linguistic features. In discussing Mr. Kobayashi's use of "too much stoplight" in Chapter 5, for example, we referred to the semantic distinction between [+count] nouns and [−count] (or mass) nouns in our hypothesis about plural formation in this variety of English.

To review from Chapter 2, there are three different kinds of linguistic features:

- Some of the features represent the **semantics** of the word (the pieces of its definition or meaning); for example, the feature [+human] plays a role in the formation of Mandarin Chinese plural nouns, with [+animate] playing a role in Cherokee.
- Some features represent the **phonology** of the word – the way it is pronounced and perceived; for example, the number of syllables a word has is a feature that plays a role in the formation of Mandarin Chinese plurals. Other phonological features play a role in Cherokee.
- Some features represent the **grammatical categories** of the word. Is the word a noun or a verb, for example? And if it is a noun, is it a pronoun or not? This latter distinction is another feature that plays a role in the formation of Mandarin Chinese plurals.

All of these linguistic features are at work in Mandarin Chinese noun pluralization. Let us now step through Problem Set 8, examining much more closely how plurals are formed in this language.

Formulating a hypothesis

Given the data (1–11) in Problem Set 8, repeated below, it is clear that the underlying morpheme {plural} has two surface forms in Mandarin Chinese: in some cases, {plural} is realized as the suffix /-men/, while in other cases, {plural} has zero phonological form. Let us assume that the underlying morpheme is /-men/, which is suffixed to all nouns. We must then explain the conditions under which the suffix /-men/ remains on the noun or the conditions under which it is deleted.

	singular		plural		
(1)	/hai.zi/	'child'	/hai.zi.men/	'children'	or
			/hai.zi/	'children'	
(2)	/jie/	'elder sister'	/jie/	'elder sisters'	but not
			/*jie.men/	'elder sisters'	
(3)	/xue.sheng/	'student'	/xue.sheng.men/	'students'	or
			/xue.sheng/	'students'	
(4)	/shu/	'book'	/shu/	'books'	but not
			/*shu.men/	'books'	
(5)	/xiong.di/	'brother'	/xiong.di.men/	'brothers'	or
			/xiong.di/	'brothers'	
(6)	/peng.you/	'friend'	/peng.you.men/	'friends'	or
			/peng.you/	'friends'	
(7)	/jing.yu/	'whale'	/jing.yu/	'whales'	but not
			/*jing.yu.men/	'whales'	
(8)	/gou/	'dog'	/gou/	'dogs'	but not
			/*gou.men/	'dogs'	
(9)	/nian.tou/	'idea'	/nian.tou/	'ideas'	but not
			/*nian.tou.men/	'ideas'	
(10)	/guan/	'official'	/guan/	'officials'	but not
			/*guan.men/	'officials'	
(11)	/bing/	'soldier'	/bing/	'soldiers'	but not
			/*bing.men/	'soldiers'	

The patterns in the data (1–11) suggest that two features of a Mandarin Chinese noun determine whether the {plural} suffix /-men/ may remain on a noun in order to express its plural:

- whether the noun has one syllable or more than one, a phonological feature:

    /jie/   'elder sister'   vs.   /hai.zi/   'child'

- whether the noun denotes a human being or not, a feature of its meaning:

    /hai.zi/   'child'   vs.   /shu/   'book'

But these features are not equally ranked in Mandarin Chinese plurals. The semantic feature [+human] dominates the phonological one – the length of the word in syllables. That is, regardless of the number of its syllables, a [–human] noun may not retain the plural suffix /-men/, as we see from the data in (7) and (9).

Setting the [−human] nouns aside and looking only at the [+human] nouns, we see that those with one syllable <u>never</u> allow /-men/ to indicate plurality at the surface in speech; while those with two syllables, <u>may optionally</u> allow /-men/ to do so.

Thus we formulate the following hypothesis, assuming that the underlying {plural} /-men/ is added to the singular form of all nouns as the first (morphological) step in the formation of Mandarin Chinese plural nouns:

Hypothesis I:
Delete /-men/ from all [−human] nouns and from [+human] nouns: necessarily if the [+human] singular form has but one syllable; otherwise /-men/-deletion is optional.

This hypothesis makes the following correct predictions for examples (12–18). Let us go through this set of data case by case:

- (12) /tong.bao.men/ 'countrymen' is well-formed because the singular /tong.bao/ is a two-syllable, [+human] noun; however, /tong.bao/ with a plural meaning would also be well-formed;
- (13) /*kuai.zi.men/ 'chopsticks', (15) /*ji.men/ 'chickens', and (16) /*ya.zi.men/ 'ducks' are ill-formed, for regardless of their syllable length, they are all [−human] nouns;
- (14) /xiong/ 'elder brothers' is well formed, for although it is [+human], the singular /xiong/ has but one syllable and thus is not compatible with /-men/;
- (17) /*mei.men/ 'younger sisters' is not well-formed, for although the singular noun /mei/ is [+human], it has but one syllable;
- (18) /ke.ren/ 'guests' is well-formed because although the singular /ke.ren/ is a two-syllable, [+human] word and thus <u>may</u> allow /-men/, it needn't retain it to form its plural.

Testing and sharpening the hypothesis

Turn now to the personal pronouns. Here we have one-syllable, [+human] words that <u>must</u> pluralize by adding /-men/. These forms <u>appear</u> to be counter-examples, which might lead us to reject or abandon Hypothesis I. But before we do that we want to ask: Is it possible to reformulate or revise Hypothesis I in order to account for all the data in (1–20)?

(19) /wo/   'I, me'   /wo.men/   'we, us'
                                      /*wo/   'we, us'

(20) /ni/   'you – singular'   /ni.men/   'plural you'
                                      /*ni/   'plural you'

The answer to this question lies in the fact that not only do the words /wo/ and /ni/ share the semantic feature [+human], but they also belong to a sub-category of noun that we designate with the grammatical category feature [+pronoun]. Thus we can revise the hypothesis by taking the feature [+pronoun] into account, assuming once again that /-men/ is first added to all singular forms:

Hypothesis II:
Delete /-men/ from all [−human] nouns and from [+human, −pronoun] nouns: necessarily if the singular form has but one syllable; otherwise /-men/-deletion is optional.

The predictive power of hypotheses

According to the reformulated Hypothesis II, (21) is ill-formed and (22) is well-formed, correct predictions given the grammaticality judgments of Mandarin Chinese speakers:

(21)   /*ta/   'they = plural she/he' (formed from /ta/ 'she/he, her/him')
                    'them = plural her/him'

(22)   /ta.men/ 'they = plural she/he' (formed from /ta/ 'she/he, her/him')
                    'them = plural her/him'

Turn now to the question of the well-formedness of (23–25):

(23)   /ta.men/   'they = plural it'   (formed from /ta/ 'it')
                                    'them = plural it'

(24)   /wu.li.xue.jia.men/   'physicists'   (formed from
                                                         /wu.li.xue.jia/ 'physicist')

(25)   /*san.ge lao.shi.men/ 'three teachers'   (formed from /san.ge/
                                                         'three', /lao.shi/ 'teacher')

Hypothesis II gives different predictions for (23) depending on whether [−human] or [+pronoun] is the dominant feature. If we assume the dominance of the semantic feature [−human] over the grammatical category feature [+pronoun], Hypothesis II predicts that (23) is ill-formed:

(23)   a   /*ta.men/   'they = plural it'
                            'them = plural it'

However, if we assume the primacy of the grammatical category feature [+pronoun], Hypothesis II predicts that (23) is well-formed:

(23)   b   /ta.men/   'they = plural it'
                            'them = plural it'

From our conversations with Mandarin Chinese speakers, it has been difficult to determine which of these predictions is correct. Although we suspect that (23a) presents the correct judgment – with the feature [–human] dominating the feature [+pronoun] – it is possible that /-men/ has spread and become a pluralizer for all pronouns, regardless of whether they are [+human] or [–human].

Turn now to (24) and (25), where we do have clear judgments from speakers of the language:

(24) /wu.li.xue.jia.men/   'physicists'
(25) /*san.ge lao.shi.men/   'three teachers'

Since Hypothesis II allows /-men/ for [+human, –pronoun] nouns unless they have but one syllable, it correctly predicts the well-formedness of (24). Note that if we had stated the hypothesis in a more restricted form:

> *Hypothesis II, restricted form* (highlighted by the underlining):
> Delete /-men/ from all [-human] nouns and from [+human, -pronoun] nouns: necessarily if the singular form has but one syllable; <u>/-men/-deletion is optional if the singular form has two syllables.</u>

then the hypothesis would predict (24) to be ill-formed, and we would have to revise it in the light of the data.

The ill-formedness of (25), however, is not predicted by Hypothesis II. Yet its ill-formedness is not unexpected, for speakers of Mandarin Chinese appear to want to express the concept 'plural' as little as possible morphologically. Since in (25) the plurality of the noun phrase is unambiguously expressed by /san.ge/ 'three', it is not surprising that /-men/ cannot be retained by /lao.shi/ in such cases.

Cross-Linguistic Similarities and Language Change

Recall that our analyses of the phonology of noun pluralization in English, Spanish, and Brazilian Portuguese revealed several cross-linguistic similarities, particularly in vowel epenthesis and voicing assimilation. From our analysis of Mandarin Chinese noun pluralization, we now discover another way in which languages resemble one another once we look beyond their obvious phonological differences. Mandarin Chinese /-men/ behaves syntactically and semantically somewhat like Nicaraguan English -*dem*, with /-men/ being deleted when plurality is satisfied by the presence of a number word (like /san.ge/ 'three') in a noun phrase.

Beyond these similarities, it is worth noting some interesting differences between how the {plural} -*dem* and the {plural} /-men/ are used across varieties of Caribbean English and varieties of Chinese, respectively. For example, in some varieties of Caribbean English, -*dem* is constrained (as /-men/ is in Mandarin Chinese) to being the plural marker for [+human] nouns only (O'Neil, 1993, p. 295). But we know that this is not true of Nicaraguan English, for in this variety of Caribbean English, -*dem* is the plural suffix for all nouns. Moreover, we learn from Li and Thompson (1981, p. 83, n. 5) that "some dialects [of Chinese, other than Mandarin Chinese] allow the suffix /-men/ to occur with [−human] nouns, including inanimate nouns." An explanation of the presence or absence of constraints on the {plural} suffix across varieties of Caribbean English and of Chinese might very well lie in language change: in infants and bilinguals, who – in their acquisition of language – are the agents of change, ridding grammar of its constraints where possible and adding others.

We thus hypothesize that in some varieties of Chinese and in some varieties of Caribbean English (Nicaraguan English among them), the plural suffixes (/-men/ in one case; -*dem* in the other) generalized at some point in time from being plural suffixes constrained to [+human] nouns to being plural suffixes for nouns of all types. This sort of generalization, which removes constraints on rules – even getting rid of rules, is an expected kind of language change.

Constructing a Feature Hierarchy

Finally, notice that this investigation of Mandarin Chinese plural nouns reveals that features can relate to one another hierarchically; that is, one feature can dominate, or take precedence over another feature. For example, the data given in (1) through (11) reveal that the semantic feature [+human] dominates the number of syllables that a word contains. Other data in (1) through (11), the data in (19) and (20), and our suspicion about (23) reveal that the semantic feature [+human] dominates the grammatical category feature [pronoun]. A **feature hierarchy** determining the formation of plural nouns in Mandarin Chinese, assuming (23) to be ill-formed, can be expressed in the form of the following tree. If /ta-men/ 'it plural' is well-formed, then the primary split in the hierarchy is between [±pronoun], with [±human] being a relevant division only under [−pronoun].

(26)

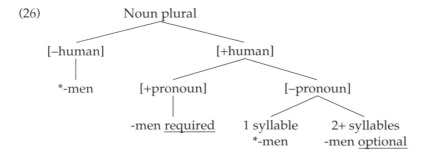

We assume that a feature hierarchy of some sort exists whenever there is an interaction of linguistic features for a phenomenon in language, any language.

Terms

semantic feature
syllabary
infix
semantics
phonology
grammatical category
feature hierarchy

Further Reading

Feeling's (1975) *Cherokee-English Dictionary* (which moves from Cherokee to English, as well as from English to Cherokee) also contains a 120-page outline of Cherokee grammar. Li and Thompson's (1981) *Mandarin Chinese: A Functional Reference Grammar* is a comprehensive and accessible grammar of the language. In these books, the pieces of Cherokee and Mandarin Chinese grammar examined in this chapter, as well as other parts of their grammars, can be pursued further.

Chapter 7

Noun Pluralization: A Summary

As we stated in the introduction to this book, linguists who examine the structure of language focus their attention on the unconscious knowledge of language that a person has when we say that she or he knows a language. Our knowledge of the structure of language, referred to as mental grammar, is comprised of the following four computational components or modules together with a lexicon (or mental dictionary):

- phonology: the structure of the sounds of language;
- morphology: the structure of the words and forms of language; '
- syntax: the structure of the phrases and sentences of language;
- semantics: the structural contribution to the meaning of the phrases and sentences of language.

In the preceding chapters and problem sets, we have examined the structural complexity and acquisition of one seemingly simple phenomenon of language: how plural nouns are formed. As we have seen from our investigations of noun pluralization in a variety of languages, there is a good deal of interaction between and among the modules of grammar – knowledge of which must be developed by infants acquiring their first language and by children and adults acquiring a second language.

From the outset of our investigations, we have assumed that the concept 'plural' is always represented in mental grammar as a single underlying morpheme that merges with a noun phrase. The morpheme {plural} may or may not be realized at the surface in speech, as determined by the phonological, syntactic, and/or semantic constraints on noun pluralization in a particular language. Forming plural nouns is then a morphological process, one that may involve other components of grammar.

Let us now review the interactions among the modules of grammar that are found cross-linguistically in plural noun formation and discuss their implications for language acquisition.

Morphophonology: The Morphology–Phonology Interaction

At its simplest, there would be no morphology–phonology interaction in a morphological process. In Nicaraguan English, for example, the morpheme {plural}, when realized as the suffix -dem, never undergoes any phonological change, nor does the noun to which it is attached. As we have seen, there are constraints on the use of -dem, but these are syntactic and semantic constraints, not phonological ones.

In standard English, however, there is morphology–phonology interaction in noun pluralization, one in which the surface or pronounced forms of the {plural} /s/ are a consequence of the phonological structure of the final sound of the singular noun:

- /ɪz/ if the word ends in a sibilant – the effect of vowel epenthesis and voicing assimilation;
- /z/ if it ends in a [+voice] sound – the effect of voicing assimilation;
- /s/ elsewhere.

The Semantics–Morphology–Phonology Interaction

We turn now to the threefold interaction of semantics, morphology, and phonology that is found in some languages.

We have found the semantic features [animate] and [human] at work in two languages. In Mandarin Chinese, for example, the retention of the suffix /-men/ is conditioned not only by the syllable length of the singular noun, but also by the value assigned to the feature [human]. Only [+human] nouns consisting of two or more syllables may be pluralized by /-men/; that is, retention of /-men/ at the surface for these nouns is optional, as illustrated below:

(1) /hai.zi/   'child'   /hai.zi.men/   'children' or
                                     /hai.zi/   'children'
     /jie/   'elder sister'   /jie/   'elder sisters' but not
                                     /*jie.men/   'elder sisters'
     /shu/   'book'   /shu/   'books' but not
                                     /*shu.men/   'books'
     /jing.yu/   'whale'   /jing.yu/   'whales' but not
                                     /*jing.yu.men/   'whales'

In Cherokee, the semantic feature [animate] is crucial to noun pluralization. In this language, nouns that are [+animate] are pluralized by **infixing** /-ni-/ after the first vowel of the singular form; [–animate] nouns are pluralized by **prefixing** /di-/ to the singular form; for example:

(2) /achuja/   'boy'   /anichuja/   'boys'
     /taluja/   'basket'   /ditaluja/   'baskets'
     /uguku/   'hoot owl'   /uniguku/   'hoot owls'
     /kanesa?i/   'box'   /dikanesa?i/   'boxes'

There are further complications for the pluralization of nouns in Cherokee, phonological ones. For example, for some [−animate] nouns the prefix /di-/ is realized in speech as /j-/:

(3) /ulogi/   'cloud'   /julogi/   'clouds'
     /egwoni/   'river'   /jegwoni/   'rivers'

The [+continuant] effect on [−continuant] consonants of the vowels that immediately follow them is widely exhibited in the languages of the world – in English, for example. Thus, compare (for many speakers of North American English) the /j/ of *residual* with the /d/ of *residue*, the noun from which the adjective is derived; here, as we can see, stress plays a role as well. We return to a full explanation and derivation of Cherokee plurals later in this chapter in the discussion of the acquisition of plural morphology.

But let us first consider a new case, that of Yakima, a member of the Sahaptin subset of the Shahaptian family of languages. In her book, *The Languages of Native North America*, Marianne Mithun observes that "Sahaptin speakers now live on the Warm Springs and Umatilla reservations in Oregon, the Yakima reservation in Washington, at Rock Creek, Priest Rapids, and Nespelem, Washington, and at Celilo, Oregon" and that the language of each of these Sahaptin communities is spoken by only a handful of persons (Mithun, 1999, pp. 477–478).

In the Yakima language, suffixation and **reduplication** (affixation through the repetition of all or part of a word) are both involved in noun pluralization, and in ways that reveal a semantics–morphology–phonology interaction that is interestingly different from what we have observed thus far. Whether there is reduplicative suffixation or suffixation of the by-now familiar kind in noun pluralization depends on whether the noun is [animate], or not.[1]

For example, the [+animate] nouns *tnun* and *ayat* are pluralized by **suffixing** -ma, while the [−animate] noun *lataam* is pluralized by full reduplicative suffixation of the noun, as shown in (4):

(4) *tnun*   'mountain goat'   *tnun-ma*   'mountain goats'
     ayat   'woman'   *ayat-ma*   'women'
     lataam   'table'   *lataam-lataam*   'tables'

---

[1] This analysis of Yakima was carried out by Virginia Beavert (Yakima), Erwin Sice, and Hope Lynn in the Workshop in Linguistics at the 21st Annual American Indian Language Development Institute, University of Arizona, Tucson, June 5–30, 2000.

There are other complications in Yakima, for this language also has a **dual** suffix -in (distinct from the word for *two*) whose use is restricted by a further refinement of the feature [+animate]. The use of the dual suffix appears to be based on whether the [+animate] noun is [+human] or not. If it is [+human], then it can be "dualized"; for example:

(5)   *ayat*   'woman'   *ayat-in*   'two women'
      nusux   'salmon'   **nusux-in*   'two salmon'
      lataam   'table'   **lataam-in*   'two tables'

Note, however, that **dualization** is complicated by the fact that it does not strictly distinguish [+human] animates from [−human] animates. *Tnun* 'mountain goat', for example, <u>can</u> be dualized:

(6)   *tnun-in*   'two mountain goats'

Perhaps, then, there is a cultural factor at work based in Yakima legend and lore, one that picks out some [−human] animates and attributes to them [+human] characteristics. Alternatively, it is possible that some [−human] nouns have simply joined the class of nouns originally restricted to [+human] nouns. Clearly, further investigation is needed in order to answer this question.

Note that the concept 'dual' adds an important third dimension to the two-way singular/plural distinction found in many languages. For languages with dual forms, such as Yakima, plurals <u>must</u> be interpreted to mean 'three or more'. Thus in Yakima, *ayat* is used to refer to one woman; *ayatin* to refer to two women; and *ayatma* to refer to three or more women. Morphologically marked dual requires that we divide the contrast 'singular/plural' into two features: [singular] and [plural]: a singular noun will be marked [+singular] and a plural noun will be marked [+plural]. A dual noun is [−singular, −plural]; that is, it is neither singular nor plural.

The Morphology–Syntax Interaction: The Role of Quantifiers

Finally – as we have seen, syntax can also be involved in noun pluralization. For example, in both Nicaraguan English and Mandarin Chinese, we saw that the morpheme {plural} – the suffixes -dem and /-men/, respectively – can not be retained if the noun phrase containing the noun is otherwise plurally quantified. For example, (7) is well-formed in Nicaraguan English, but (8) is not, where the square brackets mark off the beginning and the end of the pluralized noun phrase (NP):

(7) *I did see* [_NP_ *the turtledove-dem*].
'I saw the turtledoves.'

(8) *I did see* [_NP_ **two turtledove-dem*].

Instead, given the cardinal-number word *two*, a speaker of Nicaraguan English would say:

(9) *I did see two turtledove.*
'I saw two turtledoves.'

   In the same way, a speaker of Mandarin Chinese, cannot pluralize /lao-shi/ 'teacher' with the suffix /-men/ in a quantified noun phrase, such as:

(10) /*san.ge lao.shi.men/   'three teachers'

She or he would have to say:

(11) /san.ge lao.shi/   'three teachers'

   Finally in Nicaraguan English, the suffix *-dem* appears at the <u>end</u> of the noun phrase if the Determiner of that noun phrase contains a pluralizing measure word; *-dem* is not suffixed on the measure word itself. Thus, (12) is not well-formed and cannot mean what (13) does:

(12) *He did see* [_NP_ **the case-dem of beer*].

(13) *He did see* [_NP_ *the case of beer-dem*].
'He saw the cases of beer.'

Plural Noun Formation and Its Acquisition

From our investigations, we have seen that noun pluralization can be done in various ways, for example:

- directly through prefixes, suffixes, and reduplication – all forms of **affixation**;
- indirectly through quantifiers.

We have also learned that at least two semantic features, [animate] and [human], can be crucial to noun pluralization, as in Cherokee, Yakima, and Mandarin Chinese; and that there can be a third distinction in addition to the singular/plural one: the dual, as in Yakima – representative of many other languages.

The phonological characteristics of the singular noun are also often important for the phonological form of the morpheme {plural}: for example, the number of syllables that the singular noun has (as in Armenian and Mandarin Chinese), the stress pattern of the noun (as in Spanish), and the distinctive features of the initial or final sounds of the noun (as in English and Cherokee).

Looking further afield, an analysis of other languages reveals that noun pluralization can be expressed almost entirely in the <u>verb</u> morphology of a language. In Western Apache,[2] for example, "the plural is shown in the verb, not in the noun, except for [a handful of nouns denoting prepubescent persons] 'boys', 'girls', 'children', etc." (Perry et al., 1972, p. xi). Thus, in the first set of Western Apache sentences that follows (14a–c), whether the noun *gósé* 'dog' is singular, dual, or plural only shows up in the morphology of the verb; while in the second set (15a–c), the noun *ishkiin* 'boy' has a [–singular] form *ishikín* which is then realized as either dual or as plural – in the verb morphology. The question of exactly how number "migrates" from the NP to the verb is a matter of great interest since subject-verb agreement is characteristic of many languages, one which we will not, however, deal with in this text.

(14) a *Gósé higaal.*
         'The dog is walking.'

      b *Gósé hi'ash.*
         'Two dogs are walking.'

      c *Gósé hikah.*
         'Three or more dogs are walking.'

(15) a *Ishkiin higaal.*
         'The boy is walking.'

      b *Ishikín hi'ash.*
         'Two boys are walking.'

      c *Ishikín hikah.*
         'Three or more boys are walking.'

A central question for us to consider is: What does all this variety mean for infants acquiring their first languages and for children and adults acquiring second languages? Two characteristics of noun pluralization stand out as

---

[2]   "The Western Apache language belongs to the Athapaskan family of languages. Others in the Southwest speaking these languages are Mescalero, Chiracahua and Jicarilla Apaches, and Navajos" (Perry et al., 1972, p. 91). Mithun (1999, p. 358) adds, "Western Apache is spoken in Arizona on the San Carlos and Fort Apache reservations. . . . It is considered the most viable of the Apachean languages, with 12,000 speakers of all ages reported in 1982."

morphological alternatives whose values must be determined and fixed by the language learner:

- Does the morpheme {plural} have phonological form or not; that is, is it spoken?
- If it has phonological form, is the morpheme prefixed or suffixed to the singular form of the noun (assuming that reduplication is a type of affixation)?

Say that these values are set at [+phonological form], [+prefix]; Cherokee is such a language. Then, a person acquiring Cherokee must arrive at an under-lying {plural} form, the prefix /di-/, and the rules for deriving the phonolo-gical (or spoken) forms: /di-/, /j-/, and /-ni-/. The rules are relatively simple, involving the semantic feature [animate] and the initial vowel of the singular noun. This is a possible set of rules:

A   The morphological rule: Prefix /di-/ to the singular form of a Cherokee noun.
B   Semantic and phonological rules:

    1   For [+animate] nouns, infix /di-/ after the first vowel of the singular noun, the /d/ of /di-/ becoming [+nasal] as a consequence of infixation;
    2   /di-/ → /j-/ if followed by a [−low] vowel;
    3   /a/ → Ø following /di-/.

Following the prefixation of /di-/, plural nouns would be derived in Cherokee as follows:

A	di + a?da	'young animals'	di + uweji	'eggs'	di + atelido	'plates'
B1	ani?da		diuweji		diatelido	
B2	ani?da		juweji		diatelido	
B3	ani?da		juweji		ditelido	

In a fascinating case of what we might call regular-irregulars, the plural forms of /usdi/ 'baby' and /ayohli/ 'child' are /junisdi/ and /diniyohli/, respectively. These nouns are doubly pluralized, perhaps reflecting some cultural hesitation over where to place infants and children with respect to animacy; that is, they are treated as both [−animate], with the prefixation of /di/, and [+animate], with the infixation of a second /di/. The doubly pluralized /junisdi/ and /diniy-ohli/ are then derived by rules B1 and B2 and by B1 and B3 respectively:

A	di + di + usdi	'babies'	di + di + ayohli	'children'
B1	di + unisdi		di + aniyohli	
B2	junisdi		dianiyohli	
B3	junisdi		diniyohli	

Assume a slightly different setting of values: [+phonological form], [–prefix]; that is, suffixation; Mandarin Chinese is such a language. A person acquiring this language has to arrive at the underlying {plural} form, the suffix /-men/. Suffixing /-men/ to all nouns (pronouns included) would then require arriving at rules that delete /-men/:

A   The morphological rule: Suffix /-men/ to the singular form of a Mandarin Chinese noun.
B   Semantic and phonological rules:

  1   /-men/ → Ø if suffixed to [–human], leaving only [+human] nouns under further consideration;
  2   /-men/ → Ø if suffixed to monosyllabic [–pronoun], leaving only polysyllabic nouns under further consideration;
  3   /-men/ → Ø (optionally) if suffixed to [–pronoun].

After the suffixation of /-men/, plurals nouns would be derived as follows:

A	kuai.zi.men	ji.men	ke.ren.men	guan.men	wo.men	ta.men
	'chopsticks'	'chickens'	'guests'	'officials'	'we'	'it – plural'
B1	kuai.zi-Ø	ji-Ø	ke.ren.men	guan.men	wo.men	ta-Ø
B2	kuai.zi	ji	ke.ren.men	guan-Ø	wo.men	ta
B3	kuai.zi	ji	ke.ren-Ø, or ker.ren.men	guan	wo.men	ta

Knowing a language means having unconscious knowledge of rule systems like those for Cherokee and Mandarin Chinese; it is systems like these that must be acquired in both first and second language acquisition. Moreover, if we assume that the rule system for suffixing and then deleting /-men/ is in the mind of a speaker of Mandarin Chinese, we can then readily see how the conditions for deleting /-men/ might be simplified by both people acquiring the language as a second language and by infants acquiring it as their first language. As we discussed briefly in Chapter 6, infants and second language learners are, in fact, the primary agents of language change.

Knowing a language also means having chosen from among the alternatives available in Universal Grammar (unconsciously, to be sure) in the course of acquiring a language. Let us refer to these points of choice as **parameters**. The difference between whether a language suffixes or prefixes morphemes to words is an example of a parameter fixed one way or the other by the language learner based on linguistic experience. Looking ahead to the chapters on question formation that follow, we will again learn that whether something happens at the left edge or the right edge of a linguistic structure constitutes a striking parametric difference between languages.

In examining how questions are formed in language, we will proceed in much the same way as we have in the first part of this book: by appealing to the human instinct to construct explanations of natural phenomena – in our case, the phenomena of language. From the patterns that we saw in the problem sets on noun pluralization, we were able to formulate hypotheses and evaluate them by following through on the predictions that they made – and in the face of counterexamples, perhaps reformulating the hypothesis – ever mindful of trying to find the most parsimonious explanation of the phenomenon before us.

Terms

infixing
prefixing
reduplication
suffixing
dual
dualization
affixation
parameters

Part II

Question Formation, or How to Find Out Whether the Cat Is Sleeping in Tohono O'odham

Chapter 8
Merge

Mental grammar – the knowledge of language that a person has when we say that she or he knows a particular language – consists of four components: phonology, morphology, syntax, and semantics. In Part I of this book, our investigation of noun pluralization revealed mostly phonology, morphology, and semantics at work, but very little syntax. Here in Part II, we examine syntax in detail, focusing on a basic syntactic process in language, that of forming questions. But before we turn to question formation, we must first consider the nature of sentence structure.

The sentences of a language – its statements, questions, and commands – are made up of phrases, the phrases themselves made up of other phrases, which are themselves made up of words, suffixes, prefixes, and infixes. This suggests that sentences have a **hierarchical structure**, that they are not composed of words placed one after another like beads on a string.

We can begin to understand the structure of sentences by considering the following sentences:

(1) *Emma looked over the fence.*

First, why do we say "sentences"? Because sentence (1) is really two sentences. It is structurally ambiguous; its words can hang together in two different ways, yielding two different interpretations or meanings. Is Emma inspecting the fence, or is she looking across the fence – perhaps into the next yard? On the first interpretation, let's call it (1a), *looked over* is a two-part, or compound, verb whose object is the noun phrase (NP) *the fence*. On the second interpretation (1b), *look* is a simple verb and *over the fence* is a **prepositional phrase** (or **PP**), consisting of the preposition *over* and the object of the preposition, the NP *the fence*. This much of sentence (1) can be seen to have the following structures – shown by the square brackets:

(1)   a   *Emma* [[*looked over*] [*the fence*]].
       b   *Emma* [[*looked*] [[*over*] [*the fence*]]].

Since *looked over* and *looked* are verbs, we call the structure that contains them a **verb phase** (or **VP**). The hierarchical nature of these VP structures is visually clearer when presented in **tree** form, below.

(2)   a   b

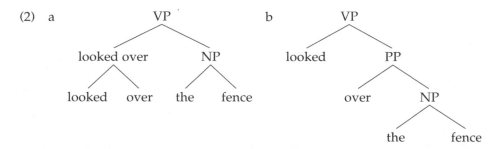

Starting at the base and moving up through the VP trees in (2a) and (2b), notice that <u>pairs</u> of elements merge at every level. In (2a):

- *the* and *fence* merge to form the NP;
- *looked* and *over* merge to form the compound verb; and
- the VP is formed through the merger of *looked over* and the NP.

In tree (2b), the following pair-wise mergers take place:

- *the* and *fence* form the NP;
- *over* and the NP form the PP; and
- *looked* and the PP form the VP.

Ultimately, of course, the VPs themselves are knit together with *Emma* to form complete sentences. This pair-wise or **binary structure** is a basic characteristic of language.

Roots and Morphemes

The basic elements of language that merge to form structured phrases such as those in (2a) and (2b) above are drawn from the **lexicon**, or mental dictionary. By basic lexical elements, we mean not only words, but also the **roots** and **morphemes** that go into the making of a word; that is, not just *look*, for example, but also the suffix that represents the morpheme {past}.

Since it is essential to what follows in this chapter, let us examine what it means for something to be a **root**. Here is a definition:

Definition:
A basic lexical element is a **root** if its grammatical category is determined
by the mergers it completes.

By linguistic convention, we will use the square root symbol, √ , to denote a
root form.

Consider the word *editor*, for example. It consists of the root √*edit* and a nominalizer or "noun-making" morpheme, abbreviated as {nmnl}. The particular
nominalizer, *-or*, denotes the person or thing (agent or instrument) doing
whatever the meaning of the root is. The agent-instrument {nmnl}, which in
one form is realized in English as the suffix *-or* (also spelled *-er*, but with no
difference in pronunciation or in meaning), cannot exist on its own. It can only
merge with a root to generate a noun.

However, √*edit* could have become something different, which is why it is
a root. Paired with the past tense morpheme {past}, √*edit* would, by the process presented in Chapter 4, end up as a verb: *edited*. Thus, we can at least see
that there are morphemes that generate verbs through merger and others that
generate nouns; let us call them **verb generators** and **noun generators**. There
are other kinds of generators, but in what follows, we concentrate on verb generators, leaving the generation of nouns aside – for the most part.

Merge

Merge is the operation by which sentences and complex words are generated.
Think of building sentences as a kind of construction project. Basic elements
are taken from the lexicon and then the operation Merge pairs them blindly.
Sometimes, the pieces fit together; other times, they do not.

For example, let us start simply by taking the following array of elements
from the lexicon: *the* (two of them), the root √*chase*, the morpheme {past}, and
two nouns: *rat* and *cat*. We now try to merge them pairwise. There are, of course,
mergers that will not work; for example, merging *the* with *the* is a bad fit, as
is merging *the* with {past}. These mergers will crash because they are ill-
formed, generating ungrammatical and uninterpretable structures, indicated,
as usual, by an *:

(3)

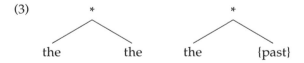

But merging *the* with *rat*, the other *the* with *cat*, and √*chase* with *the rat* does
work well. Thus, we say that these successful mergers reach **convergence**, resulting in two well-formed noun phrases (NPs) and a **root phrase** (√P). √*chase the*

rat is a root phrase because nothing yet indicates whether it is a verb phrase or a noun phrase:

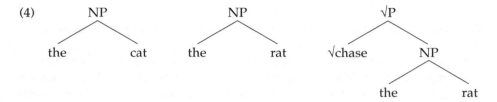

(4)

We now continue to merge these results, pairing {past} with the √P (√*chase the rat*), which converges in a VP, as in (5):

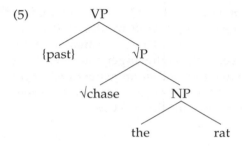

(5)

We then merge this VP with the NP *the cat*. Now everything converges in the viable structure (6), a sentence (S):

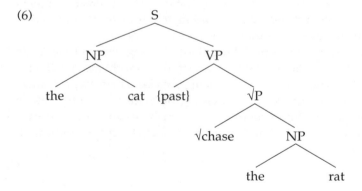

(6)

The tree shown in (6) is an **underlying structure** (sometimes referred to as a deep structure). No one talks underlying structure; it is the syntactic representation closest to thought. So some grammatical processes must take place for this and any mental structure to be realized at the **surface** in speech. From our analysis of English morphophonology, we know that for a regular root like

√chase, {past} will be realized phonologically in a regular way, as /t/, and this together with further phonological rules that assign primary stress / ´/ and lighter secondary stresses / ` / yields sentence (7):

(7)   *The cat chased the rat.*
       /ðə kæt čèst ðə ræt/

There are some questions still to be answered about the structure of the tree given in (6). For example, why is the verb generator {past} merged to the <u>left</u> of the root? Notice that its <u>effect</u> on the root is unchanged by the <u>position</u> of {past}: merging {past} with *chase* results in *chased* /čest/. Justification of the position of {past} in the tree, however, will have to wait until we move on to the later discussion of syntactic movement.

The question of why the mergers of *the* and *rat* and *the* and *cat* are labeled NP <u>can</u> be answered: because *rat* and *cat* are nouns. In general, a phrase type will be named in honor of its **head**, or dominant partner. The generation of verbs is the centerpiece of language, and the merger of verb generators like the morpheme {past} with a √P (root phrase) begets a VP.

Merging, transforming, and reaching convergence

Roots require one or more elements, each playing a separate part or **role** in a sentence. These roles directly affect the operation Merge and the successful mergers of roots with other elements that reach convergence. For √chase, the roles are these:

- a subject NP in the role of **agent** (or actor); in the case given above in (6), *the cat*; the term **subject** refers to the NP immediately below S;
- an object NP in the role of **patient**, the NP affected by the chasing; in the case given above, *the rat*; the term **object** refers to the NP immediately below √P.

On the other hand, a root like √give must surround itself with three elements:

- a subject NP in the role of **agent**;
- PP in the role of recipient or **goal** – the role that most clearly distinguishes √give-type roots from √chase-type roots;
- an object NP in the role of **theme**: something that moves from the agent to the goal.

So let's put Merge to work with this array drawn from the lexicon: √give, {past}, three determiners (*a, his, the*), a preposition (*to*), and three nouns: *book, man,* and *friend*.

Merging *his* and *friend* yields an NP, and merging this NP with *to* yields a PP (prepositional phrase), the potential goal that a root like √*give* requires:

(8)

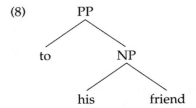

Roots like √*give* are identified and inherently distinguished in the lexicon from other types of roots by the fact that they take a goal. This fact is standardly captured in dictionary definitions of *give* and words like it, in *The Oxford English Dictionary* (1989, s.v. *give*), for example: "To make another the recipient." In recognition of this intuition, we first merge this root and the previously merged PP, which identifies the goal, generating a √P (root phrase):

(9)

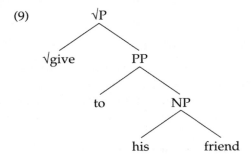

This √P in its turn successfully merges with the NP that results from a previous merger of *a* and *book*, yielding an even bigger √P, which satisfies √*give*'s need for a theme:

(10)

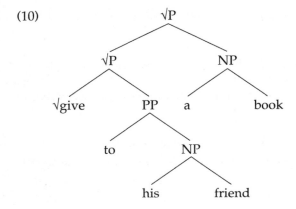

Then merging the √P in (10) with {past}, we generate a VP (verb phrase):

(11)

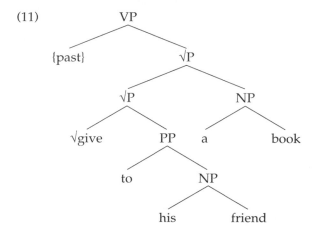

Finally, the merger of this VP and the NP that results from the merger of *the* and *man*, converges in the sentence (S) structure given in (12), satisfying all of √*give*'s required roles:

(12)

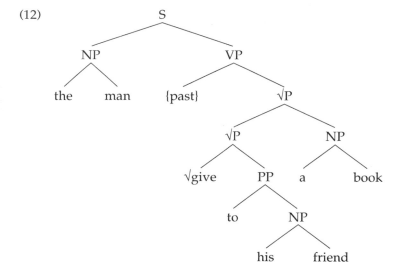

The underlying structure in (12), with the irregular interpretation of {past}, gives us sentence (13):

(13) *The man gave to his friend a book.*

While (12) is an interpretable structure, (13) is not a good sentence either phono-logically or in its word order – close, but rather like a sentence that might be produced by a person who had come to English from another language, perhaps Spanish or Italian. But for (12) to surface as a well-formed sentence in English, it needs to be affected by operations that are different from the structure-building of Merge: by operations that change the underlying structure of (12) by transforming it into a well-formed **surface** (ultimately spoken) **structure**. For example, deleting *to* would make it structurally well-formed at the surface:

(14)   *The man gave his friend a book.*
        /ðə mæn gèv hɪz frɛ̀nd ə búk/

Alternatively, moving the PP beyond the NP *a book*, to the right edge would also render a well-formed surface structure:

(15)   *The man gave a book to his friend.*
        /ðə mæn gèv ə bù̀k tu hɪz frɛ́nd/

Having been transformed through **movement** and **deletion**, the underlying structure shown in (12) converges on the well-formed sentences (14) and (15).

Why not assume that the underlying structure is *The man gave a book to his friend*, with the mergers shown in (16)?

(16)

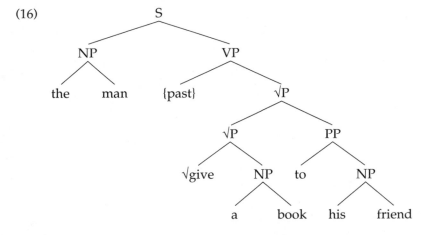

Note that the following **transformations** would then be necessary to produce the well-formed sentences (14) and (15) from (16): The NP *a book* must move to the right edge of the sentence and *to* must be deleted.

In order to choose between (12) and (16), we appeal once again to Occam's razor. For assuming the underlying structure to be (12) (*the man gave to his friend a book*) requires doing one thing or another in order to yield both the well-formed sentences (14) and (15): moving *to his friend* or deleting *to*. But assuming the underlying structure of (14) and (15) to be (16) requires doing one thing and another – in short, <u>two</u> things: moving *to his friend* <u>and</u> deleting *to*. The structure in (12) is thus more parsimonious.

Enough said about these matters for now. Later, we will examine in detail movement and deletion, operations that transform structures into other structures.

To sum up: As we have seen, more complicated sentences require more extensive mergers, but in all cases, the operation called Merge relentlessly pairs lexical elements until there is convergence in well-formed underlying syntactic structures.

Structural Ambiguity

A sentence can be ambiguous for a variety of reasons, because of an ambiguous word, for example. The sentence *Alex married Emma* is ambiguous for this reason because of the ambiguity of the verb *marry*. Either Alex performed a marriage ceremony for Emma, or Alex and Emma were married. If we reverse the positions of *Alex* and *Emma* in this sentence, then the second interpretation is unchanged. The first interpretation is radically changed, for it is now Emma who is performing the marriage ceremony for Alex. Ambiguity of this kind is called lexical ambiguity.

Other sentences are ambiguous because of the different possible grammatical relationships that exist between the words the sentences contain. For example, in *Visiting relatives can be boring*, the word *relatives* can be taken as either the subject of *visiting* (the persons who are visiting) or its object (the persons who are being visited).

And then there is structural ambiguity of the type that results from the different ways in which words can be grouped into phrases. To illustrate this type, we return to sentence (1) of this chapter, slightly altered:

(17)   *The woman looked over the fence.*

As we saw earlier, sentence (17) can mean either 'the woman inspected the fence' or 'the woman looked across the fence' – perhaps into the next yard.

Let us now examine in greater detail how this ambiguity can be explained by the different structures that Merge allows.

Take these elements from the lexicon: *the* (two of them), the root √*look*, {past}, the preposition *over*, and two nouns: *woman* and *fence*. The merger of the *the*'s, one with *fence* and the other with *woman*, gives us the NPs, *the fence* and *the woman*:

(18)

But the merger of the preposition *over* is freer: It can merge with *the fence* to form the PP *over the fence*; or it can merge with the root to form the compound root *look over*:

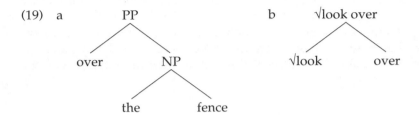

(19)   a   PP

over   NP

the   fence

b   √look over

√look   over

The PP can then merge with the root √*look*, while the compound root √*look over* can merge with *the fence* – yielding two different root phrases (√Ps):

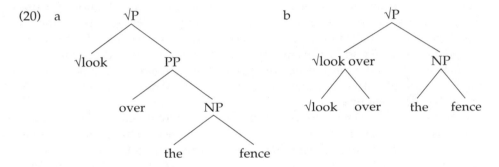

(20)   a   √P

√look   PP

over   NP

the   fence

b   √P

√look over   NP

√look   over   the   fence

Merging these √Ps with {past} then results in these well-formed VPs:

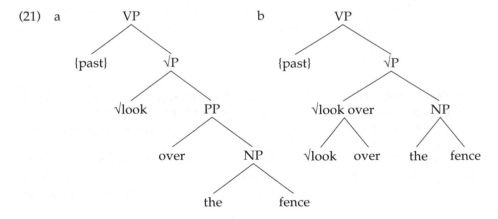

(21)   a   VP

{past}   √P

√look   PP

over   NP

the   fence

b   VP

{past}   √P

√look over   NP

√look   over   the   fence

Finally, merging (21a) and (21b) with the NP from the merge in (18) of *the* and *woman* results in convergence on two different underlying sentence structures, (22) and (23):

(22)

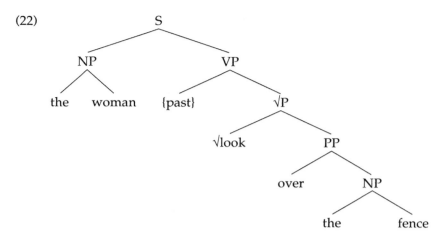

(23)

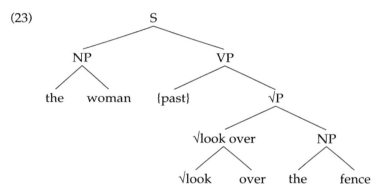

The underlying structures in (22) and (23) lead to the same surface or spoken form represented by (24), but they have different meanings, the result of slightly different sets of mergers.

(24)   *The woman looked over the fence.*
       /ðə wùmən lùkt ovər ðə féns/

One of the structures allows *over* to be moved past *the fence* to the right edge of the sentence <u>without</u> changing the meaning of the sentence. Which one – (22) or (23)? And for which meaning?

More about Transforming Underlying Structure

Let us return to the root √*give*. In (11) above, we saw that when the √P containing √*give* merges with the verb-generating morpheme {past}, the result is a verb: *gave*. But say that the √P containing √*give* were to be merged with a nominalizer {nmnl} – a noun generator, realized phonologically as /t/; then the result would be an NP containing *gift*:

(25) $\sqrt{give}$ + /t/ = *gift*[1]

Notice, moreover, that *gift* <u>may</u> surround itself with the same set of roles that *gave* <u>must</u> surround itself with: an agent, a goal, and a theme – though perhaps all three roles are implied in the word *gift*, whether they are explicitly expressed or not. Merging all of the same basic elements of the structure given in (11), but replacing the morpheme {past} with the morpheme {nmnl}, yields the following NP structure in (26), which is point by point parallel to the sentence structure in (12). Thus, in (26), the highest NP = the S of (12); the Determiner of (26) = the highest NP of (12); and the next lower NP of (26) = the VP of (12):

(26)

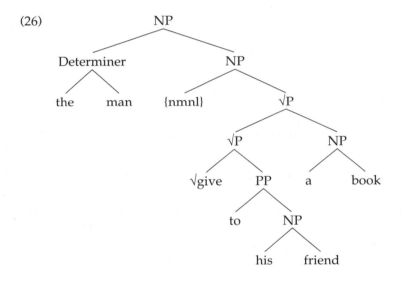

(27)   **The man gift to his friend a book.*

Hopeless? Not quite, for the kind of transformations that NPs require generally (because they <u>are</u> NPs, <u>not</u> Ss) give us the following well-formed, though perhaps not very elegant, NP:

---

[1]   The phonological effect of {nmnl} is to suffix a /t/ to the root $\sqrt{give}$. The [+voice] /v/ of the root is then assimilated to the [−voice] /t/, resulting in the /f/ of /gɪft/. Notice that this voicing assimilation is different in direction from the voicing assimilation of the English plural and past tense rules. In the formation of /gɪft/ from /gɪv + t/, assimilation is regressive in that it moves back from right to left, while in the plural and past tense rules, assimilation is progressive, moving forward from left to right: *robbed*, for example, is /rabd/ from /rab + t/.

(28)   *The man's gift of a book to his friend*

Compare the underlying structure in (26) with the transformed phrase in (28). In (28), the PP *to his friend* has been moved beyond the NP *a book*, to the right edge of the phrase; *a book* has merged with *of* into the PP *of a book*; and an *'s* has merged with the Determiner *the man*. These transformations yield the NP structure given in (29):

(29)

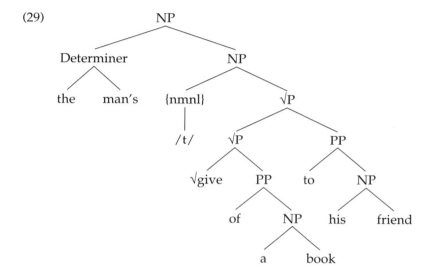

We can see that the additions of *of* and *'s* are simply structural rather than meaningful additions to the NP by asking ourselves what exactly these added elements mean. Neither the *'s* nor the *of* indicate possession, as you might be led to suspect if you were to consult a dictionary or a school grammar to answer the question, for *the man* does not necessarily possess *the gift*; he could have ordered it online, for example. And certainly *a book* cannot possess *the gift*. The answer to the question is that *'s* and *of* add nothing to the meaning of the NP; they simply have <u>structural</u> significance as markers of the agent (the person doing the giving: *the man*) and the theme (the thing being given: *the book*) in an NP based on a root like √*give*.

Importantly, transformations do not change the meaning of a structure: They take a well-formed underlying structure and transform it into a well-formed surface structure in preparation for its being spoken. And in the case of (26), the structural changes required are different from those made on (11) simply because (26) is an NP and (11) is an S.

However, unless (26) – even as transformed in (29) – merges with other elements from the lexicon, it will not be well-formed at the surface; for as an instructor might indicate in the margin of your paper, (29) is a sentence fragment (*frag*).

So to rescue (29), let us merge it with (30) – a VP, which is itself the result of merging the following array of elements from the lexicon: √*surprise*, {past}, *his*, and *mother*:

(30)

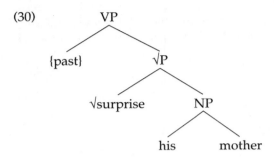

The merger of the VP in (30) with the NP in (29) (both structures now somewhat simplified) converges on (31). Note that here and elsewhere, a tree branch like △ means that further detailed treeing is not necessary or relevant to the analysis.

(31)

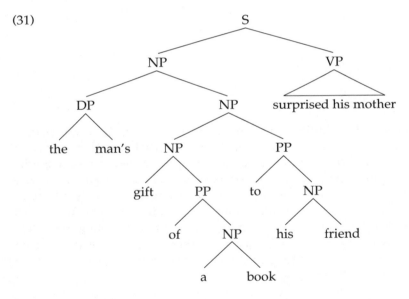

The structure shown in (31) underlies the well-formed sentence (32):

(32)   *The man's gift of a book to his friend surprised his mother.*

Notice, however, that the exact interpretation of this sentence is left open by the second *his*. Is the mother the friend's mother or the man's mother or the mother of some male person not even mentioned in (32)?

Phrase Structure and Tests of Constituency

The parts of a sentence that hang together under a label in syntactic structure are the **constituents** of that structure. In (31), for example, *his* and *friend* are the constituents of the NP that they hang from, and that NP and the *to* on its left are constituents of the PP that dominates them. But how do we know that the constituent structure shown in the phrase structure trees given above are the right structures? Intuitively speaking, they <u>feel</u> right, but we need something better than intuition. Here is something better, manipulations of the structures – sometimes referred to as tests – that provide another kind of data in support of the analyses given above: the **sentence-fragment test**, the **pronoun substitution test**, and the **movement test**.

The sentence-fragment test

When we express surprise about something that we hear, we can express it with fragments of sentences, but these fragments have to be made up of legitimate phrase-structure constituents and not of discontinuous pieces of a sentence. For example, if you were to say to someone:

(33)   *The cat chased the rat.*

she might reply with (34), but not with (35) or (36):

(34)   *Chased the rat? What's so strange about that?*
(35)   **Cat chased the? What's so strange about that?*
(36)   **The cat √chase? What's so strange about that?*

An examination of the phrase structure tree for (33), shown here as (37), reveals that the VP *chased the rat* and the NP *the rat* are constituents of sentence (33) and that *cat chased the* and *the cat √chase* are made up of pieces of constituents, but are not themselves constituents:

(37)

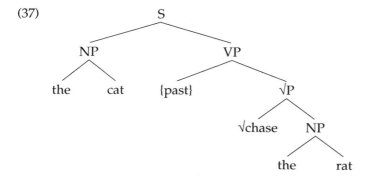

You can and do express surprise, as well as other thoughts, in fragments of sentences, but the fragments must be whole constituents of a sentence, as in (34).

The pronoun substitution test

This test mainly involves **pronouns**, basic lexical elements that can substitute for NPs and some PPs. For example, any and all of the NPs in (38) can be replaced by an appropriate pronoun, as in (39–41):

(38)   *The man gave a book to his friend.*
(39)   *He gave a book to his friend.*
(40)   *He gave it to his friend.*
(41)   *He gave it to him.*

Notice, however, that the pronouns actually replace the NPs – phrase-structure constituents – of (38). This does not fit well with a long-standing school-grammar definition of a pronoun (see, for example, Reed & Kellogg, 1889, p. 26):[2]

(42)   *Definition:*
         A *Pronoun* is a word used for a noun.

A literal reading of definition (42) would permit us to say,

(43)   **The he gave an it to his him.*

which is clearly not what we do! However, a pronoun may substitute for a single word when that is all there is for it to substitute for, as in sentence (45) for sentence (44) – with *her* substituting for *Emma*:

(44)   *The man gave a book to Emma.*
(45)   *The man gave a book to her.*

We see, then, that pronouns can substitute for NPs, even for really big and complex NPs like the one in sentence (32), repeated here as sentence (46) with pronoun substitution in (47):

(46)   *The man's gift of a book to his friend surprised his mother.*
(47)   *It surprised his mother.*

---

[2]   One hundred and twelve years later, the *Little Brown Compact Handbook* can do no better than "17b Recognizing pronouns[:] Most pronouns substitute for nouns and function in sentences as nouns do" (Aaron, 2001, p. 155). The word *function* is used here to refer to notions like 'subject of', 'object of', and so on.

The "pronouns" *there* and *then* also substitute for constituents, for **locative** prepositional phrases (locational PPs) – as in (48–51), and **temporal** prepositional phrases as in (50) and (51):

(48)   *The woman looked over the fence.*
(49)   *The woman looked there.*
(50)   *The teacher is in her office on Wednesdays.*
(51)   *The teacher is there then.*

But the substitution for (48) is only possible given the structure shown in (52), in which the PP *over the fence* is a phrase-structure constituent:

(52)

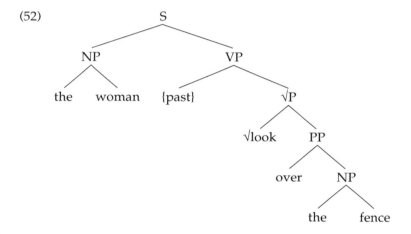

The structure shown in (53) – in which *over the fence* is <u>not</u> a constituent – only allows a pronoun to substitute for *the fence*, which <u>is</u> a constituent, as illustrated in sentence (54):

(53)

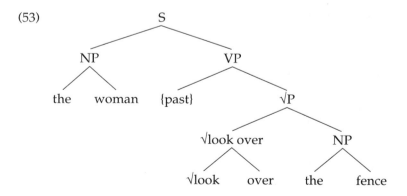

(54)   *The woman looked over it.*

In fact, for the structure shown in (53), speakers of English prefer – for prosodic reasons – sentence (55), in which *over* has been moved past *it* to the right edge of the sentence:

(55)   *The woman looked it over.*

These examples show that pronoun substitution picks out constituents of a sentence, and that these constituents are exactly those that appear in the structural trees built through Merge.

Although we'll not go into this matter in any detail, there is also "pro-verb" substitution. In (56), for example, the pro-verb *did* substitutes for the VP of the first clause *went to Chicago*:

(56)   *Emma went to Chicago and Alex did too.*

The movement test

A third test depends on movement, which we have already seen at work in sentences (13) and (15), repeated here as (57) and (58). In (58), the entire PP *to his friend* (not just some part of it) has been moved to the right edge of the sentence as a transformational operation on (57):

(57)   **The man gave to his friend a book.*
(58)   *The man gave a book to his friend.*

Quasi-poetic sentences (that is, sentences employing syntactic devices often used in poetry) also exhibit movement, but only **constituent movement** – as in (58). Compare (59) with (60), for example:

(59)   *To his friend, the man gave a book.*
(60)   **Friend, the man gave a book to his.*

Or compare sentence (61) with (62) and (63) and sentence (64) with (65) and (66):

(61)   *Let's row up this pleasant stream . . .*
(62)   *Up this pleasant stream, let's row . . .* (Thoreau, "The Assabet," line 1)
(63)   **Pleasant stream, let's row up this . . .*

(64)   *The woman looked over the fence.*
(65)   *Over the fence, the woman looked.*
(66)   **Over, the woman looked the fence.*

And finally, recall the children's song, in which two locative prepositional phrases and a directional phrase are moved to the left edge of the sentence, as in (67) and not left in place, as in (68), where they would be fine but less song-like:

(67)   *Over the river and through the woods, to grandmother's house we'll go.*
(68)   *We'll go over the river and through the woods to grandmother's house.*

These examples show that movement, like pronoun substitution, picks out constituents in a sentence.

Summing Up

Our analyses of sentences and phrases assume that they are hierarchically structured, the result of successful mergers of words, roots, and morphemes drawn from the lexicon. Successful merges converge on well-formed underlying syntactic structures that then undergo movement or deletion or other transformations in order to arrive at well-formed surface or spoken structures.

The tests we have examined all provide support for the constituent structures (NP, VP, PP) illustrated in the tree diagrams that resulted from successful merges. Since the tests provide no evidence against these structures, we will assume that the phrase structure analyses provided in this chapter are on the right track.

Now, for a problem set, after which we will be ready to move on to question formation and a closer examination of syntactic movement.

Problem Set 10: Merging, Transforming, and Converging

A   Merge the following arrays of basic lexical elements into trees that converge on well-formed English sentences. At least one tree per lexical array, and no crashes – please!

(1)   Lexical array: √send, to, a, a, the, child, {past}, friend, card
(2)   Lexical array: the, her, girl, √load, with, wagon, hay, {past}

  Hint: When in doubt about phrase structure, remember the constituency tests.

B   Draw the trees that represent the underlying structures of the following sentences. Then identify how they need to be transformed in order for them to be well-formed English sentences at the surface.

(3)   *The woman placed on the shelf a book.*
(4)   *The girl baked for her mother a cake.*

C   In the following sentence, what basic lexical element does the √P containing √go merge with that allows it to converge on a well-formed VP? That is, what is the **verb generator** here that merges with the √P to build the VP for sentence (5)?

(5)   *The boy will go to the Burlington Mall.*

Before you move on to Chapter 9, be sure to think through and construct reasoned trees and answers for this problem set.

Terms and Linguistic Conventions

hierarchical structure	agent
prepositional phrase, PP	subject
verb phrase, VP	patient
tree	object
binary structure	goal
lexicon	theme
root	movement
morpheme	deletion
verb generator	transformation
noun generator	constituent
Merge	sentence fragment test
convergence	pronoun substitution test
root phrase √P	movement test
underlying structure	pronoun
surface structure	locative
head	temporal
role	constituent movement

√   The square root symbol precedes lexical items that are roots

*   An asterisk indicates that a form is ill-formed.

△   This tree branch means that further detailed treeing is not relevant to the analysis.

Further Reading

See Chomsky (2004, pp. 152ff.) for discussion of Merge.

Chapter 9

An Introduction to the Syntax of Question Formation

All languages distinguish questions from **declarative sentences** (or statements), and all languages have question words that distinguish content questions from yes/no questions. A **yes/no question** is one that can be answered by responding "yes" or "no" – or "maybe"; for example:

(1) *Is it hot today?*
(2) *Yes, it's hot today.*

A content or **WH-question** is one that can be answered by supplying some new piece of information in place of the question word, for example:

(3) *Where have you been?*
(4) *I've been in Tucson.*

In a clear case of English-language hegemony, linguists use the term **WH-question** to refer to content questions, because of the fact that most of the question words, or **WH-words**, in English begin with *wh* in their <u>spelled</u> form.[1]

Different languages form questions in structurally different ways, but – as we shall see – Universal Grammar (UG) allows only a small number of structurally different ways.

We turn now to how questions are formed in language by first analyzing Mandarin Chinese yes/no questions.

---

[1] Notice, however, that English WH-question words differ in the <u>pronunciation</u> of their initial sounds: *Who* and *how* begin with /h/, while *why, what, where* begin with /w/ or /hw/, depending on a particular speaker's dialect.

Investigating Yes/No Question Formation in Mandarin Chinese

The full answer to a yes/no question may be preceded by *yes* or *no* (or *maybe*), but since these words are not <u>structurally</u> important for our analysis, we leave them out of consideration in our investigation of yes/no questions in Mandarin Chinese[2] and other languages in this and the following chapters.

The following data, (5–8), illustrate Mandarin Chinese yes/no questions and possible answers to them. Sentence (6) is a possible answer to question (5), and sentence (8) is a possible answer to question (7):

(5)   *Ni   kaixin   ma*
      you happy ?
      'Are you happy?'

(6)   *Wo kaixin.*
      I   happy
      'I am happy.'

(7)   *Zhu De shi laoshi   ma*
      Zhu De be teacher ?
      'Is Zhu De a teacher?'

(8)   *Zhu De shi laoshi.*
      Zhu De be teacher
      'Zhu De is a teacher.'

The structural difference between these two pairs of questions and answers – (5) and (6), and (7) and (8) – is simply that the question has a <u>spoken</u> question mark, *ma*. We refer to this spoken question mark for yes/no questions as a **yes/no question particle**, **Y/N**. In Mandarin Chinese, Y/N is realized as *ma*.

We diagram the relationship of *ma* to the rest of the question and the relationship between yes/no questions and their full answers below. Note that in these syntactic trees:

- **Y/N Q** labels a yes/no question.
- ⟋⟍ means that further detailed treeing of that constituent is not relevant to the analysis.

---

[2]   For background information on Mandarin Chinese – the language and its speakers – see Problem Set 8 in Chapter 6. The Mandarin Chinese data in this chapter are from Li and Thompson (1981) and Cheng (1991), or projected from these sources.

The trees for question (5) and answer (6), given in (9) and (10), respectively, show that a Mandarin Chinese yes/no question contains a statement (S) – one that has the <u>same</u> structure as a possible answer and that merges with the particle *ma*:

(9)   (10)

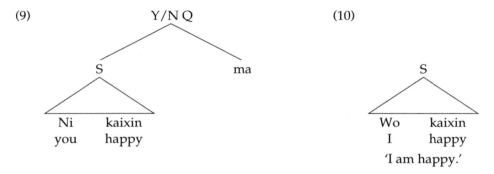

This generalization about Mandarin Chinese yes/no questions is also shown in (11) and (12), the syntactic trees for question (7) and answer (8), respectively:

(11)   (12)

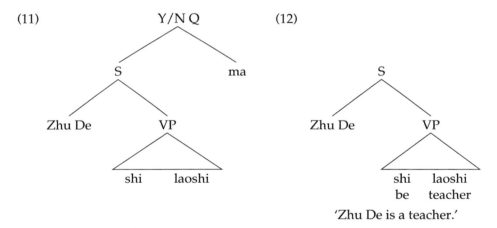

Thus, in Mandarin Chinese, the structural difference between a yes/no question and a declarative sentence (or statement) simply comes down to this: A yes/no question has the yes/no question particle *ma* attached at the right edge of the tree. Otherwise, a statement and a yes/no question exhibit the exact same structure.

As the trees above reveal, what the question particle *ma* does is "project" a question **mood** <u>over</u> the entire structure of a statement. **Mood** is a grammatical term used to refer to the attitude a speaker has toward the action or condition being expressed – in this case, an interrogative mood, as opposed to a declarative or imperative mood.

Let us now examine how WH-questions are formed in Mandarin Chinese.

Problem Set 11: WH-Question Formation in Mandarin Chinese

Here are two Mandarin Chinese WH-questions with possible replies to them – question (1) with its reply, sentence (2), and question (3) with its reply, sentence (4):

(1) *Ta   yao   shenme ne*
    she/he want what   ?
    'What does she/he want?'

(2) *Ta   yao   xiaobing.*
    she/he want bread
    'She/he wants some bread.'

(3) *Ni   kanjian-le shei ne*
    you see   who ?
    'Who did you see?'

(4) *Wo kanjian-le Li Yafei.*
    I   see   Li Yafei
    'I saw Li Yafei.'

A   Compare WH-questions (1) and (3) with their possible answers (2) and (4). What structural differences and similarities do you observe between (1) and (2)? Between (3) and (4)?

B   Formulate a hypothesis that accounts for how WH-questions are formed in Mandarin Chinese.

C   After you have formulated a hypothesis, think through and then state the form(s) that counterexamples to your hypothesis would have to take.

Before you move on to D, be sure to think through and construct reasoned answers to A–C.

D   Does your hypothesis predict the well-formedness of the additional data below?

(5) *Shei yao   xiaobing ne*
    who want bread   ?
    'Who wants some bread?'

(6) *Li Yafei yao   xiaobing*
    Li Yafei want bread
    'Li Yafei wants some bread.'

If so, show how it does. If not, reformulate your hypothesis so as to account for these data as well as the data given in the question-answer pairs (1–4). Then demonstrate how your revised hypothesis works, discussing specific examples.

E   Draw a syntactic tree for each member of the question-answer pair (1) and (2), and for each member of the question-answer pair (5) and (6).

F   An answer to a WH-question requires new information. How does a speaker of Mandarin Chinese know <u>where</u> to place that new information in a full answer (that is, in a declarative sentence)? In answering this question, refer to the syntactic trees that you drew in E.

Before you move on to Chapter 10, be sure to think through and construct reasoned, convincing trees and answers to D–F.

Terms

declarative sentence
yes/no question, Y/N Q
WH-question
WH-word
yes/no question particle, Y/N
mood

10

Syntactic Movement and Question Formation

It is a striking characteristic of language that a constituent of a sentence can be found <u>displaced</u> from its **point of interpretation**. As we saw in Chapter 8, we can observe displacement even in quite simple sentences:

(1)   *Emma looked over the fence.*

Let us assume that this sentence has the meaning 'Emma inspected the fence'. Here, *looked over* is a compound verb with a meaning ('inspect') greater than the sum of its parts. Given this interpretation of (1), it is possible to move the preposition *over* to the right edge of the sentence and still have a well-formed sentence with the same meaning:

(2)   *Emma looked the fence over.*

We refer to processes of **syntactic movement** as **transformations** – processes that explain the displacement that we observe in languages. We can then say that sentence (2) is a <u>transformed</u> version of sentence (1). Importantly, as we will see below, movement transformations move and raise a constituent to a higher level in the tree structure of a sentence, leaving a copy of that constituent behind in its "original" underlying position. The **copy** of the moved constituent is a "mental reminder" of where the moved element is to be interpreted.

We can see how movement has transformed the structure of sentence (1) into the structure of sentence (2) by examining their respective tree diagrams (3) and (5) below:

(3)

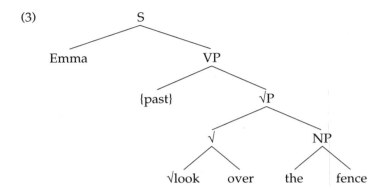

(4) *Emma looked over the fence.*

(5)

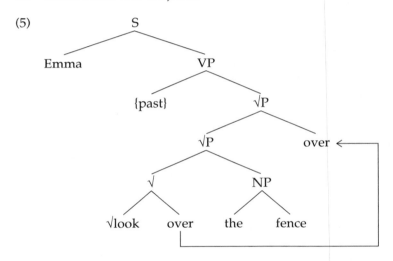

(6) *Emma looked the fence over.*

Although up until now we have informally said that the preposition *over* in sentence (2), repeated here as (6), has moved to the right edge of the sentence, more has happened structurally. We see from (5), the tree for sentence (6), that *over* has actually been <u>raised</u> up within the root phrase (√P) and has created a position for itself in the structure by merging to form a higher √P. From this higher point, *over* dominates its copy in its underlying position within the root (√). The copy of *over* is a reminder that it is to be interpreted as part of the root √*look over*. In speech, the copy of *over* must, of course, be deleted since only the moved preposition *over* is pronounced.

From this example, we see that movement always involves **raising** to a position in the syntactic structure that <u>dominates</u> the copy of the moved constituent. The technical term for this relationship is **c-command**, **c** standing for **constituent**. C-command is a syntactic relationship defined on structural trees:

Definition:
A constituent c-commands another constituent if the constituent that <u>immediately</u> dominates it also dominates the other constituent.

We illustrate c-command by moving through (5), the tree structure of sentence (6), beginning at the top:

- *Emma* and VP (verb phrase) mutually c-command one another because the S (sentence) that immediately dominates (that is, lies directly above) *Emma* also immediately dominates the VP.
- Moving lower in the tree, we see that the morpheme {past} c-commands the √P (root phrase), as well as each constituent within that √P: the root (√) and the NP *the fence*.
- {past} also c-commands each constituent of the √: √*look* and *over*; as well as each constituent of the NP: *the* and *fence*.

Constituents that are mutually c-commanded – as *Emma* and VP are by S, and as {past} and the √P are by VP, for example – are called **sisters**. Constituents that are not mutually c-commanded are not sisters. For example, although {past} c-commands √*look*, these two constituents are not sisters since they do not mutually c-command one another.

Returning now to the preposition *over*, which has been raised by movement, we see in (5) that *over* c-commands its copy, *over*, since it immediately dominates the √P of which the copy is a constituent. A moved constituent will <u>always</u> c-command its copy because of its movement to a higher, dominating position in a structural tree.

To understand a transformed sentence like (6), we mentally reassemble the pieces of the sentence so as to get the right interpretation. In this case, the lower copy of the moved preposition *over* prompts us to reassemble *looked* with *over* so that the two are interpreted as the compound verb *looked over*, with the meaning 'inspected'.

Preposition movement (or **P-movement**) is one possible transformation in language, one that relates the underlying structure and the surface structure of sentences. English is among the few languages that have P-movement. There are, however, other, more common types of movement rules in language, as we shall see.

In order to explain the relationship between questions and their answers, we look now at the movement that is characteristic of question formation in three languages, English, Tohono O'odham, and Brazilian Portuguese. We begin with English yes/no question formation.

Investigating English Yes/No Question Formation

By way of introduction, let us recall how yes/no questions are formed in Mandarin Chinese. From the linguist's point of view, as well as from the infant's point of view as a language learner, the simplest and most parsimonious assumption is that Mandarin Chinese yes/no question formation is the way in which yes/no questions are formed in language: The yes/no question particle simply projects a question mood over a statement; nothing moves.

Can we apply this analysis to English yes/no questions? By making this tightly constrained hypothesis, we will soon learn if we are wrong. With this hypothesis in mind, consider the following English yes/no questions and the statements that answer them:

(7)   *Is Emma moving to Buffalo?*
(8)   *Emma is moving to Buffalo.*

(9)   *Has Emma moved to Buffalo?*
(10) *Emma has moved to Buffalo.*

Comparing the question and answer pairs reveals that something has been moved in forming these yes/no questions. Focusing on (7), we assume that what has been moved is the **auxiliary** verb *is*, a verb generator that merges with a √P (root phrase) to form a VP (verb phrase). This particular *is* is the **progressive** form of the verb *be*, which expresses an ongoing action or condition and in (7) places √*move* in its progressive form, *moving*. Progressive is one of a number of **grammatical aspects** that mark the relation of the verb to concepts like duration, completion, and so on.

Thus we hypothesize the following underlying structure for the yes/no question (Y/N Q) in (7):

(11)   a

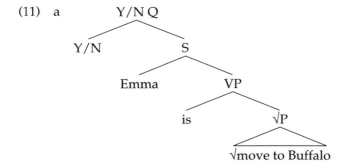

Notice in (11a) that we assume that English, like Chinese, has a yes/no question particle, which we label **Y/N**. In English, however, the **yes/no question particle** has zero phonological form at the surface; that is, it is not expressed in pronunciation. It is in the mind but not in the mouth.

We also assume that underlying the structure of a yes/no question is a statement (or declarative sentence, S), one that has the structure of a possible answer and that merges with the question particle, Y/N.

Although it has no phonological form, the yes/no question particle in English has syntactic effect. Acting like a magnet, Y/N attracts and raises the progressive auxiliary *is* to its position:

(11) b

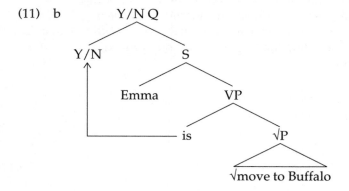

Recall that movement always leaves behind a copy to remind us of the point of interpretation of the moved constituent. Thus, when *is* is attracted to and fills the empty yes/no question particle position (empty because Y/N has no phonological form in English), a copy of *is* remains in its underlying structural position. The movement of *is* to the position of Y/N results in the following structure for (7):

(11) c

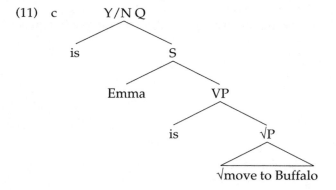

In the example of tree (11c), we again see that movement requires that a constituent be raised to a higher position in the syntactic structure, one that c-commands the copy of that moved element. The particular type of movement represented in (11c) is called **auxiliary movement,** another possible transformation in language.

In addition to attracting the progressive auxiliary *is* to itself, the English yes/no question particle, Y/N – while having no phonological content itself – does have phonological effect. The particle imposes an intonational contour over a yes/no question that is different from the corresponding statement. The pitch of the yes/no question rises through the final word *Buffalo*, while the pitch of the corresponding statement falls through the final word.

(12)   *Is Emma moving to Buffalo?*

(13)   *Emma is moving to Buffalo.*

A parallel analysis can be made of (9) with Y/N attracting the perfective auxiliary *has* and imposing a rising intonation across the yes/no question:

(14)   a

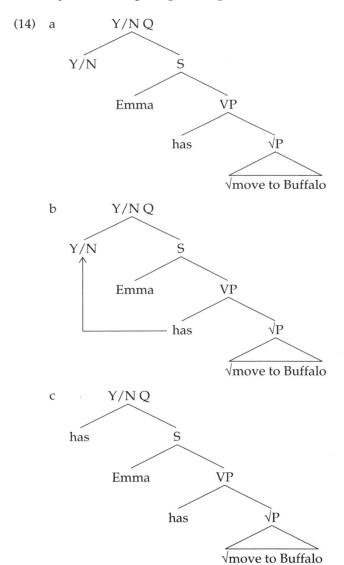

(15)   Has Emma moved to B̄uffalo?

The auxiliary *has* is the perfective form of *have* and is a verb generator like the progressive auxiliary *is*, merging with a √P to form a VP. **Perfective** is a grammatical aspect that expresses completion and that in question (9), repeated in (15), places the √*move* in its perfective form, *moved.*[1]

Indirect Yes/No Questions

Note that auxiliary movement is found only in independent, "free-standing" yes/no questions in English. If a yes/no question is a **subordinate clause** that is embedded in a sentence, a so-called **indirect question**, then neither its word order nor its intonation is different from that of a statement. For example, compare the intonational contour of question (12) and statement (13) above with that of the indirect question in (16):

(16)   *I wonder whether Emma is moving to Buffalo.*

Notice, however, that indirect yes/no questions contain a <u>spoken</u> yes/no question particle (*whether*), and it is this question word that occupies the Y/N position and prevents the auxiliary from raising to this position:

(17)

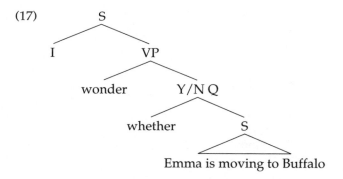

(18)   *I wonder whether Emma is moving to Buffalo.*

In this sense, indirect yes/no questions in English are like direct yes/no questions in Mandarin Chinese (examined in Chapter 9). Both have a spoken yes/no question particle (*whether* and *ma*), differing over whether the position of the particle is at the left edge or right edge of the Y/N Q structure.

---

[1]   The analysis here of the auxiliary forms is actually somewhat more complex than we allow, for *is* and *has* result from the merging of tense and person/number (in this case {present, 3rd singular}) and the roots √*be* and √*have*.

Interestingly, however, Mandarin Chinese must use a different type of yes/no question for indirect questions, the so-called A-not-A type. A-not-A yes/no questions take the following form – both as a free-standing alternative to a *ma*-type yes/no question, as in (19), and as an indirect (or embedded) yes/no question, as in (20):

(19) *Ta   zai jia   bu zai jia*   (alternatively: *Ta zai jia ma*)
      she/he be home not be home
      'Is she/he home?'

(20) *Wo bu zhidao ta   zai jia   bu zai jia*
      I   not know she/he be home not be home
      'I don't know whether she/he is home (or not).'

In (20), if we were to replace *ta zai jia bu zai jia* ('Is she/he home?') with its alternative *ta zai jia ma* ('Is she/he home?'), as in (21), the sentence would take on an entirely different meaning from that given for (20):

(21) *Wo bu zhidao ta   zai jia   ma*
      I   not know she/he be home ?
      'Don't I know whether she/he is home (or not)?'

This is because *ma* can only impose a yes/no question mood over the entire sentence structure that precedes it; that is, *ma* calls in question the <u>whole</u> statement (*Wo bu zhidao ta zai jia* 'I don't know whether she/he is home'), rather than the embedded one (*ta zai jia* 'she/he is home'). Thus, *Wo bu zhidao ta zai bu zai ma?* can only have the meaning given in (21) – a rather odd questioning of one's knowledge.

The Role of Movement in Yes/No Question Formation

Different languages form questions in structurally different ways. What possibilities have we learned about so far? Let us concentrate our attention on yes/no questions – the direct kind – first.

In Mandarin Chinese, we see that yes/no questions are formed by the merger of a question particle *ma* – one that has phonological content – and that this particle imposes or projects a yes/no question mood over the structure of a statement. Otherwise, a Mandarin Chinese yes/no question and the corresponding statement that answers it have exactly the same structure. There is no syntactic movement.

In English, the merger of a question particle with no phonological form also imposes a yes/no question mood over the structure of a statement. In addition, in contrast to Chinese, the question particle in English attracts the auxiliary verb, moving it to the yes/no question particle position and leaving a copy of the auxiliary behind in its underlying structural position. Moreover, the particle, though lacking phonological content, has phonological <u>effect</u>: It imposes a rising intonational contour over a yes/no question that is different from a statement's falling intonational contour.

Are there other possibilities? Would we ask such a yes/no question if there weren't? With this broad hint in mind, let us now examine yes/no question formation in Tohono O'odham.

Problem Set 12: Yes/No Question Formation in Tohono O'odham

In the introduction to her *Papago Grammar* (1983, pp. xiii–xiv), Ofelia Zepeda writes about O'odham, the people and the language, as follows:

> The Papago people – or as they call themselves, the 'O'odham – reside in south-ern Arizona and northern Mexico, where they have lived for centuries. Most of the 'O'odham live on four reservations in southern Arizona. The main reservation, with its Indian agency at Sells, covers the largest area . . . Not all of the 'O'odham live on the reservations; many live in towns near them – such as Ajo, Maricopa, and Casa Grande – as well as in the cities of Phoenix and Tucson.
>
> Covering more than two and a half million acres, the main Papago Indian re-servation is the second largest (after the Navajo) in the United States. Since there are approximately twelve thousand Papagos,[2] the population density relative to the land area is small; however, the Papago actually constitute a relatively large tribal population as compared to other American Indian . . .
>
> [T]he best estimate as to the number of Papagos who still speak Papago fluently in the early 1980s is more than two-thirds of the population, or approximately seventy to seventy-five percent . . .

Zepeda notes, however, that "many young Papagos appear to be less fluent in Papago than their elders; many say that they speak only a little, others that they don't speak Papago at all, but understand it."

Tohono O'odham has now replaced the word *Papago* to refer to both the people and their language.

Investigating Tohono O'odham Yes/No Question Formation

Turning now to yes/no question formation in Tohono O'odham, consider the following data (derived from Zepeda, 1983, pp. 14–15). Note that {**impf**} labels the verb generat-ing morpheme *o*, an **imperfective** auxiliary verb that indicates "*ongoing action* in the *pre-sent* or *past*" (Zepeda, 1983, p. 8 – italics hers).

---

[2]   "According to U.S. Census figures, 1980." According to US Census 2000 figures, the main reservation alone now has a population of 10,787 (*Tucson Citizen*, June 5, 2001, p. 1).

(1)   *No g mi:stol ko:s?*
      'Is/was the cat sleeping?'

(2)   *G³ mi:stol o   ko:s.*
      the cat   {impf} sleep
      'The cat is/was sleeping.'

(3)   *No g gogogs hihink?*
      'Are/were the dogs barking?'

(4)   *G gogogs o   hihink.*
      the dogs   {impf} bark
      'The dogs are/were barking.'

A   Compare question (1) with statement (2), and question (3) with statement (4). What differences do you observe between these pairs? What similarities?

B   Draw a syntactic tree for each member of the pairs (1) and (2); (3) and (4).
       Hint: Recall auxiliary movement in English yes/no question formation and its consequences.

C   Based on your analysis of the data, formulate a hypothesis that explains how yes/no questions are formed in Tohono O'odham. Demonstrate how your hypothesis works, discussing specific examples.

D   How does yes/no question formation work in a language (other than English) that you know?

Before you move on in this chapter, be sure to think through and construct reasoned, convincing trees and answers for A–C.

The Role of Movement in WH-Question Formation

How are WH-questions formed in Mandarin Chinese? From Problem Set 11 (in Chapter 9), we can conclude the following:

- that Mandarin Chinese has a WH-question particle *ne* that merges with the structure of a statement and projects a WH-question mood over the entire structure;[4]
- that WH-words and the new information contained in a possible answer to a WH-question are located in the <u>same</u> structural positions.

---

[3]   The determiner *g* in (2) and (4) is in fact always deleted sentence-initially at the surface. Its deletion follows from Zepeda's second rule for Tohono O'odham: "Rule 2: Always drop the *g* determiner at the beginning of a sentence" (Zepeda, 1983, p. 13). Zepeda's Rule 1, however, is the relevant one at this point: "Rule 1: The aux[iliary, in this case, *o*] occurs in second position in a sentence" (p. 8). There are no further rules of this sort in Zepeda's grammar of Tohono O'odham.

[4]   Later we will see that *ne* may or may not be spoken. It is not unusual for languages to have elements that are optionally spoken. Compare, for example, the optionality of English *that*, as in *I think that Emma is tired* versus *I think Emma is tired*.

We illustrate this analysis of Mandarin Chinese WH-questions in (22) and (23) below, the syntactic trees of the question-answer pair (3) and (4) of Problem Set 11:

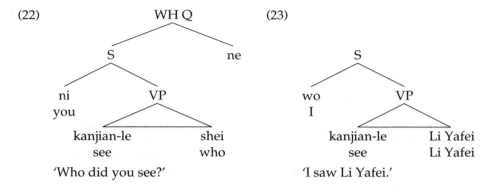

(22)

'Who did you see?'

(23)

'I saw Li Yafei.'

From this structural analysis we see that there is no syntactic movement in Mandarin Chinese WH-question formation, just as there is no syntactic movement in Mandarin-Chinese yes/no question formation.

We now turn to an investigation of how WH-questions are formed in English, which is obviously quite different from how they are formed in Mandarin Chinese.

Problem Set 13: WH-Question Formation in English

Consider the following data, consisting entirely of English WH-questions:

(1) *What will Emma put on the table?*
(2) *Where can he put the book?*
(3) *Where will she go tomorrow?*
(4) *Who must Emma talk to?*

A   Your goal is to explain WH-question formation in English. How would you proceed in your investigation given the WH-questions in (1–4)? What other data would you need to collect in order to proceed and why?
     Hint: Recall that questions and their possible answers are structurally related.
B   Proceed to collect more data.
C   Does English WH-question formation involve movement? How do you know? Draw trees to support your answer.
D   Based on the data you have collected and your analysis of them, formulate a hypothesis about how WH-questions are formed in English. Demonstrate how your hypothesis works, discussing specific examples.
E   How does WH-question formation work in other languages that you know?

Before you move on in this chapter, be sure to think through and construct reasoned, convincing trees and answers to A–D.

The Syntax of Question Formation

Thus far, we have seen that all languages have question particles – some with phonological content or effect, and that the merging of these particles projects a question mood over the structure of a statement. But how do languages differ? Recall the syntactic tree diagrams.

From these trees, we see that languages differ as to whether the question particle is merged at the left edge of the structure of the question, as in English and Tohono O'odham, or at the right edge of the structure, as in Mandarin Chinese.

Languages also differ over whether the question particle forces syntactic movement by attracting and raising elements to itself:

- In Tohono O'odham and English yes/no questions, the question particle acts like a magnet, attracting auxiliary verbs. In English WH-questions, WH-words are also moved to the question particle position. And where there is movement, a copy of the moved element is always left behind in its underlying structural position.
- In Mandarin Chinese yes/no and WH-questions, question particles do not act as magnets. There is no syntactic movement.

We now ask the expected WH-question: What other structural possibilities are there for WH-question formation?

Problem Set 14: WH-Question Formation in Brazilian Portuguese

Consider, now, the following WH-questions from Brazilian Portuguese,[5] the variety of Portuguese spoken in Brazil:

(1) *Maria visitou quem?*
     Maria visited who
     'Who did Maria visit?'

(2) *Quem Maria visitou?*
     who   Maria visited
     'Who did Maria visit?'

To which one could only – from the point of view of structure – answer with (3), not (4):

(3) *Maria visitou Paulo.*
     Maria visited Paulo
     'Maria visited Paulo.'

---

[5] For background information on Brazilian Portuguese – the language and its speakers – see Problem Set 6 in Chapter 3. This problem set is based on our work with Filomena Sandolo (Universidade de Estadual de Campinas, Brazil).

(4)   *Paulo Maria visitou.
      Paulo   Maria visited
      'Maria visited Paulo.'

Consider also:

(5)   Com quem Paulo conversou no   supermercado?
      to   who Paulo talked   in-the supermarket
      'Who did Paulo talk to in the supermarket?'

(6)   Paulo conversou com quem no   supermercado?
      Paulo talked   to   who in-the supermarket
      'Who did Paulo talk to in the supermarket?'

To which one could only answer – structurally:

(7)   Paulo conversou com Pedro no   supermercado.
      Paulo talked   to   Pedro in-the supermarket
      'Paulo talked to Pedro in the supermarket.'

A   On the basis of these sets of questions and their possible answers, formulate and clearly
    state a hypothesis about how WH-questions are formed in Brazilian Portuguese. Also,
    demonstrate how your hypothesis accounts for the data, using syntactic trees of the
    questions and possible answers in (1–4).
B   After you have formulated a hypothesis, think through and then state the forms that
    counterexamples to your hypothesis would have to take.
C   Languages form questions in structurally different ways, but Universal Grammar (UG)
    allows only a small number of structurally different ways. Summarize the ways that
    WH-questions are formed in the languages that we have investigated thus far.

Before you move on to Chapter 11, be sure to think through and construct reasoned,
convincing trees and answers to A–C.

Terms

point of interpretation
syntactic movement
transformation
copy
raising
c-command
constituent
sister
preposition movement, P-movement
auxiliary

progressive
grammatical aspect
yes/no question particle, Y/N
auxiliary movement
perfective
subordinate clause
indirect question
imperfective, {impf}

Chapter 11

Question Formation: A Summary

Languages fall into different types. The linguistic study of such language differences is referred to as **typology**. For example, on the phonology side, we can ask whether or not a language is primarily a **tone-accent** language like Navajo and Mandarin Chinese, in which words are distinguished one from another by relative tone – pitch essentially. In Mandarin Chinese, for example, /mén/ with a rising tone means 'gate'; /mèn/ with a falling tone means 'bored'; and /men/ with neutral tone is the plural morpheme encountered in Problem Set 8. On the other hand, there are **stress-accent** languages like Tohono O'odham and English, in which words are distinguished from one another by relative stress – manifested as syllable loudness or length. For example, English /ri.jékt/ *reject* with stress on the second syllable is a verb, while /rí.jɛkt/ *reject* with stress on the first syllable, is the related noun. Or looking at syntax, in particular the order of grammatical elements in a sentence, we can ask whether a language is a Subject-Object-Verb or **SOV** language like Western Apache, illustrated by the sentence *Ishkiin lii yizloh* 'The boy the horse caught', or a **SVO** language like Mandarin Chinese, illustrated by the sentence *Li Yafei yao xiaobing* 'Li Yafei wants some bread'.

In this summary chapter, we will examine the typology of question formation on the basis of the languages we analyzed in Chapters 9 and 10.

The Universal Elements of Question Formation

Consider first what we assume to be true of questions – for all languages:

- All languages have a **yes/no question particle**, **Y/N**, and a **WH-question particle**, **WH**, that merge and project a question mood over the structure of a statement (or declarative sentence).
- All languages have **WH-words** (or question words) for WH-questions.

Of course, it is obvious that the phonological form of question particles and WH-words differs from language to language. For example, the yes/no question particle in Tohono O'odham is *n* and in Mandarin Chinese it is *ma*, while in English the particle Y/N has no phonological content. Furthermore, the WH-word for 'who' is *shei* in Mandarin Chinese, but *que(m)* in Brazilian Portuguese.

Nevertheless, while such differences are noteworthy, what is important is the fact that question particles and WH-words <u>exist</u> in all languages. This is a fact of Universal Grammar. The phonological form of the particles, or whether they have phonological form at all, is another matter: facts of Particular Grammars.

The Typology of Question Formation

At the end of Problem Set 14, we wrote that different "languages form questions in structurally different ways, but Universal Grammar (UG) allows only a small number of structurally different ways." We now examine the precise ways in which question formation differs from language to language. Briefly, these are the ways – presented as a set of yes/no questions:

- Is the question particle located at the left edge of the structure, or at the right edge?
- Is the question particle a magnet; that is, does it attract elements to itself, causing them to move to the question particle position?
- Is attraction (or movement) obligatory or optional?
- Does the question particle have any phonological, perhaps intonational or **prosodic effect**?

We hypothesize that these four questions constitute universal **parameters** that frame the acquisition of question formation in a particular language: Based on their experience with a language, infants developing a first language and children and adults acquiring a second language set each parameter one way or another.

For example, we have seen that for Mandarin Chinese, language learners must set the first two parameters as follows: question particles are located at the right edge of the structure, but they are <u>not</u> magnets; thus, there is <u>no</u> syntactic movement in Mandarin Chinese question formation.

In English WH-questions and in English and Tohono O'odham yes/no questions, however, the question particles are located at the left edge. Moreover, in both languages, the particles <u>do</u> act like magnets; thus, there is syntactic movement to the location of the question particle. Acquiring these languages requires setting the question formation parameters quite differently from Mandarin Chinese.

The structure of English yes/no questions was presented in detail in Chapter 10, but analyses of Tohono O'odham yes/no question formation and of English WH-question formation have not been given in detail, so let us now do that, examining Tohono O'odham yes/no question formation first.

Yes/No Question Formation in Tohono O'odham

Consider the following Tohono O'odham examples, taken from Problem Set 12:

(1) *No g gogogs hihink?*
     'Are/were the dogs barking?'

(2) *G gogogs o   hihink.*
     the dogs   {impf} bark
     'The dogs are/were barking.'

Recall that questions are structurally related to statements that possibly answer them. On the basis of this question-answer pair and other data in the problem set, we conclude:

- that Tohono O'odham has a yes/no question particle *n* that merges at the left edge and projects a yes/no question mood over the structure of a statement;
- that this particle attracts the verb-generating morpheme {impf}, the imperfective auxiliary verb *o*, causing it to move and <u>attach</u> to *n*.

We illustrate this analysis in the following set of tree diagrams (3a) through (3c) for the question in (1), treeing the underlying structure first:

(3) a

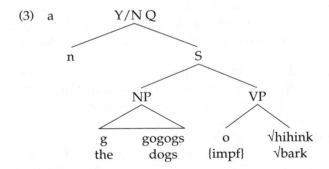

As illustrated in (3b), the yes/no question particle *n* then attracts {impf} *o*, raising it to itself:

(3) b

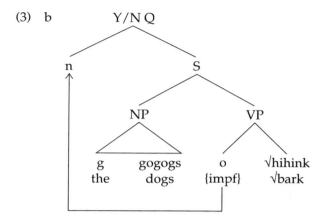

The raising of *o* and its <u>attachment</u> to *n* results in the syntactic structure illustrated in (3c), with a mental copy of *o* in the position from which {impf} *o* has been moved:

(3) c

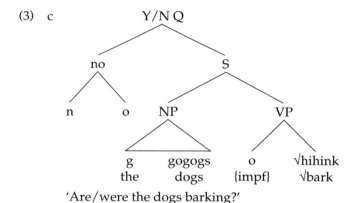

'Are/were the dogs barking?'

The copy of {impf} *o* is not realized at the surface in speech. It does, however, occupy the underlying structural position where {impf} *o* is mentally interpreted.

While our analysis of Tohono O'odham yes/no questions tells us much about that phenomenon, it tells us nothing about whether there is movement of WH-words and the auxiliary in WH-questions in Tohono O'odham. In order to address these questions, we would need to examine the language more deeply: reading further in Zepeda (1983), doing field work, collecting more data, and analyzing that data. Or doing another problem set, perhaps Problem Set 15 at the end of this chapter. Our initial investigation of yes/no question formation in this language does, however, hint at what the structure of Tohono O'odham WH-question formation might be.

WH-Question Formation in English

We now turn to the analysis of English WH-question formation, illustrating it with the following question from Problem Set 13 and a statement that is a possible answer to the question:

(4)   *Who must Emma talk to?*
(5)   *Emma must talk to Peter.*

We conclude on the basis of these and other data in the problem set that, like the English yes/no question particle, the English WH-question particle (WH) has zero phonological form in English. In contrast to English yes/no question formation where only the auxiliary verb moves, we see that the WH-word <u>and</u> the auxiliary verb move in the formation of a WH-question: *who* and *must*, respectively in question (4). Moreover, the WH-word and the auxiliary are moved and raised to the left – evidence that the particle WH is at the left edge of the structure.

How then can we represent the underlying structure of (4) and these movement transformations?

Let us begin by assuming that the question particle WH acts like a magnet, attracting and raising the WH-word *who* to its empty position (empty because WH has no spoken form). Since *must* and *who* do not constitute a phrasal unit in underlying structure, they must fill separate positions in the syntactic tree. Thus, a second position must be created for *must*. We do this by creating an empty "landing site," Ø, in a higher sentence (S) for the auxiliary to move to, as shown in (6a):

(6)   a

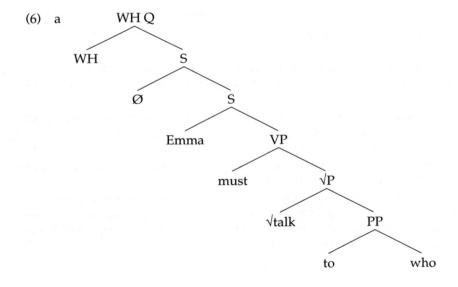

The WH-word *who* is then attracted and raised to WH, the WH-question particle position, and *must* is attracted to Ø, as illustrated in (6b):

(6)   b

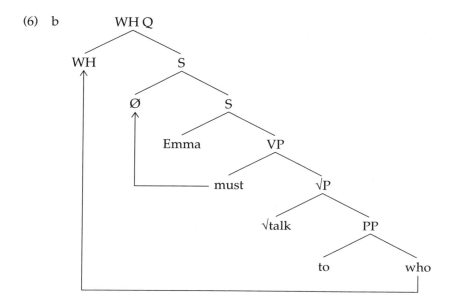

The movement of *who* and *must* results in the structure illustrated in (6c), with a copy of *must* in the position from which the auxiliary *must* has moved, and a copy of *who* in the position from which the WH-word *who* has been moved:

(6)   c

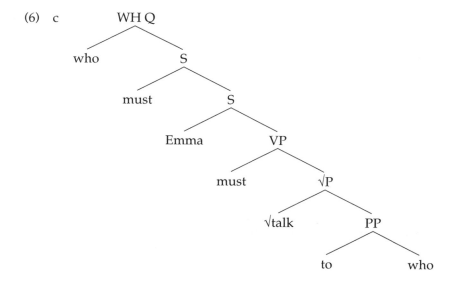

Note that the copies of the moved elements in (6c) are not realized in speech. Nevertheless, the copies are computed in the mind. The tree in (6c) makes a claim about what is in the mind of a speaker of English. For example, an English speaker knows just where *must* has been moved from, for its copy mentally occupies *must's* underlying point of interpretation.

In ordinary, direct English WH-questions, the WH-word and verb generator (like the auxiliary *must*) <u>always</u> move, as illustrated above in (6a) through (6c). However, there is a pseudo-question in English in which there is no movement, either of the WH-word or the auxiliary verb. Say, for example, that a person asks question (4), repeated below as (7), and receives a surprising answer, (8):

(7)   *Who must Emma talk to?*
(8)   *Emma must talk to the Queen of England.*

The person might then respond with a surprise or **echo question**, in which both the WH-word and the auxiliary remain in their <u>underlying</u> structural positions:

(9)   *Emma must talk to who?!*

The new information in the full answer in (8) (*the Queen of England*) is, of course, in the same position as the WH-word *who* in the echo question in (9); likewise, the auxiliary *must* is in the same position in both (8) and (9). Thus, for English at least, constructing full answers to WH-questions and their corresponding echo questions is an excellent way to test for the structural location of copies of the moved WH-word and verb generator in ordinary WH-questions.

Finally note that if a WH-question is asked in English about two constituents, <u>only one</u> of them is moved to the question-particle position; the other one remains in its underlying position:

(10)   *Where will Emma be when?*
(11)   *When will Emma be where?*

But not:

(12)   **When where will Emma be?*

Auxiliary movement in English WH-questions

It should be noted that auxiliary movement in English WH-questions is different from auxiliary movement in English yes/no questions in that it appears to be unrelated to WH-question formation itself and may simply be a remnant in English of a very general characteristic of language: the tendency for the first constituent of the verb phrase to appear in second position, the so-called verb-second phenomenon. Recall in this connection, Zepeda's "Rule 1 [for Tohono O'odham]: The aux[iliary *o*] occurs in second position in a sentence" (Zepeda, 1983, p. 8).

Note that the parallel between indirect yes/no questions and indirect WH-questions is not exact. Although the WH-word moves in indirect WH-questions, auxiliary verbs like *must* remain in their underlying structural position and cannot be moved – presumably because a landing site cannot be created in indirect question constructions:

(13)   *I wonder who Emma must talk to.*
(14)   **I wonder who must Emma talk to.*

As further evidence that auxiliary movement in the formation of English WH-questions is perhaps unrelated to question formation, we see that there is no such auxiliary movement in WH-questions in other varieties of English while there is such movement in yes/no questions – in Nicaraguan English, for example:

(15)   *Where they will catch fish?*
(16)   *Do you want buy a horse skin?*

WH-Question Formation in Brazilian Portuguese

From our examination of the data in Problem Set 14, we see that, like English, Brazilian Portuguese has a null WH-question particle. However, in Brazilian Portuguese, WH-words <u>may</u> move to the question particle position, but they need not move. Thus questions (17) and (18) have the same meaning. Both can be answered with (19), but not with (20):

(17)   *Maria visitou quem?*
       Maria visited who
       'Who did Maria visit?'

(18)   *Quem Maria visitou?*
       who   Maria visited
       'Who did Maria visit?'

(19)   *Maria visitou Paulo.*
       Maria visited Paulo
       'Maria visited Paulo.'

(20)   **Paulo Maria visitou.*
       Paulo Maria visited
       'Maria visited Paulo.'

We illustrate Brazilian Portuguese WH-question formation with the following trees for question (17). The tree in (21a) is its underlying structure; (21b) illustrates optional movement (or attraction); and (21c) illustrates the surface structure that results from the optional movement of *quem* to the position of the WH-question particle.

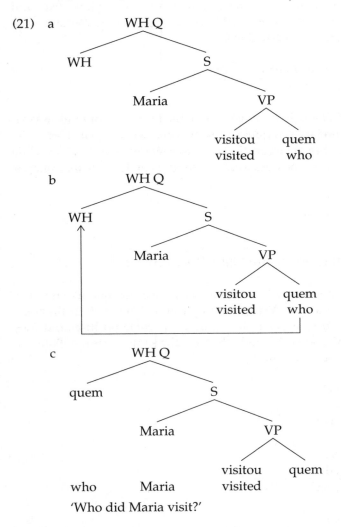

'Who did Maria visit?'

Finally, we note that in Brazilian-Portuguese WH-questions, if a WH-word is spoken in its underlying position, the WH-question particle imposes a rising intonation over the question.

An alternative way of explaining Brazilian-Portuguese WH-question formation is to say that there is <u>always</u> movement and that the difference between questions (17) and (18) results from deleting <u>one or the other</u> of the *quem*'s so that only one of them survives as a spoken WH-word, which one being optional. This line of analysis raises a number of questions. For example, should Mandarin Chinese WH-questions then be reanalyzed from this point of view? Does *ne* attract WH-words but leave them always spoken in their underlying positions? However, intriguing as it is, we will not pursue this line of questioning further at this point.

Question Formation: A Typological Hierarchy

Based on our analysis of question formation in a variety of languages, we present the following typological hierarchy:

(22)

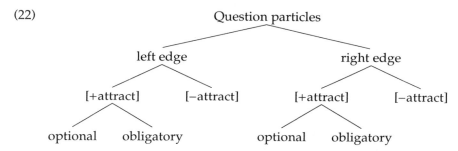

Two-dimensional space does not allow us to enrich this hierarchy further so as to include all the question formation parameters. For example, the hierarchy does not allow for the (unlikely) possibility that yes/no question particles and WH-question particles might occupy different edges within a language. Nevertheless, we can begin to fit the languages that we have examined into this tentative diagram. English and Tohono O'odham, for example, are languages with question particles at the left edge that attract elements to themselves. Mandarin Chinese, on the other hand, is an example of a language with question particles at the right edge that do not attract elements to themselves.

Obviously, there are some gaps in this hierarchy. Only some of the typological possibilities are illustrated in the languages that we have examined thus far. We might wonder, for example, is there a language with a question particle at the right edge that attracts WH-words? Thus, we would need to look further to see if these gaps are illustrated by other languages (perhaps by ones that you know), or whether the gaps exist because that is what Universal Grammar requires.

The hierarchy captures, in part, the unconscious decisions that infants, children, and adults must make in order to develop knowledge of question formation. Universal Grammar specifies that there are question particles and WH-words, since every language must have WH- and yes/no questions, but evidence about a particular language will determine which choices are made further down the hierarchy. It is on the basis of the positive evidence available to them about the language they are acquiring that language learners set the question formation parameters.

Problem Set 15: WH-Question Formation in Tohono O'odham

The data given in this problem set illustrate one type of Tohono O'odham WH-question and the possible answers to such questions.[1] These data are based on the analysis in Zepeda's *Papago Grammar* (1983) or projected from other material in her book.

For the data presented here, note that the following conventions are used in Tohono O'odham orthography:

- a colon (:) after a vowel indicates that it is long;
- an apostrophe (') represents a glottal stop;
- ñ represents a tongue blade sound that is [+nasal, −anterior] – as in the English word *canyon*; c is pronounced /č/; and sh is pronounced /š/;
- otherwise, all symbols represent the sounds shown in the distinctive feature matrices in Chapter 2 of this book.

Note, finally, that {impf} labels the verb generating morpheme *o*, an imperfective auxiliary verb that indicates "*ongoing action* in the *present* or *past*" (Zepeda, 1983, p. 8 – italics hers).

(1) *Do: o   g   a'ali   huhu'id?*
     who {impf} the children chase
     'Who are/were the children chasing?'

(2) *(G)[2] a'ali   o   huhu'id g   Husi.*
     (the) children {impf} chase   the José
     'The children are/were chasing José.'

(3) *Do: o   g   Mali:ya ñu:kud?*
     who {impf} the María   take-care-of
     'Who is/was María taking care of?'

(4) *Mali:ya o   ñu:kud   g   Huan.*
     María   {impf} take-care-of the Juan
     'María is/was taking care of Juan.'

---

[1] For background information on Tohono O'odham – the language and its speakers, see Problem Set 12 in Chapter 10.

[2] Recall that in Tohono O'odham, the determiner *g* is in fact always deleted sentence-initially. Its deletion follows from Zepeda's second rule for Tohono O'odham: "Rule 2: Always drop the *g* determiner at the beginning of a sentence" (Zepeda, 1983, p. 13). Zepeda's Rule 1, however, is the relevant one at this point: "Rule 1: The aux[iliary, in these cases, the {impf} *o*] occurs in second position in a sentence" (p. 8).

Constituent order in Tohono O'odham is actually much freer than shown in this problem set and in Chapter 10, Problem Set 12. Zepeda's Rule 1 always obtains, but around the auxiliary, there is a great deal of constituent-order freedom that we ignore for the purposes of these problem sets, looking instead only at the basic, underlying constituent order in Tohono O'odham.

(5) *Ba:*   *o*   *g*   *ceoj cipkan?*
    where {impf} the boy work
    'Where is/was the boy working?'

(6) *Ceoj o*   *cipkan g*   *kui weco.*
    boy {impf} work   the tree under
    'The boy is/was working under the tree.'

(7) *Sha:cu o*   *g*   *Klisti:na ñeid?*
    what   {impf} the Christina look-at
    'What is/was Christina looking at?'

(8) *Klisti:na o*   *ñeid*   *g*   *mi:sa.*
    Christina {impf} look-at the table
    'Christina is/was looking at the table.'

A   Draw the underlying and surface structural trees for at least two of the Tohono O'odham questions given in (1), (3), (5), and (7). On the basis of your analysis of these structures, formulate and state a hypothesis for how WH-questions are formed in Tohono O'odham, giving the rules that explain the relationship between the underlying and surface trees.

B   How does Tohono O'odham fit into the typological hierarchy for question formation given here in Chapter 11?

Before you move on to C, be sure to think through and construct reasoned, convincing trees and answers to A and B.

C   How can you incorporate the following additional data into your analysis of Tohono O'odham WH-question formation?

(9) *Do: mamagina o*   *g*   *Husi wapkon?*
    who cars   {impf} the José wash
    'Whose cars is/was José washing?'

(10) *Husi o*   *wapkon g*   *Huan mamagina.*
    José {impf} wash   the Juan cars
    'José is/was washing Juan's cars.'

(11) *Do: kawyuga o*   *g*   *gogogs huhu'id?*
    who horse   {impf} the dogs   chase
    'Whose horse are/were the dogs chasing?'

(12) *Gogogs o*   *huhu'id g*   *Mali:ya kawyuga.*
    dogs   {impf} chase   the María   horse
    'The dogs are/were chasing María's horse.'

D   Consider the following data in (13) and (14) (repeated from (7) and (8) above) and (15–20). These data reveal that there are two words for *what* in Tohono O'odham, *sha:* and *sha:cu*.

(13) *Sha:cu o*   *g*   *Klisti:na ñeid?*
    what   {impf} the Christina look-at
    'What is/was Christina looking at?'

(14) *Klisti:na o   ñeid   g   mi:sa.*
      Christina {impf} look-at the table
      'Christina is/was looking at the table.'

(15) *Sha:cu o   g   ali   huhu'id?*
      what   {impf} the child chase
      'What is/was the child chasing?'

(16) *Ali   o   huhu'id g   Mali:ya kawyuga.*
      child {impf} chase   the María's horse.
      'The child is/was chasing María's horse.'

(17) *Sha: o   g   Huan kaij?*
      what   {impf} the Juan say
      'What is/was Juan saying?'

(18) *Huan o   kaij nakoshdag.*
      Juan {impf} say foolishness
      'Juan is/was saying foolish things.'

(19) *Sha: o   g   Klisti:na elid?*
      what {impf} the Christina think
      'What is/was Christina thinking?'

(20) *Klisti:na o   elid pi has.*
      Christina {impf} think no thing
      'Christina is/was thinking nothing.'

This difference is clearly a principled one since *sha:* and *sha:cu* are not interchangeable. Thus, (21–24) are not grammatical questions in Tohono O'odham.

(21) **Sha: o g Klisti:na ñeid?*   cannot mean   'What is/was Christina looking at?'
(22) **Sha: o g ali huhu'id?*   cannot mean   'What is/was the child chasing?'
(23) **Sha:cu o g Huan kaij?*   cannot mean   'What is/was Juan saying?'
(24) **Sha:cu o g Klisti:na elid?*   cannot mean   'What is/was Christina thinking?'

What semantic feature distinguishes between the objects of verbs like those in the grammatical questions (13) and (15) (*ñeid* 'looking at'; *huhu'id* 'chasing') and those in the grammatical questions (17) and (19) (*kaij* 'saying'; *elid* 'thinking')? How does that semantic feature explain why *sha:cu* is grammatical for questions (13) and (15), but not for (23) and (24) and why *sha:* is grammatical for questions (17) and (19), but not for (21) and (22)?

E   Focusing <u>only</u> on the structure and rules of WH-question formation, which language (or languages) analyzed thus far in this book do you believe would be less difficult to acquire for a speaker of Tohono O'odham? Which language (or languages) would be more difficult to acquire? Why do you answer as you do?

Before you move on to Chapter 12, be sure to think through and construct reasoned, convincing answers to C–E.

Terms

typology
tone-accent
stress-accent
SOV
SVO
yes/no question particle, Y/N
WH-question particle, WH
WH-words
prosodic effect
parameters
echo question

Chapter 12

The Acquisition of WH-Question Formation

As we have seen from our investigation of a variety of languages, there is a question formation typology. While all languages have question particles and question words, languages can be sorted into types based on several universal parameters: whether question particles are at the left edge or the right edge of the syntactic structure, whether question particles attract and raise elements through movement, whether movement is optional or obligatory, and whether question particles have any phonological effect. The hierarchy of parameters at the end of Chapter 11 represents, in part, the task of acquiring question formation in a particular language. Infants acquiring their native language and children and adults acquiring a second language must set each of the question formation parameters on the basis of the positive evidence available to them about the language.

In this chapter, we examine how this parameter-setting task is accomplished in the acquisition of WH-question formation, focusing mostly on second language learners. Before turning to this topic, let us review and extend the discussion of language acquisition models presented in Chapter 4.

Modeling First and Second Language Acquisition

An infant is surrounded by language at least from birth and exposed to elements of prosody, or the rhythmic characteristics of language, *in utero* (see Jusczyk, 1997). Given this experience in the ambient language, the infant develops knowledge of that language with remarkable ease and speed. Within four or five years, the infant will acquire mature knowledge of the structure of the language (or languages) of its family and community; this is true of children in every language community, despite very different social and linguistic experiences. And despite severe cognitive deficiencies, language is acquired (see Blank, Gessner, & Esposito, 1979; Yamada, 1990). Language acquisition can, in fact, only be prevented by severely depriving an infant of sufficient language experience, though even under the most deprived conditions, language-like behavior manifests itself (see Curtiss, 1977; Goldin-Meadow, 2003).

We assume that native language acquisition proceeds quickly and uniformly across infants and young children because they are equipped with **Universal Grammar**, the innate knowledge of structural features of all languages that enables human beings to acquire any language. In Chapter 4, we modeled the growth of the infant's knowledge of language as follows, where UG stands for Universal Grammar and PG for **Particular Grammar**:

Experience in a language → UG → PG of that language

On the basis of the interaction between UG and the infant's experience with **positive evidence** about a language (or languages), knowledge of the PG of that language (or those languages) <u>grows</u> quite naturally.

On this view, the infant's linguistic knowledge develops in a UG-compatible way; that is, at every stage of development, what the infant knows is always a **possible language**, but this knowledge is only imperfectly reflected in what the infant produces. For example, recall Berko's (1958) study of noun pluralization in young English-speaking children. Our analysis of the data presented in Chapter 4 revealed that nearly all of the children's errors involved omitting the plural suffix /s/, /z/, or /ɪz/. We argued that omitting the plural suffix could be due to the pluralizing presence of a cardinal number in Berko's probes ("This is a wug. Now there's another one . . . There are two – ?"), a choice that many languages, Nicaraguan English and Mandarin Chinese among them, make. Thus, the children's "errors" reflect a <u>possible</u> way for languages to mark noun plurality, one that is an option within UG.

We now return to the models of second language acquisition by people older than five or six years of age that were outlined in Chapter 4. First, there is the model that claims that there is no difference between an infant acquiring its native language (L1) and a child or an adult acquiring a second language (L2):

Model 1:
Experience with L2 → UG → PG2

Or we could factor interference of the child's or adult's first language knowledge into the model, the minus sign indicating that PG1 has "subtracted" or used up some of UG – what was once available to the learner in L1 acquisition:

Model 2:
Experience with L2 → UG – PG1 → PG2

Another suggestion is that only knowledge of the first language is available for second language acquisition; that is, UG – having been "spent" getting a first language – is no longer directly available:

Model 3:
Experience with L2 → PG1 → PG2

A useful analogy is to think of Model 3 as the "instant-coffee model" of L2 acquisition: A spoonful of instant coffee (UG), once stirred into hot water (experience with L1), is gone forever. This contrasts sharply with the tea-bag metaphor: after one use (for L1 acquisition), a tea bag (UG) placed in a cup of hot water will give you another cup of tea (Model 1), but perhaps not so strong a cup of tea, the strength of the tea leaves having been diminished (Model 2).

Still another possible model suggests that second languages are acquired, at least by adults, through general problem-solving strategies – in sharp contrast to the language-specific strategies outlined above. We signify 'general problem-solving strategies' by X:

Model 4:
Experience with L2 → X → XG of L2

Each of these four models makes different predictions about the form that knowledge of a second language will take. Model 4 predicts that such knowledge could take forms not exhibited in the languages of the world, since L2 knowledge is not constrained in this model either by UG or by PG1 (knowledge of the first language, which is itself constrained by UG). For without any constraints based in UG on L2 acquisition, the second language learner would likely depart markedly from the grammar of the L2 or from the grammar of any language. However, there is abundant evidence that the grammars that people develop in second language acquisition are possible languages. Thus we discard Model 4 as a viable hypothesis for L2 acquisition.

In Model 3, a second language learner would be completely "trapped" by her or his first language, able only to analyze the positive evidence about the L2 through PG1. This model predicts that the language learner would develop L2 knowledge that is very heavily if not totally influenced by the phonology, morphology, and syntax of the L1. For example, the language learner, while using the words and perhaps the forms of the L2, would place them in the syntactic structures of her or his native language. We also know that this is not the case, for children and adults do UG-compatible things in the L2 that are not in evidence in their native languages, nor necessarily sanctioned by the grammar of the L2 either.

Nevertheless, Model 3 may play a role in explaining the initial stages of L2 acquisition. Perhaps the second language learner begins by trying out the new language's forms and structures through the grammar of her or his first language (PG1) – unconsciously hopeful that the acquisition of a second language will be this easy. However, in the face of positive evidence about the L2, the language learner will soon give up this pursuit, unconsciously following Model 2.

In Model 2, UG is available for L2 acquisition except insofar as the grammar of the first language (PG1) has universal parameters set in ways that make them inaccessible to resetting. At the end of Chapter 4, we gave an explanation of this sort for the imperfect Catalan phonology of Spanish-Catalan bilinguals whose native language is Spanish. We observed that the phonological feature [ATR] is not active in Spanish; not being distinctive in the language, we hypothesized that it has been "lost" from Spanish speakers' UG. On this view, [ATR] is not available to Spanish speakers acquiring Catalan and this results in the imperfect phonology of their PG2.

Model 2 is, then, a _partial_ interference model, PG1 standing in the way of acquiring some parametric settings in the L2, which ones or kinds remaining to be determined.

Recall from Chapter 4 that in addition to the partial and total interference of PG1 predicted by Model 2 and Model 3, another source of L2-acquisition interference may be that there is a critical period for language acquisition; that is, there is a window of opportunity for the perfect acquisition of an L1 and the closing of this window prevents the perfect acquisition of an L2. The critical period may well be the basis for Model 3's prediction that L2 learners are captive of their PG1. In Model 2, the subtractive effect of PG1 on universal parametric settings could be influenced by the critical period or periods that may exist for phonology, morphology, and syntax.

Turn, finally, to Model 1: The implication of this model is that L2 acquisition would be perfect, no different from an infant's acquisition of its ambient language. Implausible as it seems, there is some evidence for Model 1 from research on stress-accent (reviewed in O'Neil, 1998b). This work has revealed that speakers from a wide variety of first languages all behave in much the same way with respect to the acquisition of English stress-accent, and in much the way that children developing English as their first language behave, except that adults do not "bother" to get the exceptions (or irregularities). Note, however, that these data are derived from just one submodule of the phonology of English: stress-accent. Other modules of grammar and their submodules would have to behave in the same way as stress-accent for Model 1 to be fully supported – again an unlikely prospect.

Child vs. adult second language learners

At the outset, we note an important difference between the L2 development of children and adults: Adults generally end up with less than perfect knowledge of their second languages, while a child's PG2 will be very close to perfect. Thus you can nearly always tell an adulthood-learner from a childhood-learner. For there seems to be a perceptible and permanent gap between what adults <u>know</u> of a second language and what they are able to <u>do</u> with that knowledge. For some reason that we do not understand, adults seem to be forced by nature to settle for less than children do. Perhaps, though, we should look not only at an adult's imperfect knowledge of her or his second language, but also at the effect of the second language on the first; for it may be that adults are unconsciously collapsing the points of difference between their languages in order to ease the mental burden of knowing more than one language. In part, we know that this is the way languages change: under the influence of the accommodations that bilinguals make between languages that come into contact, whether through conquest, trade, or migration.

We now turn to an extensive discussion of L2 acquisition of WH-questions and to a very brief discussion of L1 acquisition of WH-questions. Research on this matter constitutes tests of the models of L2 acquisition reviewed above.

Second Language Acquisition of WH-Question Formation

Our investigation of WH-question formation in a variety of languages revealed a parametric difference in the position of the WH-words in WH-questions: either WH-words are attracted by and moved to the position of the WH-question particle, or they remain *in situ* – a Latin phrase, meaning 'in its original place'. What are predictable consequences of this parametric difference for second language acquisition? The models of second language acquisition predict different outcomes for individuals acquiring English WH-questions as a second language if their native language is Chinese or if their native language is Brazilian Portuguese (or French, which is similar to Brazilian Portuguese in this respect).

Note that hereafter we will ignore the difference between child and adult L2 learners, letting adult = child/adult.

Chinese to English: A case of dissimilar languages

What do the models of adult second language acquisition predict for native speakers of Chinese learning English WH-question formation?

- Model 1 – the UG-only model – predicts that Chinese speakers would acquire English WH-movement without any first language interference.
- Model 2 makes at least two predictions. If the universal question formation parameters are among those that cannot be reset, then Model 2 predicts permanent interference from the native language since Mandarin Chinese question formation parameters are set differently from those of English: [+right edge] question particles vs. [−right edge]; [−attract] WH-words vs. [+attract]; on this view, the parameter settings of Mandarin

Chinese have subtracted the English settings from UG, rendering them unavailable. On the other hand, if both of these question formation parameters can be reset, then Model 2 predicts little or no PG1 interference.
• Model 3, in which adults have only their PG1 available to them and no access to UG, predicts that adults coming to English from Chinese would never acquire English WH-movement.

Regardless of model, we assume that adults acquiring a second language – like infants acquiring their first language – have only **positive evidence** of grammatical forms; they do not have **negative evidence** available to them in their experience. That is, they do not have evidence of which forms are ungrammatical and why – in this case, evidence that the WH-word *in situ* of Chinese cannot occur in English.

What are the facts of Chinese-to-English WH-question formation? The facts of the matter are these: Moving between the two languages in this respect only appears to offer little difficulty for Chinese speakers learning English (see White & Juffs, 1998; Hawkins, 2001). Thus, Model 3 is not supported by these data. However, the data can be taken as support for either Model 1 or Model 2, [±attract] and [±right edge] being among parameters that can be reset in Model 2.

How do we explain these results? Perhaps Chinese and English are so dissimilar in question formation that the difference is not a problem for L2 acquisition, under the assumption that 'dissimilar' is easier to acquire than 'similar' (Borer, 1996, p. 720). On this view, narrowly drawn differences (the small distinction between Catalan /ε/ and /e/ and Spanish /e/, for example) defy acquisition; broadly drawn parametric differences don't. This may distinguish those parameters that cannot be reset from those that can. In any case, all the linguistic evidence that the Chinese speaker gets indicates that WH-movement is the only option in English. (On the other hand, an English speaker learning Chinese would only get evidence that Chinese WH-words are required to stay in their underlying structural positions.) Where there are such striking parametric differences between language, such as [±attract], there may be few acquisition difficulties. The WH-movement parameter would simply need to be reset from [−attract] to [+attract].

There is, however, a problem with this line of reasoning: Given evidence that WH-words are moved, it does not follow that they must be moved. The way out of this apparent difficulty lies in this additional fact about Chinese WH-question formation: in contrast to English, Chinese WH-questions not only have a WH-word *in situ*, but they also have *ne*, an optionally spoken WH-question particle. Thus, rather than the parametric difference in WH-question formation being dependent on whether the language has WH-movement or not, it might depend on whether the language has a question particle with potentially phonological form or not, or whether the particle is a left-edge particle or a right-edge one. WH-movement would then follow from a language not having a question particle with phonological form, or from the particle being at the left edge. That is, there would be an interaction between the type or position of the WH-particle and WH-movement. (A similar hypothesis is examined and supported in detail in Cheng, 1991.)

On Model 1 or Model 2, Universal Grammar would prepare an adult acquiring an L2 – like the infant acquiring its native language – for either the presence of overt question particles or their absence, or their left/right-edge position. The relationship between these alternatives could well be that having a right-edge question particle like *ne* in a language precludes WH-movement, but as we have seen for English, the left-edge position of a question particle forces WH-movement, though optionally in some languages, as in Brazilian Portuguese.

French to English: A case of similar languages

In French, there is WH-movement, but it is optional: WH-words may move, or they may remain *in situ*. French is like Brazilian Portuguese in this respect. The difference between these two languages is that French (like English) has auxiliary movement if there is WH-movement, while Brazilian Portuguese does not.[1]

Compare the French examples (1) and (2) (Crain & Lillo-Martin, 1999, p. 202) with the Brazilian Portuguese examples (3) and (4):

(1)   *Qui as-tu   vu?*
      who have-you seen
      'Who did you see?'

(2)   *Tu as   vu   qui?*
      you have seen who
      'Who did you see?'

(3)   *Quem está Maria visitando?*
      who   is   Maria visiting
      'Who is Maria visiting?'

(4)   *Maria está visitando quem?*
      Maria is   visiting who
      'Who is Maria visiting?'

Returning to the models of adult second language acquisition, we again ask what they predict for native speakers of French (or Brazilian Portuguese) who are acquiring English WH-question formation.

---

[1]   It is possible that the optionality of WH-movement in French and Brazilian Portuguese is evidence that these languages are in the process of changing from being [+attract] languages to [−attract] languages, ones in which WH-words remain *in situ*.

On Model 1, in which only UG is available, French speakers will acquire English WH-movement. Under the alternatives – Models 2 and 3, in which PG1 plays a partial and a total role, respectively – French speakers will continue to believe that WH-words can be left *in situ*, as in their native language.

If this latter prediction were true, it would be a case of 'similar' being harder to acquire than 'dissimilar'. Speakers of French acquiring English WH-questions will get evidence that WH-words move, but nothing in the data will tell them that WH-words must always move.

However, if optionality is among the parameters that can be reset, then Model 2 predicts its resetting; there will be no PG1 interference.

The facts of this matter are these: French speakers acquiring English do <u>not</u> leave English WH-words *in situ*; they move them (see White et al., 1991; Grondin & White, 1996). That is, they end up with obligatory WH-movement for English.

Here, the facts again support Model 1 or Model 2, offering no support for Model 3: A person's PG1 does not seem to be the sole basis for second language acquisition of WH-question formation. And evidently, rule optionality can be reset.

As far as we know, the matter has not been examined for Brazilian-Portuguese speakers acquiring English; however, we predict results similar to those of the French-to-English studies. What might we predict for English speakers acquiring French or Brazilian Portuguese?

Spanish to English: A case of very similar languages

English and Spanish are very much alike in their formation of WH-questions, since both languages require WH-movement. Thus the potential difficulties (if any) for people moving in either direction between the two languages may come at a more subtle level of analysis than whether there is WH-movement or not.[2]

Consider the following data. In forming a WH-question out of a prepositional phrase (PP) in English, a speaker of English can either move the NP out of the PP, **stranding** the preposition in its original position as in (5) below, or move the whole prepositional phrase that contains the WH-word as in (6):

(5)   *Who did the man give a book to?*
(6)   *To who(m) did the man give a book?*

A native Spanish speaker's judgments of the analogous Spanish versions of questions (5) and (6) would be that (7) is ill-formed and (8) is well-formed (where Spanish *a* is a preposition meaning 'to'):

---

[2]   In Spanish – as in French, all verbs move in WH-questions, not simply the auxiliary verbs as in English.

(7)   *¿Quién dio   el   hombre un libro a?
          who   gave the man   a   book to

(8)   ¿A quién   dio   el   hombre un libro?
         to who(m) gave the man   a   book
         'To who(m) did the man give the book?'

This means that for English declarative sentences of the type illustrated in (9), a speaker of English has available two well-formed WH-questions that ask for information about the goal or direction of the giving: questions (5) and (6). A speaker of Spanish, on the other hand, has one question available for declarative sentences of the type illustrated in (10): question (8).

(9)   *The man gave a book to the woman.*

(10)   *El   hombre dio   un libro a la   mujer.*
          the man   gave a   book to the woman
          'The man gave a book to the woman.'

In light of these data, the following questions again arise:

- First, what difficulty (if any) would a speaker of English have in developing knowledge of Spanish WH-question formation that would be grammatically acceptable to a native speaker of Spanish?
- Second, what difficulty (if any) would a speaker of Spanish have in developing knowledge of English WH-question formation acceptable to a native speaker of English?

Under the assumption that some version of Model 2 is correct, we might expect English speakers to form WH-questions in Spanish as they do in English, producing questions of types (7) and (8). In fact, we would expect them to prefer WH-questions of type (7) since stranding prepositions is very common in spoken (and written) English. Moreover, there is nothing in the data they get from Spanish that tells them they cannot form WH-questions in this manner; that is, there is no negative evidence. If these expectations are correct, then an English-speaking person acquiring Spanish will make many Spanish errors of the type shown in (7), repeated below as (11), in which the preposition is stranded:

(11)   *¿Quién dio el hombre un libro a?*

Speakers of Spanish, however, would have little difficulty producing well-formed WH-questions in English because first of all, they would get positive evidence that prepositions <u>can</u> (but do not have to) be stranded. Moreover, it is always acceptable in English to move the preposition along with the WH-word in forming a question (as in Spanish). In fact, while preposition stranding is proscribed in school grammar, moving the preposition along with its object to the left edge of a question is prescribed. However, questions of type (6), repeated below as (12):

(12)   *To who(m) did the man give a book?*

are quite formal in English. Native speakers of a language sometimes have this sort of thing in mind when they think foreign speakers of their language "sound like a book" in their obedience to the rules of prescriptive grammar.

Surprisingly, there is little linguistic research on the question of preposition **stranding** versus what is called **pied-piping**: moving prepositions to the left edge of the question along with the WH-word – that is, moving the entire PP. Moreover, despite the assertion of Lipski (1996, p. 161) that "English-speaking learners of Spanish routinely attempt preposition stranding," they actually experience little long-term difficulty: "the phenomenon usually disappears within the first semester" (Lipski, 1996: e-communication).[3]

Preposition or P-stranding is very rare among the languages of the world. It appears to be a parameter for which UG <u>favors</u> one setting over the other: [–P-stranding] over [+P-stranding] in this case. Here, we say that [+P-stranding] is the **marked** value of the parameter, the value triggered by positive evidence in the data. With no positive evidence in support of it, [–P-stranding] – the **unmarked** value – comes 'free'. An adult acquiring a second language and an infant acquiring its native language simply unconsciously assume, in the absence of evidence to the contrary, that the ambient language is a [–P-stranding] language.

Thus, the fact that speakers of English acquiring Spanish as a second language assume that Spanish is [–P-stranding] provides support for either Model 1 or Model 2, in which UG plays a role in second language acquisition.

---

[3]   A construction that appears to offer real difficulty for English speakers learning Spanish is revealed in the following:

(i)   *¿Quién conoces?
       who   know-you

rather than:

(ii)   ¿A quién conoces?
       to who know-you
       'Who do you know?'

This error of omitting the preposition is quite likely due to the rule of 'personal *a*' in Spanish, which requires that the animate direct object of a verb be preceded by the preposition *a*, which in this case has no meaning.

The Role of Markedness in Model 2

Unmarked and marked differences between grammars may in fact be <u>the</u> difference crucial to understanding the interaction of UG and PG1 in second language acquisition. Assume that languages prefer pied-piping: for their prepositions not to be stranded; that they prefer the phonological feature [ATR] to be inactive: for there to be a smaller number of vowels rather than a greater number; that they prefer WH-movement (in fact, rules in general) to be obligatory, not optional; and so on – UG exhibiting <u>a bias toward economy,</u> favoring fewer structures over a greater number. Assume further that in acquiring a second language, moving from an unmarked to a marked preference should be relatively difficult, while moving from a marked to an unmarked one should be relatively easy. Given these assumptions, we infer from Model 2 that marked settings of UG are not available in second language acquisition. This reading of Model 2 would then explain why English speakers do not strand Spanish prepositions; why Spanish speakers do not activate [ATR] in acquiring Catalan vowels; and why French speakers do not optionally leave WH-words *in situ* in English WH-questions.[4]

This line of argument cannot, however, be carried over to the acquisition of English WH-questions by speakers of Mandarin Chinese since there is no way to argue on the basis of economy that overt question particles are the marked or unmarked preference or that left-edge particle position is preferred over right-edge. Perhaps markedness does not hold of these and other right/left differences between languages: for example, post-positional v. pre-positional phrases. However, in the absence of a deep understanding of these matters, notions of markedness do give us a way to begin to investigate such differences further (but see Kayne, 1994, for another approach).

Preposition-deletion: Further support for Model 2

A well-documented difficulty with P-stranding for adults acquiring English, Spanish speakers included, is this: Rather than stranding prepositions, L2 learners of English prefer to delete them, with a result that is unacceptable in English – and for which they certainly get <u>no</u> positive evidence.

For example, while sentences like (13) and (14) are judged grammatical by both native speakers and by adults acquiring English, the corresponding questions (15) and (16) are <u>also</u> acceptable to people coming to English from a wide variety of native languages (though clearly unacceptable to native speakers of English):

---

[4]   Moreover, under the assumption that the stress parameters of English have, for the most part, their unmarked values, then second language learners' successful acquisition of English stress patterns also appears to be explained by markedness (O'Neil, 1998b).

(13)   *We talked about the movie last night.*

(14)   *She waited at the station for the train.*

(15)   **What did you talk last night?*   with the meaning:
       'What did you talk about last night?'

(16)   **What did she wait at the station?*   with the meaning:
       'What did she wait for at the station?'

Thus instead of stranding English prepositions, adults acquiring English as their second language – and, interestingly, infants developing it as their native language – generally prefer to delete prepositions in sentences like (15) and (16), and in relative clause structures as well; for example:

(17)   **This is the movie that we talked last night.*   with the meaning:
       'This is the movie that we talked about last night.'

(18)   **I missed the train that I waited at the station.*   with the meaning:
       'I missed the train that I waited for at the station.'

These errors of P-deletion are likely due to a strong UG-driven resistance to P-stranding. In languages that have prepositions, P-deletion is made possible by the fact that the prepositions commonly associated with verbs are often implicit in the meaning of the verb: For example, *go* implies *to*; *wait* implies *for* (unless otherwise indicated, as in *wait on*); and so on. (For details on this phenomenon, see Klein, 1993.)

These errors also provide further evidence for Model 1 or Model 2 – the models for which UG plays a primary or the only role.

First Language Acquisition of WH-Question Formation

Since infants re-entered the discussion two paragraphs ago, we now turn briefly to the consequences of the parametric differences among languages for first language acquisition of WH-question formation. About this we can be brief, for the evidence indicates that infants "have" the syntax of questions at the very earliest stages of productive language development (Guasti, 2002, chapter 6).

Research on infants raised in English-speaking families shows that WH-question formation is well established in their earliest WH-questions – at two and a half years on average, as the following examples show (Crain & Lillo-Martin, 1999, p. 210; the asterisks now indicating that these questions are not well-formed with respect to the <u>mature</u> speaker's knowledge of English):

(19)   *Who make that?
(20)   *What mommy eating?
(21)   *Where Daddy's going?

Infants raised in an English-speaking setting always move WH-words from their underlying structural positions to the left edge of the question. For them, the complexities of English questions lie not in moving the WH-word, but rather with the position of other elements of questions, such as the verb-generating 's (contracted *is*) of (21).

They even move the WH-word to the left edge of a question when they leave a copy behind in a hierarchically lower position. This is illustrated in the following examples from a child aged 3;3 (Crain & Lillo-Martin, 1999, p. 238):

(22)   *What do you think what's in that box?
(23)   *What do you think what the baby drinks?

Since the infant only gets positive evidence for WH-movement in its experience with English, it is not surprising that WH-movement is found in the very earliest stages of language production in the English-speaking infant – especially if we assume WH-movement is tied to a language having either a WH-question particle with no phonological content or a left-edge WH-question particle. On the other hand, infants raised in a Mandarin-Chinese-speaking environment always leave WH-words *in situ*, in their underlying structural positions (Cheng, personal communication).

Finally, what can be said about infants raised in French-speaking or Brazilian-Portuguese-speaking families, who get evidence that WH-words may either move or remain in their underlying structural position? Research on first language acquisition of French is relevant. Crain and Lillo-Martin report that "children learning French initially use only moved WH-elements" (1999, p. 210). Thus we might safely predict that infants acquiring Brazilian Portuguese would do the same and that optionally leaving WH-words *in situ* (that is, in their underlying structural positions) develops later.

Summing Up

Evidence from studies of second language acquisition of English WH-questions strongly supports a model of L2 acquisition that incorporates UG, either Model 1 or Model 2:

Model 1:
Experience with L2 $\rightarrow$ UG $\rightarrow$ PG2

Model 2:
Experience with L2 $\rightarrow$ UG – PG1 $\rightarrow$ PG2

Apparently, UG <u>is</u> available to adults. However, this discussion, which has been limited to acquisition of WH-question formation and related phenomena, cannot be the whole story of L2 acquisition. But it does point to the central role of UG in L2 acquisition. The interaction between UG and PG1 is, in fact, the focus of a good deal of current research on L2 acquisition. The extent to which there is interference from the first language remains to be specified, though it does appear that markedness plays an important role.

As for first language acquisition, the following model is the only viable candidate:

Experience in a language $\rightarrow$ UG $\rightarrow$ PG of that language

---

Problem Set 16: Indonesian Speakers' Acquisition of English WH-Question Formation

Research on the acquisition of English WH-movement by native speakers of Indonesian has focused on whether the difference between WH-question formation in the two languages results in PG1 interference, or not (Mirizon, 1998).[5] Before we turn to examining what the results of this research tell us about L2 acquisition, let us first consider the role of WH-movement in Indonesian WH-question formation.

WH-Question Formation in Indonesian

Indonesian is the official language of Indonesia, but it is only one of the many languages of that country. According to *Ethnologue: Languages of the World* (2005), Indonesian is the native language – chiefly in Bali and Java – of approximately 23,000,000 persons, and there are more than 140,000,000 second language users. The language is spoken throughout Indonesia as well as in the Netherlands, the Philippines, Saudi Arabia, Singapore, and North America.

To understand the role of WH-movement in this language, we begin as usual by comparing the structure of WH-questions and statements that are possible answers. Given the question-answer pair (1) and (2) and the pair (3) and (4), we see that Indonesian WH-questions are formed by leaving the WH-word *in situ*, as in (1) and (3):

(1) *Ahmad men-ulis   apa?*
     Ahmad {active}-wrote what
     'What did Ahmad write?'

(2) *Ahmad men-ulis   laporan itu.*
     Ahmad {active}-wrote report   that
     'Ahmad wrote that report.'

---

[5] This problem set, with the data somewhat simplified, is adapted from Hawkins (2001, pp. 318–319), citing the work of Mirizon (1998). Additional data is from Cole, Hermon, and Tjung (2002).

(3)   *Siti akan   membeli apa?*
       Siti {future] buy   what
       'What will Siti buy?'

(4)   *Siti akan   membeli buku ini.*
       Siti {future} buy   book this
       'Siti will buy this book.'

The WH-word also remains *in situ* in indirect WH-questions, such as (5):

(5)   *Saya tidak tahu Siti akan   membeli apa.*
       I   not   know Siti {future] buy   what
       'I don't know what Siti will buy.'

   However, looking further into the language, we find that <u>not all</u> WH-words remain *in situ* in WH-questions. In particular, if the WH-word is the <u>subject</u> of a sentence, then it must be raised to the left edge where it is immediately followed by the WH-question particle (WH) *yang* – in direct questions, as in (6) and (7), as well as in indirect questions, as in (8). Subject WH-words may not remain *in situ*, as in the ungrammatical (9). Moreover, a WH-word may <u>not</u> be raised to the left edge if it is the <u>object</u> of the underlying statement, as in the ungrammatical (10). Note that in the following examples, the underlying position of the WH-word is shown as a copy in parentheses.

(6)   *Siapa yang (siapa) akan   menjadi wasit   pertandingan itu?*
       who   WH (who)   {future} become referee match-of   that
       'Who will become referee of that match?'

(7)   *Siapa yang di-rampok (siapa) tadi   malam?*
       Who WH   was robbed (who) just-now night
       'Who was robbed last night?'

(8)   *Saya heran   apa yang (apa) membuatmu demikan gembira hari ini*
       I   surprised what WH (what) makes-you   so   happy   day this
       'I wonder what makes you so happy today.'

(9)   **Siapa akan   menjadi wasit   pertandingan itu?*
       who   {future} become referee match-of   that

(10)   **Apa   yang Ahmad men-ulis (apa)?*
       What WH   Ahmad wrote   (what)

   With these facts about WH-question formation in Indonesian in mind, we – or rather, you – are now in a position to examine research on native Indonesian speakers' acquisition of English WH-question formation.

Indonesian Speakers' Judgments of English WH-Questions

Mirizon (1998) investigated whether the contrast between WH-question formation in Indonesian and English interfered with native Indonesian speakers' acquisition of English WH-movement. Using a grammaticality judgment task, Mirizon tested two groups of native speakers of Indonesian: intermediate- and advanced-level English language learners. A control group of native speakers of English was also tested. The L2 learners were all adults who had begun studying English in Indonesian schools at age 12–13 years and had then spent about a year in England as graduate students.

In the following data from Mirizon's study, the proportion of responses in which subjects accepted a specific type of grammatically well-formed English WH-question is given. Note that in the data:

- square brackets enclose the indirect WH-question that is embedded after verbs like *say, believe, think,* and so on;
- parentheses enclose the unspoken copy of the moved WH-word.

Table 12.1   WH-movement from the embedded subject position

Sample item: *What did Sue say [(what) was on sale in the Union Shop]?*

Intermediate L2 Learners	Advanced L2 Learners	L1 Control Subjects
67.5% accepted	72.5% accepted	90.0% accepted

Table 12.2   WH-movement from the embedded object position

Sample item: *Who does the journalist believe [Tom saw (who)]?*

Intermediate L2 Learners	Advanced L2 Learners	L1 Control Subjects
67.5% accepted	72.5% accepted	90.0% accepted

A   Consider the models of L2 acquisition presented in Chapter 12. Which model best explains the results of Mirizon's research? Explain why you answer as you do.
B   Why don't the other models provide as strong an explanation of the results?

Before you move on to Chapter 13, be sure to think through and construct reasoned, convincing answers to A and B.

Terms

Universal Grammar, UG
Particular Grammar, PG
positive evidence
possible language
in situ
positive evidence
negative evidence
stranding
pied-piping
marked
unmarked

Further Reading

Baker (2001), culminating in chapter 7 "Why parameters?", is a thorough explication of parametric theory.

Crain and Thornton (1998) summarize much of their research on first language acquisition in *Investigations in Universal Grammar: A Guide to Experiments on the Acquisition of Syntax and Semantics,* and, in the course of critiquing earlier research and experimental methods, present strong and clear arguments for the research methodology they employ. Crain and Lillo-Martin's (1999) *An Introduction to Linguistic Theory and Language Acquisition* covers many of the same topics as Crain and Thornton (1998) at an introductory level but provides as well an introduction to the linguistic theory on which the research is built. Guasti (2002) is a comprehensive guide to current research on L1 acquisition and to the thinking that underlies it. For the argument against a role for negative evidence in language acquisition, see Marcus (1993).

Hawkins' (2001) *Second Language Syntax: A Generative Introduction* provides a comprehensive introduction to research on L2 syntax and its acquisition in the theoretical framework developed in this book.

Part III

Constraints, or Why You Can't Say *Wanna* Whenever You Wanna

Chapter 13

Syntactic Constraints on Contraction in English

In Part II of this book, we examined the syntax of question formation in several languages. From our investigation, we learned that question particles can act as magnets, attracting and raising elements to their positions in the syntactic structures of questions. In particular, we found that WH-movement, which results from the WH-question particle's magnetic force on WH-words, is characteristic of WH-question formation in some but not all languages: Brazilian Portuguese and English have WH-movement, for example, but Mandarin Chinese does not.

For languages with WH-movement, the **WH-copy** left behind by movement is crucial to the interpretation of what or who a WH-question is about. Consider two examples from English. In (1) below, *who* has moved to the WH-question particle position at the left edge of the question, leaving a copy of itself in its "original" or underlying position – as indicated by the parentheses. While the WH-copy is not realized in speech, we compute its presence in our minds: the WH-copy informs us that the question is about the object of the preposition, more specifically, the goal of the giving:

(1) *Who did Emma send letters to (who)?*

But in (2), the copy of *what* informs us that the question is about the object of the verb *give*, the theme of the giving:

(2) *What did Alex give (what) to Emma?*

WH-copies allow a listener to reconstruct a question's underlying structural relationships and thus to comprehend the question and the straightforward part of the speaker's intention.

WH-copies also allow the listener to construct an answer to a WH-question, if an answer is known. In a full answer to a WH-question, the information being sought after is placed in the underlying position of the WH-word, as shown in (3), a possible answer to (1), and in (4), a possible answer to (2):

(3)   *Emma sent letters to Alex.*
(4)   *Alex gave Peter's book to Emma.*

   To reiterate: In languages with WH-movement, the WH-copies left behind by movement are the mental images crucial to interpreting and answering WH-questions.

Looking Ahead

In Part III of this book, we explore WH-copies further and introduce related syntactic phenomena of English contraction. Our investigation begins in this chapter and focuses on the surprising role these syntactic elements play in constraining or restricting contraction in English. In the next chapter, we examine the acquisition of syntactic **constraints** on contraction in English and also, in a return to earlier concerns, the phonology of contraction in English.

Problem Set 17: The Syntax of *Wanna*-Contraction in English

In normal speech, native speakers of English generally contract *want to* to *wanna*, as in the following example:

   I wanna see you later.   Contracted from: *I want to see you later.*

   In fact, it seems speakers of English are always able to say *wanna* for *want to*. We can test this informal hypothesis by trying to generate a well-formed contraction of *want to* whenever the occasion arises. For example, in negotiating with a landlord, a person might say:

   I wanna pay you at the end of the month. When do you wanna get paid?

That works fine, but in response to the landlord's saying:

   I don't wanna have that couple around here anymore as tenants.

The person can't then ask,

   Yeah-but, which tenants do you *wanna stay?

   The ill-formedness of this second question indicates that English speakers can<u>not</u> contract *want to* to *wanna* whenever they wanna. Why is this so?

Investigating *Wanna*-Contraction

Let's proceed to investigate this phenomenon further by collecting **grammaticality judgments** from native speakers of English on the contractibility of *want to* to *wanna* in the following WH-questions (1–9):

		Is wanna OK?
(1)	When do you want to get paid?	OK
(2)	Which tenants do you want to stay?	*
(3)	Who do you want to talk to?	
(4)	Who do you want to visit?	
(5)	Where do you want to go?	
(6)	When do you want to speak?	
(7)	Who do you want to speak?	
(8)	Who do you want to go?	
(9)	Who do you want Emma to speak to?	

A   On the basis of these data and the patterns displayed in them, formulate a hypothesis that explains the **constraint** on *wanna*-contraction: that is, under what condition or conditions is a speaker of English constrained or prevented from contracting *want to* to *wanna*?

   In formulating your hypothesis, consider the grammaticality judgments for (1–9), as well as other data you can gather about these WH-questions.

B   Once you have formulated your hypothesis, think the matter through and then state the forms of possible counterexamples to your hypothesis. That is, what conditions would new data have to meet in order to falsify your hypothesis?

C   Try to construct counterexamples to test your hypothesis. If you find counterexamples, then you will need to decide what the consequences are for your hypothesis: leading perhaps to revising or reformulating the hypothesis and then to further testing of the reformulated hypothesis; or perhaps to rejecting the hypothesis altogether.

D   Can you **generalize** <u>beyond</u> your hypothesis to explain the following data? If so, restate your hypothesis and demonstrate how it works, discussing specific examples.

(10)   *I want to pay you on the first of the month.*
       I wanna pay you on the first of the month.

(11)   *I wonder what Emma used to free Alex from prison.*
       I wonder what Emma *useta free Alex from prison.

(12)   *I wonder how Emma used to get to the prison to visit Alex.*
       I wonder how Emma useta get to the prison to visit Alex.

(13)   *What kinds of subs do you have to go?*
       What kinds of subs do you *hafta go?

(14)   *Why do you have to eat subs?*
       Why do you hafta eat subs?

Before you move on to Problem Set 18, be sure to think through and construct reasoned, convincing answers to A–D.

Problem Set 18: The Syntax of *Is*-Contraction in English

There are other kinds of contraction in English besides the *wanna*-contraction type. For example, contraction occurs when certain verbs are phonologically weakened and attached to the word preceding them. The contractible verbs of this sort include some forms of the main verb *be* and forms of the auxiliary verbs *have*, *be*, *will*, and *do*. Here are some examples:

(1) *Emma is an anarchist.*	→	*Emma's an anarchist.*
(2) *Emma has been here before.*	→	*Emma's been here before.*
(3) *Peter is acting weird again.*	→	*Peter's acting weird again.*
(4) *Alex will leave at noon.*	→	*Alex'll leave at noon.*
(5) *Where did Emma go?*	→	*Where'd Emma go?*

Given our experience with *wanna*-contraction, we might suspect that it is not possible to contract these verbs under all conditions.

Investigating *Is*-Contraction

To investigate this phenomenon, we focus initially on the contraction of *is* to *'s*, under the expectation that explaining the syntax of *is*-contraction will generalize to all cases of this sort of contraction, whether it involves auxiliary verbs or other forms of *be*. Consider, then, the following set of sentences, and collect grammaticality judgments from native speakers of English about the contractibility of *is* in (6–15).

Is it okay to contract *is* to *'s*?

(6)   *Alexander wonders when Emma is at home.*
(7)   *Alexander wonders what Emma is looking at.*
(8)   *Alexander wonders who he is sometimes.*
(9)   *Alexander wonders where Emma is.*
(10) *Emma is at home on Tuesdays.*
(11) *Emma is looking at the Moon.*
(12) *Alexander thinks he is Napoleon sometimes.*
(13) *Emma is at home.*
(14) *Do you know what that is on the table?*
(15) *That is a book on the table.*

A   Look for patterns in these data that correlate with the ungrammaticality of *is*-contraction. Then formulate a hypothesis that explains the constraint on *is*-contraction. That is, under what condition or conditions is a speaker of English constrained or prevented from contracting *is*?

   Hint: Notice that some of the sentences (6–15) contain an **indirect WH-question**, that is, a question contained within a statement or question.

B   Demonstrate how your hypothesis works for all of the sentences (6–15).

C   Having formulated a hypothesis, test it by looking for counterexamples. State clearly and precisely the forms that counterexamples must take in order to falsify your hypothesis. If you find counterexamples, reformulate your hypothesis to account for them.

D Consider the following data. In sentences (16) and (18), contraction of the second *is* is not allowed; but in sentence (17), contraction of the second *is* is allowed.

(16) *Emma is fleeing from the FBI and Peter is too.* →
      *Emma's fleeing from the FBI and *Peter's too.*

(17) *Emma is tough and so is Peter.* →
      Emma's tough and so's Peter.

(18) *Emma is working harder today than Peter is.* →
      *Emma's working harder today than *Peter's.*

Are these sentences counterexamples to your hypothesis? If so, state why they are counterexamples, and then generalize or expand your hypothesis to account for them. If these sentences are not counterexamples, then demonstrate how your hypothesis explains them.

Hint: Pay close attention to the position of the 'missing' or 'understood' constituents in sentences (16–18).

E How would you further generalize your *is*-contraction hypothesis to account for sentences like (19) and (20)?

(19) *If you don't do it today, I will tomorrow.* →
      *If you don't do it today, *I'll tomorrow.*

(20) *I have seen the light, but I don't think they have yet.* →
      *I've seen the light, but I don't think *they've yet.*

Before you move on to Chapter 14, be sure to think through and construct reasoned, convincing answers to A–E.

Terms

WH-copy
constraint
grammaticality judgment
generalize
indirect WH-question

Chapter 14

Contraction in English: Its Acquisition and Related Topics

We turn now to specific details of constraints on the interaction between contraction and WH-movement in English, as well as to the acquisition of English contraction.

Wanna-Contraction

The mystery presented by Problem Set 17 is why native speakers of English cannot contract *want to* to *wanna* whenever they want to or wanna. Thus, for examples (1–9), native speakers will give the following grammaticality judgments for *wanna*-contraction:

			Wanna-judgment
(1)		*When do you want to get paid?*	OK
(2)		*Which tenants do you want to stay?*	*
(3)		*Who do you want to talk to?*	OK
(4)	a	*Who do you want to visit?*	OK
	b	*Who do you want to visit?*	*
(5)		*Where do you want to go?*	OK
(6)		*When do you want to speak?*	OK
(7)		*Who do you want to speak?*	*
(8)		*Who do you want to go?*	*
(9)		*Who do you want Emma to speak to?*	*

Note that example (4), in its uncontracted form, represents two different underlying syntactic structures with different interpretations: (4a) and (4b). These two structures (and their related meanings) emerge in our judgments about the possibility of *wanna*-contraction for (4).

In addition to grammaticality judgments, other data can be gleaned by virtue of the fact that examples (1–9) are all WH-questions. As we found in our earlier investigation of English WH-questions, the WH-word is moved to the question particle position, leaving behind a copy, which is deleted prior to the pronunciation of the sentence (see Chapters 10 and 11). It seems reasonable to ask whether the location of the WH-copies in (1–9) might be useful in accounting for the different judgments about the contractibility of *want to*.

Recall that WH-copies allow us to mentally reconstruct the underlying structural relationships between WH-words and their questions. Because of this, we can interpret and construct a full answer to a WH-question and we can also recast the question as an echo question. Thus, to repeat from Chapter 11, the location of a WH-copy can be established by these two "tests":

- by noting the position of the new information in a full answer to a WH-question;
- by noting the position of the WH-word in a corresponding echo-question – the kind of exclamatory question used when surprised by the answer to a WH-question.

These two positions are necessarily the same, as indicated by the underlining in (10–13) below. Note that we enclose WH-copies in parentheses within sentences; in (10), for example, the copy of *when* is *(when)*.

(10)   *When do you want to get paid (when)?*
        I want to get paid every hour on the hour.   (full answer)
        You want to get paid when!?   (echo question)

(11)   *Which tenants do you want (which tenants) to stay?*
        I want everybody except you to stay.
        You want which ones to stay!?

(12)   a   *Who do you want to visit (who)?*
             I want to visit the Sultan of Brunei.
             You want to visit who!?
        b   *Who do you want (who) to visit?*
             I want the President to visit.
             You want who to visit!?

(13)   *Who do you want Emma to speak to (who)?*
        I want Emma to speak to Lenin.
        You want Emma to speak to who!?

In some cases, the WH-copy is located at the end of the question, at the right edge of the structure; in others, the WH-copy is located between *want* and *to*.

We can display these data about the location of the WH-copies together with the data from the *wanna*-judgments in Table 14.1.

Table 14.1

			WH-copy
	Wanna	Wh-copy at	between
	judgment	right edge?	*want* and *to*?
(1) *When do you wanna get paid?*	OK	yes	no
(2) *Which tenants do you wanna stay?*	*	no	yes
(3) *Who do you wanna talk to?*	OK	yes	no
(4) a *Who do you wanna visit?*	OK	yes	no
b *Who do you wanna visit?*	*	no	yes
(5) *Where do you wanna go?*	OK	yes	no
(6) *When do you wanna speak?*	OK	yes	no
(7) *Who do you wanna speak?*	*	no	yes
(8) *Who do you wanna go?*	*	no	yes
(9) *Who do you wanna Emma speak to?*	*	yes	no

Formulating and testing hypotheses

Setting question (9) aside for the moment – since it is apparently different from the other examples, the following explanation of the data suggests itself. Let us call it Hypothesis I:

> *Hypothesis I:*
> You cannot contract *want to* to *wanna* if there is a WH-copy between *want* and *to*.

Note that as a matter of parsimony, once we have stated when contraction cannot happen, we have automatically given the conditions for when it can, and vice versa. Thus, you need not add a condition allowing contraction to a statement that gives the conditions for constraining it. Remember Occam's razor.

In order to falsify Hypothesis I, a counterexample must take one of two structural forms:

- one in which a WH-copy lies between *want* and *to*, yet *wanna*-contraction is still allowed;
- one in which a WH-copy does not fall between *want* and *to*, yet *wanna*-contraction is not allowed.

There are no counterexamples of the first type – though it is a good exercise to try to construct them. But question (9) is a clear counterexample of the second type. For in (9), the WH-copy is located after *want to* – definitely not between *want* and *to*; yet there can be no *wanna*-contraction.

Is this a serious counterexample – one that requires us to reject Hypothesis I entirely? Actually it is not, for counterexamples like (9) push us to reexamine what all the uncontractible forms (2, 4b, 7, 8, <u>and</u> 9) have in common and to reformulate Hypothesis I in a more <u>general</u> way – a good scientific result:

Hypothesis I':
You cannot contract *want to* to *wanna* if there is anything between *want* and *to*.

In other words, *wanna*-contraction is blocked by the presence of <u>any</u> element between *want* and *to*. This is somewhat surprising since that element need not be a word or phrase as in (9); it can also be a WH-copy on its way to deletion, the purely abstract point of interpretation that arises as a consequence of WH-movement. Clearly though, while a WH-copy is not spoken or heard, it appears to have phonological consequences since it blocks *wanna*-contraction.

Say, however, we were to approach a solution from a different direction, from the point of view of when *wanna*-contraction is allowed, not constrained. Then we would be led by the data to formulate a very different hypothesis from Hypothesis I:

Hypothesis II:
You can contract *want to* to *wanna* if a WH-copy is located at the end of the sentence.

To test this hypothesis, we need to see if it can be falsified by counterexamples. In order to find counterexamples, we begin by thinking through what we are looking for. Clearly, a counterexample that would falsify Hypothesis II must take one of the following forms:

- one in which a WH-copy is not at the end of the question (at the right edge), yet *wanna*-contraction is still allowed;
- one in which a WH-copy is located at the end of the question, yet *wanna*-contraction is not allowed;
- one in which there is no WH-copy, yet *wanna*-contraction is nevertheless allowed.

The data set contains no counterexamples of the first sort. But there is a counterexample of the second sort in (9) since there the WH-copy falls at the end and contraction is not allowed because of the presence of a word or phrase between *want* and *to*.

On the basis of this counterexample and others like it that we can easily construct, we can save Hypothesis II by revising it to:

Hypothesis II':
You can contract *want* and *to* to *wanna* if the WH-copy is at the end of the sentence and there is no word or phrase between *want* and *to*.

This reformulation makes Hypothesis II′ somewhat less parsimonious than Hypothesis I. Notice, moreover, that Hypothesis II′ also fails since we can readily find counterexamples in which the WH-copy is not at the end and no word or phrase comes between *want* and *to*, but which nevertheless allow contraction of *want to* to *wanna*. Simply take example (5), say, repeated here as (14) and make it trivially longer:

(14)   *Where do you want to go (where)?*

(14′)   *Where do you want to go (where) tonight?* →
         Where do you wanna go (where) tonight?

Moreover, Hypothesis II′ does not account for *wanna*-contraction in sentences other than WH-questions, that is, in sentences that do not contain a WH-copy. Counterexamples of this sort are found in the introduction to Problem Set 17 itself; for example:

(15)   *I wanna pay you at the end of the month.*

Still we could continue to try to save Hypothesis II′ by reformulating it further in the following way:

Hypothesis II″:
You can contract *want to* to *wanna* if the WH-copy is located after *want to*, and if there is no word or phrase between *want* and *to* regardless of whether the sentence or question contains a WH-copy.

But now Hypothesis II″ is clearly not parsimonious in the way that Hypothesis I is. Indeed, Hypothesis II is a serious target for Occam's razor, which should surely force us to set it aside.

There is, however, at least one other hypothesis, a meaning-based one that does not take account of WH-copies, one that also focuses on when contraction is allowed:

Hypothesis III:
You can contract *want to* to *wanna* if the "wanter" is the same as the subject of the **infinitive**.

This hypothesis can be made clearer by looking at some examples of how it works. Thus, consider the relationship between the "wanter" and the "speaker" (the subject of the infinitive *to speak*) in examples (16) and (17):

(16)   *When do you want to speak?*
(17)   *Who do you want to speak?*

In (16), the "wanter" is the same person as the speaker, so *wanna*-contraction is possible; in (17), however, the "wanter" is different from the speaker, so *wanna*-contraction is not possible.

Are there counterexamples to this hypothesis? The structure they would have to take is the following: We need to look for sentences in which the "wanter" and the "to-doer" (the subject of the infinitive) are the same and in which *wanna*-contraction is not possible. Consider the following sentences:

(18)   *They want themselves to speak.*
(19)   *They want, no matter what anyone says, to speak.*
(20)   *They want never to speak.*

In (18), (19), and (20), the "wanters" want to be the speaker; that is, in fact, the necessary interpretation of the reflexive pronoun *themselves* in (18). Yet there can be no contraction. Even simply pausing between *want* and *to* prevents contraction, as can be demonstrated for (16) and (17) above – where Hypothesis III predicts contractibility should always be possible.

Notice, however, that Hypothesis I' provides an explanation for the failure to contract in these examples:

> *Hypothesis I':*
> You cannot contract *want to* to *wanna* if there is anything between *want* and *to*.

We now see that the term 'anything' in Hypothesis I' means literally that, since 'anything' includes a word or phrase (*Emma, themselves, no matter what anyone says*), a WH-copy, a pause.

The failure of Hypothesis III thus further supports and strengthens Hypothesis I'. It is also support for the idea that the constraint on *wanna*-contraction is a purely <u>structural</u> one and not based in meaning. Hypothesis I' appears, then, to offer a good explanation of the facts.

What we learn from *wanna*-contraction

There are at least two important observations to make about this problem set and its solution. The first is that the sentences of English (indeed, of all languages) contain unspoken but consequential elements that are necessary for the mental computations involved in producing and comprehending sentences. WH-copies, for example, have consequences in English despite their lacking phonological content. In particular, we learn from *wanna*-contraction that a WH-copy marking the location of a WH-word in underlying structure is crucial to explaining <u>both</u> contraction and interpretation; a WH-copy blocks contraction under certain circumstances, and it establishes the grammatical and semantic relationship of the WH-word to the other constituents of the underlying syntactic structure. For example, in question (7), partially treed below in (21) – with *to* as the verb generator for the VP *to speak*:

(21)   Who do you

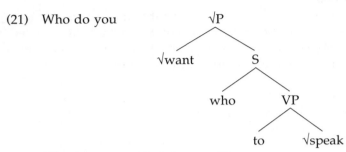

Who do you want (who) to speak?

the WH-copy of *who* both blocks contraction **and** reveals that *who* is the subject of the infinitive *to speak*. The role that WH-copies play in *wanna*-contraction complements what we have already observed about unspoken syntactic elements having phonological consequences. In English yes/no questions, for example, the question particle lacks phonological content but has phonological effect, imposing a rising intonation over the question.

The other observation to make is that no one could ever have taught a child Hypothesis I', the constraint on *wanna*-contraction that we formulated above. In fact, it was only quite recently – in the course of the intense study of syntax during the past three decades or so – that the peculiarities of *wanna*-contraction in English were noticed. The question, then, is how does a child acquire the knowledge evident in the solution to this and other problems? Further, can an adult get this sort of knowledge as she or he goes about getting English as a second, third, or nth language?

First language acquisition of *wanna*-contraction

Recent work has shown that children demonstrate knowledge of the constraint on *wanna*-contraction as early as it is ethical to bother them about such matters. In a paper entitled "Language acquisition in the absence of experience," Crain (1991) reports on some very clever experiments that he and Thornton designed to elicit *wanna*-contraction from two- to five-year old children. In summarizing their work, Crain describes interview protocols that were developed to solicit "the child's help in finding out information about rats. The child's help was sought in this task because the rat (puppet) . . . was too timid to talk to grown-ups" (1991, pp. 603–604).

A summary of the interview protocols continues below. In the protocols, the term **object extraction** refers to the fact that in questions of type (4a) above, *Who do you want to visit (who)?*, the WH-word *who* is moved from its position as the object of *visit* – where a WH-copy is left behind. **Subject extraction** refers to the fact that in questions of type (4b) above, *Who do you want (who) to visit?*, the WH-word *who* is moved from the subject position of *to visit* – where a WH-copy is left behind.

Protocol for Eliciting Object Extraction Questions

Experimenter:	The rat looks hungry. I bet he wants to eat something. Ask Ratty what he wants.
Child:	*What do you wanna eat (what)?*
Rat:	Some cheese would be good.

Complex Protocol: Subject Extraction Questions

Experimenter:	There are three guys in this story; Cookie Monster, a dog, and this baby. One of them gets to take a walk, one gets to take a nap, and one gets to eat a cookie. And the rat gets to choose who does each thing. So <u>one</u> gets to take a walk, right? Ask Ratty who he wants.
Child:	*Who do you want (who) to take a walk?*
Rat:	I want the dog to take a walk.

Working with 21 children aged 2;10 to 5;5 (mean age of 4;3), Crain and Thornton got the following results:

Table 14.2

	Want to contracted	*Want to* uncontracted	Unrelated response
Object extraction:			
What do you want to eat (what)?	59%	18%	23%
Subject extraction:			
Who do you want (who) to take a walk?	*4%	67%	29%

Note that one child out of the 21 who were tested was responsible for all of the ungrammatical *wanna*-contractions, indicated in the table by an asterisk.

In commenting on this same experiment, Crain and Lillo-Martin (1999) conclude that:

> the experiment described here shows that children do obey the constraints on "wanna" contraction in their productions at a very early age. Since there would be no way for children to retreat from a mistake if they tried to (over-)generalize the application of "wanna" contraction to all surface sequences of "want" + "to" [since no useful negative evidence is available to the child], this constraint [on WH-copies] is a prime candidate for universal, innate knowledge. (p. 253)

It is important to understand what Crain and his co-workers Thornton and Lillo-Martin are claiming to be part of Universal Grammar. It is certainly not *wanna*-contraction itself, which is particular to English. Rather, what is a universal fact of language is that purely abstract, unspoken elements like WH-copies can have the effect of spoken ones and that these elements are constrained. In English, the constraint on WH-copies blocks what to common sense appears at first glance to be a freely occurring contraction.

However, assuming this constraint is part of Universal Grammar, how are we to explain the data from the child who violated the constraint and contracted over WH-copies?

Consider the following: There are clearly three steps in the derivation of questions like *What do you wanna eat?* and *Who do you want to take a walk?* First, a WH-word moves to the question particle position at the left edge of the structure, leaving a WH-copy behind; then, if it is allowed, there is contraction; then deletion of the WH-copy prior to pronunciation. For adult speakers of English and nearly all of Crain and Thornton's subjects, these steps affect an underlying syntactic structure in the order just given:

	Object extraction	Subject extraction
Input:	*do you want to eat what*	*do you want who to take a walk*
1. WH-movement:	*what do you want to eat (what)*	*who do you want (who) to take a walk*
2. *Wanna*-contraction:	*what do you wanna eat (what)*	*who do you want (who) to take a walk*
3. WH-copy deletion:	*What do you wanna eat?*	*Who do you want to take a walk?*

Suppose, however, that the apparently unconstrained *wanna*-child ran the steps of the derivation in the following slightly different order, reversing steps 2 and 3:

	Object extraction	Subject extraction
Input:	*do you want to eat what*	*do you want who to take a walk*
1. WH-movement:	*what do you want to eat (what)*	*who do you want (who) to take a walk*
3. WH-copy deletion:	*what do you want to eat*	*who do you want to take a walk*
2. *wanna*-contraction:	*What do you wanna eat?*	**Who do you wanna take a walk?*

This would explain the data from this child. And if this were true, then the child did not violate the constraint on contracting over WH-copies, for if steps 2 and 3 are reversed then there are no WH-copies to block *wanna*-contraction.

Second language acquisition of *wanna*-contraction

As far as we have been able to determine, there is only one L2 acquisition study of the constraint on *wanna*-contraction, a dissertation on *wanna*-contraction judgments by Turkish students of English (Ellidokuzoglu, 2002), and this research generally supports Crain's conclusions about L1 acquisition. Moreover, in our own work with students who speak English fluently but as a second language, we have discovered that they give – at better than chance level – the same grammaticality judgments for sentences like (1–9) that we would expect from native speakers of English, further supporting the notion that sensitivity to the consequences of WH-movement – and WH-copies – may be part of Universal Grammar.

Thus experimental evidence from first language acquisition and evidence from second language acquisition strongly support the point made in the title of Crain's paper: The constraint on *wanna*-contraction is acquired in the absence of any relevant experience. By 'relevant' experience, we mean exposure to evidence that contraction across a WH-copy is not possible in English. But, as we have already pointed out, negative evidence about ungrammatical forms is simply not available to the language learner. The positive evidence that the child and the adult get and the universal constraints on moved elements are sufficient.

Is-Contraction

We now extend the idea that there are unspoken constituents other than WH-copies that have phonological effect into a discussion of **ellipsis** or the deletion of repeated material, and its significance for an understanding of *is*-contraction. We begin with the consequences of WH-copy ellipsis for *is*-contraction. As was the case for *wanna*-contraction, it is clearly not always possible to contract *is*, as we see from the following grammaticality judgments for sentences (6–15) from Problem Set 18, repeated here as (22–31):

		's judgment
(22)	*Alexander wonders when Emma is at home.*	OK
(23)	*Alexander wonders what Emma is looking at.*	OK
(24)	*Alexander wonders who he is sometimes.*	*
(25)	*Alexander wonders where Emma is.*	*
(26)	*Emma is at home on Tuesdays.*	OK
(27)	*Emma is looking at the Moon.*	OK
(28)	*Alexander thinks he is Napoleon sometimes.*	OK
(29)	*Emma is at home.*	OK
(30)	*Do you know what that is on the table?*	*
(31)	*That is a book on the table.*	OK

Although one should be careful not to be blinded by success, it is certainly a reasonable move to see if the hypothesis that explains *wanna*-contraction also constrains the contraction of *is*. To check this possibility, we need to locate the WH-copies for the WH-words in the indirect WH-questions in (22–25) and in (30). To do this, we extract the indirect WH-question from its larger setting by ignoring everything that precedes the WH-word (*Alexander wonders*, for example). We next run the resulting WH-question (for example, *When is Emma at home?*) through the standard tests for the location of WH-copies. And then we locate the WH-copies with respect to *is*, both where contraction fails, as well as where it is possible. Examining just two of the relevant sentences in their uncontracted form, one where *is*-contraction is possible, and one where it is not, and using the full-answer test and the echo-question test, we arrive at the following locations for the WH-copies in sentences (22) and (25).

(22)   *Alexander wonders when Emma is at home (when).*
  When is Emma at home?   (WH-question)
  Emma's at home <u>every 15th Monday</u>.   (full answer)
  Emma's at home <u>when</u>?!   (echo question)
  Alexander wonders when Emma's at home. (*is*-contraction)

(25)   *Alexander wonders where Emma is (where).*
  Where is Emma?
  Emma's <u>at the police station.</u>
  Emma's <u>where</u>?!
  **Alexander wonders where Emma's.*

It is clear from the location of the WH-copies in these two sentences that the constraint on *wanna*-contraction does <u>not</u> carry over to explain *is*-contraction. While *wanna*-contraction is blocked by an intervening WH-copy, it appears that *is*-contraction is blocked for another reason.

Formulating and testing hypotheses

Perhaps examining the syntactic trees for sentences (22) and (25), repeated below as (33) and (35) will help us uncover the structural constraint on *is*-contraction. So let us now tree the indirect WH-questions and the location of the WH-copies in these sentences:

(32)   Alexander wonders

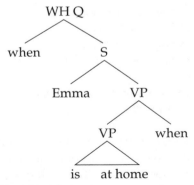

(33)   *Alexander wonders when Emma's at home.*

(34)   Alexander wonders

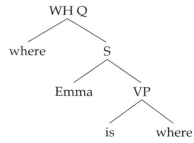

(35)   *Alexander wonders where *Emma's.*

We can see from these trees that *is*-contraction is blocked when the WH-copy is the right-hand **sister** of *is*, as in sentence (35). Recall from Chapter 10 that constituents that **c-command** one another are called **sisters**.

Thus we need to hypothesize a constraint on *is*-contraction that is different from the one that explains *wanna*-contraction, but one that nevertheless takes into account the position of WH-copies. Let us try this one out, returning later to why it might work this way:[1]

> *Hypothesis I:*
> If a WH-copy is a right-hand sister of *is*, *is* cannot be contracted onto the constituent that immediately c-commands *is*.

The partial trees (32) and (34) above illustrate how Hypothesis I constrains *is*-contraction in sentence (35) while allowing it in (33). In sentence (33), although *Emma* c-commands *is*, the WH-copy of *when* is not a sister of *is*. Since this condition is not met, *is*-contraction is possible. In sentence (35), the WH-copy of *where* is the right-hand sister of *is*, and *Emma* immediately c-commands *is*. Thus *is*-contraction is <u>not</u> possible in (35).

A careful examination of the other sentences in the relevant set ((23), (24), and (30)) reveals that the structural contrast between sentences (33) and (35) holds for these sentences as well: sentence (23) patterns like (33), and sentences (24) and (30) are like (35).

To test Hypothesis I, we next ask if there are counterexamples. Two kinds of counterexamples could falsify this hypothesis:

- sentences in which there is a WH-copy that is a right-hand sister to *is*, but which do allow *is*-contraction;
- sentences in which there is no WH-copy at all, but which do not allow *is*-contraction.

---

[1]   Note, again, that in stating the constraint on *is*-contraction, the hypothesis – by Occam's razor – automatically <u>allows</u> contraction wherever the constraint is not satisfied: both in sentences that have no WH-copy (26–29) and (31) as well as in those sentences with a WH-copy that does not fall under the constraint.

There are no examples of the first sort, but there are examples of the second type in Problem Set 18: sentences (16) and (18), repeated below as (36) and (37), with which we compare sentence (17), repeated as (38):

(36)   *Emma is fleeing from the FBI and Peter is too.* →
       Emma's fleeing from the FBI and *Peter's too.

(37)   *Emma is tough and so is Peter.* →
       Emma's tough and so's Peter.

(38)   *Emma is working harder today than Peter is.* →
       Emma's working harder today than *Peter's.

Notice that *is*-contraction is fine in (37), but not in (36) and (38). Notice further that also, since these sentences do not contain questions – direct or indirect – they do not contain WH-copies. This might lead us to suspect that there is something more <u>general</u> than WH-copy – but which includes WH-copy – that makes *is*-contraction impossible for sentences (36) and (38), as well as (24), (25), and (30). Let us keep this possibility in mind as we examine further the structure of (36), (37), and (38).

Consider, then, the uncontracted versions of (36), (37), and (38), sentences that result from **ellipsis**, the deletion of identical, repeated material (the obverse of a copy). Ellipsis leaves a **GAP** in the syntactic structure. We demonstrate this in the following pairs of trees. In (39a), (40a), and (41a), we tree the second part of the "full" versions of these sentences, restoring the material deleted from the second part because it is identical to material in the first part. In (39b), (40b), and (41b), we tree the same portion of the sentences following deletion, identifying the GAP that results from ellipsis. Note that *is* has been raised in (40a) and (40b), leaving a copy of itself in its underlying position:

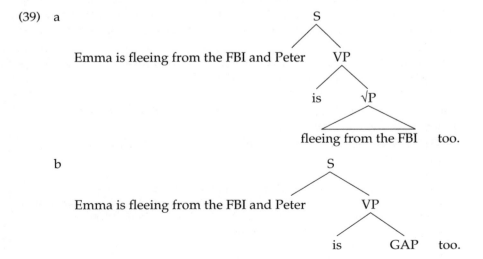

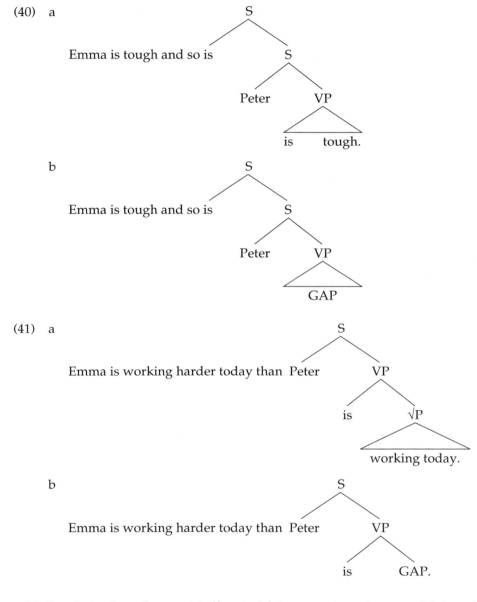

(40) a

Emma is tough and so is

Peter

is   tough.

b

Emma is tough and so is

Peter

GAP

(41) a

Emma is working harder today than Peter

is

working today.

b

Emma is working harder today than Peter

is   GAP.

Notice that when the repeated material is present, as in trees (39a) and (41a), *is*-contraction is possible. However, as we see in trees (39b), (40b), and (41b), contraction may be blocked depending on the position from which 'understood' material has been deleted. When a GAP is a right-hand sister to *is*, then *is* cannot be contracted onto the constituent that immediately c-commands *is*. Although there is also a GAP in (40b), the GAP is <u>not</u> a sister to *is*. Thus *is*-contraction is possible in sentence (37), but not in sentences (36) and (38).

A way to capture this fact, as well as the failure of contraction in sentences (24), (25), and (30), from the set (22–31) on p. 185, is to reformulate and generalize Hypothesis I as follows, letting GAP be a term that covers both deletion by ellipsis and WH-copies left behind by WH-movement:

Hypothesis I′:
If a GAP is the right-hand sister of *is*, then *is* cannot be contracted onto the constituent that c-commands *is*.

By thinking very broadly, we see that a GAP can include both WH-copies – as in sentences (22–25) and (30), or it can result from ellipsis, the deletion of identical material in a sentence – as in (36–38).

Notice that for sentences (22–25) and (30), the crucial question is not simply whether there is a GAP in the sentence: as with (36–38), we must also know the exact structural location of the GAP with respect to *is*. Thus given Hypothesis I′, it is not surprising that the points of deletion in (22) and (23) have no effect on the contraction of *is* in these sentences.

The reformulation of Hypothesis I to Hypothesis I′ shows once again how counterexamples to a hypothesis can lead to a better hypothesis – a desirable result. Hypothesis I′ is a better hypothesis than Hypothesis I because in its more general form, it explains more of the data. We must, of course, proceed to challenge this hypothesis as well – as the occasion arises.

A WH-copy in the absence of a WH-word?

Filling the gap in sentence (38) with the root phrase (√P) *working today*, as in tree (41a), does, however, seem somewhat forced and awkward. Thus, variation in English leads us to a different explanation of sentences like (38), repeated here as (42):

(42)   *Emma is working harder today than *Peter's.*

Example (42) may well be a case of WH-movement in a kind of WH-sentence (WH-S) that is different from a question, for in some varieties of English it is perfectly fine to say:

(42′) *Emma is working harder today than what Peter is.* →
       *Emma's working harder today than what *Peter's.*

As with (42), the first *is* in (42′) can be contracted, while the second *is* cannot.

The WH-word *what* in this variety of English reveals that there is WH-movement in the formation of (42′); that is, it contains a WH-copy in its underlying structure, which we tree as follows:

(43)   a

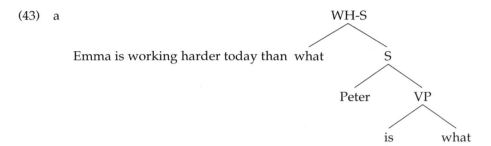

Since contraction is not allowed in this sentence, we predict the WH-copy of *what* to be a right-hand sister of *is*, which it is – as the tree in (43a) reveals. The WH-copy results in a GAP in that right-hand sister position, which constrains the contraction of *is*:

(43)   b

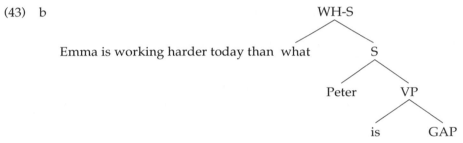

*Emma is working harder today than what *Peter's GAP.*

Standard varieties of English in which *what* does not show up in sentences of this sort might simply contain a null WH-word, represented by Ø below, with similar consequences for *is*-contraction:

(43)   c

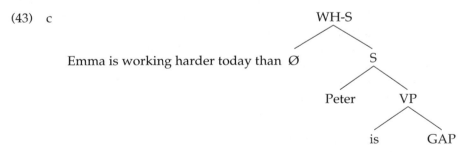

*Emma is working harder today than Ø *Peter's GAP.*

This analysis is not that far-fetched, for the null WH-word (as opposed to *who* or *that*) is generally a possibility in WH-sentences, as in a sentence such as:

(44)   *This is the person Ø I met GAP yesterday.*

To summarize this discussion: Apparently in comparative constructions such as (42), the WH-word does not surface <u>phonologically</u> in standard varieties of English, but nevertheless it does have phonological effect – the structural position of the GAP left by the WH-copy blocks *is*-contraction.

Generalizing across other auxiliary verb contractions

The following sentences, as well as some of those with which Problem Set 18 was introduced, indicate that *is*-contraction is about more than just the contraction of *is*. In (19) and (20), for example, repeated here as (45) and (46), *will*-contraction and *have*-contraction are blocked, and importantly both are elliptical sentences. The GAP that results from ellipsis is located exactly where it blocks contraction in *is*-contraction:

(45)   *If you don't do it today, I will GAP tomorrow.* →
       *If you don't do it today, *I'll GAP tomorrow.*

(46)   *I have seen the light, but I don't think they have GAP.* →
       *I've seen the light, but I don't think *they've GAP.*

Hypothesis I′ must clearly be further generalized into a hypothesis about the contractibility of English auxiliary verbs, thus covering even more data. We leave it to you to think about which auxiliaries are contractible and how to rewrite the hypothesis in its more general form.

First language acquisition of *is*-contraction

As you might expect from the earlier discussion of *wanna*-contraction, it has also been shown through careful experimentation that children have the constraint on *is*-contraction at a very young age (see Crain, 1991, reporting on work by Crain and Thornton). In research designed to try to elicit appropriate *is*-contraction from preschool children, Crain and Thornton hypothesized "that children will not produce ungrammatical questions such as . . . [*Do you know what that's GAP up there?*], despite the absence of relevant evidence from the environment," but that they will readily contract when the grammar allows, as in *Do you know what that's doing GAP up there?* (Crain, 1991, p. 604).
   Here are the simple protocols that they used:

Protocols for [*is*-]Contraction
Experimenter: Ask Ratty if he knows what that is doing up there.
Child: *Do you know what that's doing up there?*
Rat: It seems to be sleeping.

Experimenter: Ask Ratty if he knows what that is up there.
Child: *Do you know what that is up there?*
Rat: A monkey.

Working with twelve children aged 2;11 to 4;5 (mean age of 3;8), Crain and Thornton were able to elicit questions involving *is*-contraction from all of their subjects without getting "a <u>single</u> instance of contraction where it was ruled out in the adult grammar" (Crain, 1991, p. 604 – emphasis added). Here are some examples of the correctly uncontracted questions that the children produced:

> *Do you know what that black thing on the flower is (what)?* (age 4;3)
> *Squeaky, what do you think that is (what)?* (age 3;11)
> *Do you know what that is (what) on the flower?* (age 4;5)
> *Do you know what that is (what), Squeaky?* (age 3;2)

As with *wanna*-contraction, children apparently know when not to contract *is* without having had any relevant linguistic experience, and certainly no instruction. Though their experience may be rich in positive evidence about the contraction of *is* (and other auxiliary verbs), what is not available to them is negative evidence; that is, evidence that tells them when <u>not</u> to contract. Thus, such unconscious knowledge of the constraints on GAPs must follow from principles of Universal Grammar.

Although it is the mark of a second language learner to err at these very subtle levels of syntax, second language learners are generally able to make the correct grammaticality judgments of *is*-contraction, despite being unable to accurately produce the constructions in question.

The Return of Phonology: The Phonology of *Is*-Contraction

Consider, now, the phonology of *is*-contraction. Note first that contraction to /z/ results not only from the contraction of *is* but also from the contraction of the auxiliary *has*, as in *Emma's been here* (the contraction of *Emma has been here*). Thus, if we assume that contraction begins from the phonological forms /ɪz/ and /hæz/, contraction can then be phonologically understood as a <u>reduction</u> of both words to /z/. This occurs by deleting the sounds that precede the /z/ and attaching the /z/ to the preceding word, where not constrained from this by Hypothesis I':

> *Hypothesis I':*
> If a GAP is the right-hand sister of *is*, then *is* cannot be contracted onto the constituent that c-commands *is*.

We can observe this reduction of /ɪz/ and /hæz/ in the following examples:

(47)   *Dave /ɪz/ outside.*   →   *Dave/z/ outside.*
(48)   *Emma /hæz/ never been here.* →   *Emma/z/ never been here.*

But notice that if we substitute *Geoff* for *Dave* and *Emma*, the sound that represents the contracted word is different from that of (47) and (48) in a familiar way:

(49)   *Geoff /ɪz/ outside.*   →   *Geoff/s/ outside.*
(50)   *Geoff /hæz/ never been here.*   →   *Geoff/s/ never been here.*

In (49) and (50), the contracted /z/ surfaces as /s/. Why should this be?

First note the differences between the sounds that end the words to which the contraction /z/ is added: /v/ and /ə/ (the latter a vowel) in sentences (47) and (48); /f/ in sentences (49) and (50). Recall that /v/ and /ə/ are both voiced sounds, while /f/ is among the set of voiceless sounds. Remember also that /z/ is a voiced sound, and /s/ is a voiceless sound. (See the distinctive feature matrices in Chapter 2.)

The phonology of contraction thus closely resembles the phonology of regular plural noun formation in that **voicing assimilation** applies. When the contraction /z/, which is a voiced sound, is attached to the preceding word, this /z/ automatically assimilates its voicing to the sound that immediately precedes it. This means that the contraction /z/ remains a voiced sound when the word it attaches to ends in a voiced sound, like the final /v/ of *Dave* or the final /ə/ of *Emma*. But when this /z/ attaches to words ending in a voiceless sound, like the final /f/ of *Geoff*, then the contraction /z/ is devoiced to /s/. In other words, /z/ assimilates to the voiceless sound /f/ by becoming voiceless itself.

Note, however, that something different, though not unexpected, happens when the contraction /z/ attaches to a word that ends in /s/, or any other sibilant: /z/, /š/, /ž/, /j/, /č/. For *is*-contraction does not then surface as:

(51)   *Elvis /hæz/ been here before.*   →   **Elvis/s/ been here before.*
(52)   *Bush /ɪz/ a has-been.*   →   **Bush/s/ a has-been.*
(53)   *Jazz /hæz/ never been better.*   →   **Jazz/z/ never been better.*

Clearly, voicing assimilation does not apply. Instead, the **epenthetic vowel** /ɪ/ is inserted between these word-final [Tongue blade, +strident] (= sibilant) sounds and the contraction /z/ (itself a sibilant), separating them and correctly giving us:

(54)   *Elvis/z/ been here before.*   →   *Elvis/ɪz/ been here before.*
(55)   *Bush /ɪz/ a has-been.*   →   *Bush/ɪz/ a has been.*
(56)   *Jazz /hæz/ never been better.*   →   *Jazz/ɪz/ never been better.*

The result of this sort of contraction of /ɪz/ or /hæz/ after a sibilant sound is always /ɪz/.

Now particularly for (55), this may look as if we are engaging in some slight of hand for the contraction of *is*, simply taking something away by contraction and then reinserting it by another rule. But nevertheless, that is the most general way to account for <u>all</u> the facts if we keep in mind that the phonology of *is*-contraction involves *has* as well as *is*. Moreover, there is a clear but subtle phonological difference in phrasing between (57) and its contracted form, sentence (58):

(57) *Jazz /hæz/ never been better.*
(58) *Jazz/ɪz/ never been better.*

That difference lies in the timing of the syllables *Jazz* and /ɪz/. In (58), the syllables end up sounding like a word, like *fuses*, say. And that is – after all – what contraction is all about: phonological merge, making a single word out of two separate words. In (57), *jazz* and /hæz/ are separate words, with /hæz/ being lightly stressed, while in (58), *jazz*/ɪz/ is a single word phonologically.

To conclude this chapter, let us turn to the question of why auxiliary verbs contract in English at all.

To Contract or Not: The Phonology–Semantics Interaction

In general, contraction in language can only affect weakly accented, unstressed elements in a sentence, like the infinitive *to* (as in *want to → wanna*) or the negative *not* (as in *does not → doesn't*). Perhaps, then, *is*-type contractions are related to the fact that auxiliary verbs and forms of *be* generally have their stress reduced by the rules that assign stress within a sentence. When weakly stressed, the members of this set of verbs that begin with a vowel or the relatively weak glides /h/ and /w/ are candidates for contraction – the forms of *have* and *will* and *would*, for example. But for some reason that is not well understood, these verbs are blocked from stress reduction if their right-hand sister is a GAP. Not being able to be de-stressed under this condition, these verbs then fail to contract onto the constituent that c-commands them.

Why then can't the past tense forms of *be*, which begin with /w/, contract when they are not constrained from contracting? In sentence (59), for example, *was* cannot contract onto *Emma*, while past tense *had* can contract onto *Emma* in sentence (60):

(59) *Emma was singing.*   →   **Emma's singing.*
(60) *Emma had already seen the movie.*   →   *Emma'd already seen the movie.*

These data reveal a very general constraint on deletion: the necessity of being able to recover deleted information unambiguously, a universal fact of language referred to as the **recoverability of deletion**. Deletion is possible <u>only if</u> the meaning of the deleted material can be recovered from the immediate syntactic context. In (60), *had* is the only interpretation that can be given the contraction /d/ in the context of the perfect participle *seen*. But the contraction /z/ of (59) is ambiguous between the final /z/ of *is* and *was*. Thus it could not be uniquely interpreted if both *is* and *was* were to contract to /z/. The present-tense interpretation of /z/ from *is* follows from the fact that present tense is the default tense for languages that have overtly morphological tense. In English, for example, this is manifested by the fact that past tense is indicated by a spoken morpheme, present tense by Ø, an unspoken one; that is, present tense is unmarked.

This general constraint on deletion also holds for a sentence like (61), a variation on sentences (37) and (38):

(61)   *?Emma was working hard yesterday, and so's Peter.*

Because of the conflict of tenses, this can only be reconstructed as the semantically strange (62), which is why (61) and (62) are marked '??': a person cannot be presently working hard in the past tense:

(62)   *?Emma was working hard yesterday, and so is Peter working hard yesterday.*

Nevertheless, (61) and (62) are syntactically well-formed.

We have now strayed into meaning and semantics, which we will take up shortly in Part IV of this book, so let us sum up before moving on.

Summing Up

Our examination of *wanna*-contraction and *is*-contraction has led us beyond a consideration of WH-copy to the more general concept 'gap' and to constraints on contraction that are sensitive to WH-copies and to GAPs and their position in syntactic structure. Of course, *wanna*-contraction and *is*-contraction are part of the particular grammar of English and thus not universal phenomena. However, in the absence of negative evidence about when contraction is blocked, L1 and L2 acquisition of the constraints on contraction in English must follow from Universal Grammar – from the effects that WH-copies and GAPs can have on linguistic form more generally. If we were to look at languages other than English, we should expect to find that WH-copies and GAPs have similar constraining effects.

Terms and Linguistic Conventions

infinitive
object extraction

subject extraction
ellipsis
sister
c-command
GAP
voicing assimilation
epenthetic vowel
recoverability of deletion

( )   Parentheses enclose the copy of a moved element.

Further Reading

An early and detailed presentation of the experimental research on L1 acquisition of *wanna*-contraction and *is*-contraction can be found in Crain (1991). The research on *wanna*-contraction acquisition is discussed at more length in Crain and Thornton (1998, chapter 21).

The L2 acquisition study, "Wanna and Turkish Learners of English" (chapter 8 in Ellidokuzoglu, 2002), is online at http://maxpages.com/thena/Turkish_Learners.

Part IV

Meaning and – Finally – about Counting Dogs in Kiowa

Chapter 15

Meaning: An Introduction

As we stated earlier in this book, the knowledge of language that a person has when we say that she or he knows a particular language consists of:

- a **lexicon**, containing the roots, words, and morphemes that label the concepts expressed in that language;
- a **mental grammar**, or set of phonological, morphological, syntactic, and semantic rules for combining and interpreting items drawn from the lexicon.

Given this knowledge of language, how then is the meaning of a sentence constructed? Working with an array of items drawn from the lexicon, the operation called **Merge** pairs these items until they converge on a well-formed underlying structure. As we saw in Part II of this book, there are syntactic rules (such as WH-movement, Auxiliary-movement, and Preposition-movement, for example) that transform an underlying structure into its surface structure. From that point, there are rules of phonology that interpret a surface structure into its phonological form, the basis for a spoken utterance. In part, meaning derives from rules of syntax and semantics that interpret surface structure into its logical form.

Phonological Form (or **PF**) is the point at which knowledge of language meets the systems of articulation and perception, that is, the systems that allow us to speak/sign and to hear/see language. PF was dealt with in some detail in Part I of this book, and at other points as well – in the discussion in Chapter 14 of the phonological results of contraction, for example.

Logical Form (or **LF**) is the point at which knowledge of language meets systems of thought, including belief systems, real-world knowledge, and so on – aspects of what we refer to with the word *meaning*. In linguistics, PF and LF are referred to as **interface levels**, the points at which mental grammar interfaces or meets with systems external to it, yet still internal to the mind.

We diagram the relationship between underlying structure, surface structure, PF, and LF as follows:

(1)   Underlying structure

Surface structure

PF   LF

In the chapters that follow, we will investigate meaning, in particular, the narrow meaning of a sentence that is derived from syntactic and semantic rules. Let us call it simply **Meaning**: the contribution of mental grammar to the meaning of a sentence. We contrast this with the **Broad Meaning** of a sentence, which derives from Meaning plus contributions from other components of mind, such as knowledge of context, systems of belief, expectations, and so on. For example, a simple sentence like *That tree needs pruning* could be just that: a simple assertion about the condition of a particular tree; or it could be a covert request of the hearer that she or he prune the tree in question. Beyond mental grammar, it is "other stuff" in the mind/brain that allows a speaker or a hearer to determine the intended interpretation of this sentence.

We augment the previous diagram to illustrate this fact and to show that Meaning is "contained" within Broad Meaning:

(2)   Underlying structure

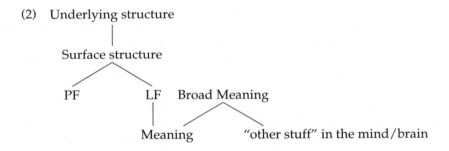

In these chapters, we focus our investigation of Meaning on NP (noun phrase) number and questions, topics dealt with in depth in Parts I and II of this book, and on NP role, a topic dealt with only informally thus far. We begin by considering the Meaning of words and morphemes.

The Compositionality of Meaning

The Meaning (hereafter, simply meaning) of a sentence is read off the meaning of its words and other morphemes and from the syntactic structure in which the words and morphemes are contained. Moreover, the meaning of a sentence is **compositional**: The meaning of a larger expression is a function of the meaning of its parts and the syntactic rules that are used to merge them into grammatical structures. These structures are then affected by transformations, but recall that although transformations may change structure, they do nothing to change the meaning of a structure, as was discussed in Chapter 8.

The composition of meaning begins, at bottom, with the meaning of the items taken from the lexicon in the formation of a sentence – its roots, words, and morphemes (like {past}, {plural}, and so on). Items from the lexicon fall into two categories:

- **lexical categories**, which include words (nouns, adjectives, verbs, and prepositions), but also roots and various suffixes and prefixes that can form new words (such as *-er, un-, re-*);
- **functional categories**, which include determiners, tense and number markers, question particles, and so on.

Lexical categories consist of what are sometimes referred to as **open class** items: "open," since new roots (and thus new nouns, adjectives, verbs, and even prepositions) are regularly added to a language. Functional categories consist of **closed class** items: "closed," since the items in each category are fixed in number by Universal Grammar (UG). Some functional categories are realized as a set of words; the definite and indefinite determiners *the, a(n),* and *some* are an example. A member of a functional category may have no phonological form, as is true of the question particles of English as opposed to those of Mandarin Chinese, for example. A member of a lexical category does not have this privilege.

Meaning and lexical categories

Now consider the following simple assertion, a quite ordinary English sentence:

(3) *The striped dishes are on a red table.*

We have already seen that the meaning of a word is partly a function of its **semantic features** and their values: for example, [±human] and [±animate] were discussed in Part I of this book. Viewed this way, *dishes* are clearly [−animate] (and thus necessarily [−human]). There are other features that contribute to the meaning of a word. For example, as well as being [−animate], *dish* and *table* are both [+count] nouns; that is, they are among the countable things of the mind and the world as opposed to *gold, milk,* and so on, which are [−count] or non-countable, mass nouns. There are further distinctions among [+count] words: Some are [+concrete], like *dish* and *table*, while others are [−concrete] or abstract, like *idea* and *dream*. Abstract [−concrete] nouns can then themselves be [+count] like *idea*, or [−count] like *integrity*. And so on. Like the distinctive features of phonology, semantic features cross-classify the words and morphemes of a language. For example, /b/ and /m/ are both [+voice], but they differ in their nasality; in the same way, *idea* and *dish* are both [+count], but they differ in their concreteness.

Quite rapidly, however, the set of semantic features gives out and what then remains of the meaning of a lexical item is an unanalyzable residue, its **kernel definition**. For example, *dish* is on the one hand an artifact – a container or an object created by human beings, but it is also what is put on or in a dish, as in the sentence *The dish we had last night was delicious*. In fact, artifactual nouns appear always to have an abstract meaning as well as a concrete one; for example, a book can be an object on a shelf or it can be an idea in the mind – as this one has been (in two minds) for over a decade and half!

Dictionaries try to lay all of this out in definitions and these definitions can be quite helpful if you already know the language in question, for dictionaries only provide the reader with hints and synonyms that circle around the meaning of a word. In order to talk about words, one must inevitably use words. This is why the discussion of meaning and defining a word often begin and end in circularity.

Meaning and functional categories

The meaning of a member of a functional category is more easily pinned down. However, these lexical items, although they have meaning, cannot "mean" on their own, but only in the context of what they relate to. The morpheme {present}, for example, cannot mean without being associated with a root. Thus, the following would be a conversation stopper:

(4)   *The* {plural} {present} *on a* {singular}.

But one can speak only in lexical categories and make a certain amount of sense (as we observe in young children acquiring their native language and adults acquiring a second language):

(5)   *Dish on table.*

We will return to the meaning of functional categories, but meanwhile let us examine in more detail the structure of sentence (3), repeated below as (6):

(6)   *The striped dishes are on a red table.*

Adjunction and the Structure of Predication

Now if the meaning of a sentence is read off the meaning of its words and other morphemes and from the structure in which the words and morphemes exist, then we can only move ahead in a discussion of the meaning of sentence (6) by examining its syntactic structure. This is no small matter since we have not yet shown any way of representing even such mildly complex noun phrases as *the striped dishes* and *a red table*. It is easy enough to get as far as (7):

(7)

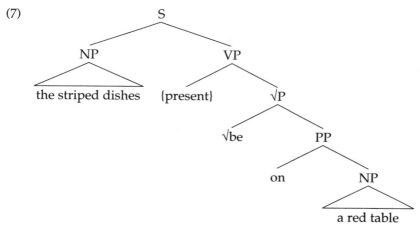

The striped dishes are on a red table.

But what is the internal structure of the two NPs? How do *striped* and *red* get into the syntactic picture? And once there, how is their meaning incorporated into the sentence?

Notice that if these words are dropped from sentence (6), we still have a well-formed English sentence with the same basic structure; the relationship between *the dishes* and *on a table* remains unchanged. Sentence (8) asserts of the dishes that they are on a table, just as sentence (6) does:

(8) *The dishes are on a table.*

But, if we drop *table* and *dishes* from sentence (6), then we have a suggestive but ill-formed sentence:

(9) **The striped are on a red.*

Sentence (9) begs us to ask, "The striped <u>what</u> are on a red <u>what</u>?" This is because *striped* and *red* are **adjuncts**; that is, they are adjoined or attached to NPs like *the dishes* and *a table* in a dependent or subordinate way. *Striped* and *red* add information to the NPs *the dishes* and *a table,* and are dependent on them for their compositional interpretation.

As we saw in Chapter 8, merging of the sort discussed there <u>creates</u> the basic syntactic structure of a sentence. For example, putting {past} and a √P (root phrase) together yields a new syntactic object: a VP. In contrast, merging an adjunct into a sentence does not result in a new kind of syntactic object, nor does it change the basic syntactic structure of a sentence. **Adjunction** does, however, embellish an already existing basic syntactic structure, NPs in the case under discussion.

In a sense, then, adjuncts are on a different plane from the unadorned sentence (8). But since speech takes place in time, what may be three-dimensional in the brain cannot remain that way in language production; the structure has to be placed along a time line in speech production – a characteristic of speech that is not necessarily true of signed sentences, since signed languages are produced in three-dimensional space.

Although linearization requires that adjectives like *striped* and *red* be on a spoken time line, notice that it is arbitrary that in English adjectives fall in place before the noun that they are adjoined to, perhaps as a consequence of a parametric setting. They could just as well follow the noun as they do in Spanish and French, languages that are in many respects quite similar to English. Other types of adjuncts in English <u>do</u> follow the nouns that they modify: *the man <u>with red hair</u>; a table <u>that is red</u>*; and so on. Moreover, in English, structurally complex adjective phrases also follow the nouns they modify. Compare the position and grammaticality of *special* and *special to linguistics* in sentences (10–13):

(10)   *Special terms are not always found in dictionaries.*
(11)   **Terms special are not always found in dictionaries.*
(12)   *Terms special to linguistics are not always found in dictionaries.*
(13)   *?*Special to linguistics terms are not always found in dictionaries.*

The multidimensionality of the mind/brain obviously cannot be represented very well in a tree diagram on a two-dimensional piece of paper. A mobile or a Tinkertoy® structure would be a better way to go. However, we can improvise, and try to capture the multidimensionality of syntax with some two-dimensional tricks as follows:

(14)

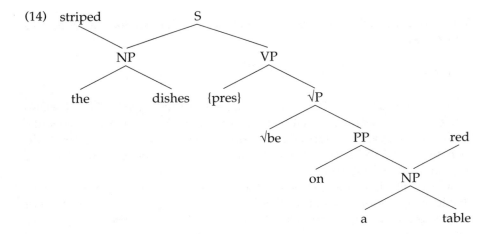

But now how is the strange object in (14) to be interpreted? How did it get put together and what is its meaning? The structure in (14) is the result of **adjunction**: the merging of additional constituents into the structure <u>from outside</u> the basic sentence. This is <u>the</u> way of enriching the expressive power of individual sentences given by Universal Grammar (Chomsky, 2001, p. 18). If adjunction were not available, then we would be restricted to speaking in a series of additive sentences like the following:

(15)   a   *The dishes are on a table.*
      b   *The dishes are striped.*
      c   *The table is red.*

The sentences (15a–c) reveal that sentence (6) *The striped dishes are on a red table* has packed into it three instances of **predication**, whereby something is expressed about something else. Here are the three instances of predication:

- First, it is predicated of these particular dishes that they are among the set of striped things in the situation: *the striped dishes* are contained in the intersection between the set of dishes in the situation and the set of striped things in the situation, with the term **set** used here in its mathematical/logical sense: any collection of distinct elements.
- Second, it is predicated of a table that it is among the set of red things in the situation: *a red table* is contained in the intersection between a set of tables in the situation and a set of red things in the situation.
- Finally – and this is the <u>primary</u> predication, it is predicated of *the striped dishes* that they are included in the set of things located on a red table.

Predication amounts to set intersection in the first two instances – the result of adjunction – and set inclusion in the third – the result of Merge. The primary predication is found in sentence (6) and in its stripped down version, sentence (15a).

Notice further that the two secondary predications that result from adjunction can also be accomplished by adjoining relative clauses to the NPs, *the dishes* and *a table*; that is, by bringing subordinate-clause versions of sentences (15b) and (15c) into sentence (15a), creating sentence (16):

(16)   *The dishes that are striped are on a table that is red.*

In this case, the adjunct clauses <u>follow</u> the phrases to which they are adjoined. In other languages (Mandarin Chinese, for example), such relative clause adjuncts <u>precede</u> the constituents to which they are adjoined.

It has, in fact, generally been argued in the theory of grammar that a sentence like (6) is derived through transformations from something like sentence (16). *That are* and *that is* must be deleted in the course of the derivation, with what remains of the predications (*striped* and *red*) being moved – in a language like English – so that they immediately precede *dishes* and *table*:

> *The dishes that are striped are on a table that is red.* = (16)

By deletion: *The dishes Ø striped are on a table Ø red.*

By movement: *The striped dishes are on a red table.* = (16)

Number and set size in noun phrases

Having dealt with the predications of sentence (6), we are now in a position to examine how the **functional categories** of sentence (6) are interpreted: the definite determiner *the* and the indefinite determiner *a*, and NP number.

Consider number first: Basically number fixes set size, with {singular} denoting a set with a single member, while {plural} – in English – denotes a set size of two members or more. Thus the NPs in sentence (6) denote sets of the following sizes:

- The plural NP *the striped dishes* denotes the set size ≥ 2: two or more striped dishes are involved in this situation;
- The singular NP *a red table* denotes the set size $= 1$: there is but one red table involved in this situation.

Set types: (in)definite

Turn, finally, to the determiners *the* and *a*. The [+definite] determiner *the* is a **universal quantifier,** fixing the set type such that it denotes what is true of the entire set of things involved; that is, for all striped dishes referred to in sentence (6), it is a fact that they are on a red table. If just one striped dish were beneath the table, it would be false to assert sentence (6). Thus:

- From the definite determiner *the*, we infer something about the entire set denoted by the set size: that what is being said about this set is true of all of its members.

The [−definite] determiner *a* sets up a different set type, for it is an **existential quantifier,** with a different meaning from that of definite determiners:

- From the indefinite determiner *a*, we infer the existence of a red table upon which the striped dishes are asserted to be.

Compare sentence (6) with sentence (17) below. In sentence (17), the plural indefinite determiner *some* has replaced definite *the* and the definite determiner *the* has replaced indefinite *a*. What is the effect of this change in determiners?

(17)   *Some striped dishes are on the red table.*

The change clearly reverses the definiteness values and asserts that there exist two or more striped dishes such that they are located on a particular red table. Although some other striped dishes might be under the table, next to the table, and/or in the pantry, these facts would not affect the truth value of sentence (17), if indeed at least two of the striped dishes were on the red table.

In addition to the universal and existential set types discussed thus far, there is also **generic**. For example, a "bare" plural, like that in sentence (18), and what looks like a [+definite] singular NP in sentence (19), are interpreted generically in English; that is, to refer to the entire species, the universal set of dogs:

(18)   *Dogs are four-legged animals that bark.*
(19)   *The dog is a four-legged animal that barks.*

In Nicaraguan English – and in many languages of the world, however, the "bare" <u>singular</u> is used to express the generic, as in the Nicaraguan English version of a classic nursery rhyme:

(20)   *What are little girl made of? Little girl made of sugar and spice and everything nice. That what little girl made of.*

Thus we see that there is interpretive interaction between number and in-/definiteness and the absence of in-/definiteness in "bare" nouns. Notice also that in a generic expressions of this sort, *is* and *are*, the present tense forms of *be*, are not used to refer to time at all, for generic statements are timeless – unless, of course, we are speaking about an extinct species.

Looking Ahead

The discussion of sentence (6) has been a running definition of the concept **'compositionality of meaning'**. As we have seen, the meaning of a sentence is composed of the meaning of its parts, from its predications and its expressions of NP number and definiteness. These are treated together for they are the basic ingredients in the meaning of simple assertions of the sort made in sentence (6).

But, as you might suspect, there is more to say about the meaning of NPs than whether they are definite or indefinite, singular or plural. For as we will see, NPs stand in relationship with other elements in a sentence, with roots in particular, and from those relationships they take on further meaning. For example, in sentence (21), the NP *the striped dishes* plays a different role than it does in sentence (6):

(21)   *Emma broke the striped dishes.*

In (21), *the striped dishes* are <u>affected</u> by Emma's consciously breaking them or at least causing them to be broken. In (6), *the striped dishes* are simply said to exist in a particular <u>location</u> specified by the **locative** PP *on a red table*, with *on* making the location precise.

In Chapter 17, we will explore the role that concepts like 'affected' and 'location' play in the meaning that NPs and PPs take on in a sentence. But first, we move on in Chapter 16 to conclude a pending discussion of NP number, turning – finally – to analyzing the compositional construction of NP number in Kiowa.

Terms

lexicon
mental grammar
Merge
Phonological Form, PF
Logical Form, LF
interface level
Meaning
Broad Meaning
compositional
lexical categories
functional categories
open class
closed class

semantic features
kernel definition
adjuncts
adjunction
predication
set
universal quantifier
existential quantifier
generic
compositionality of meaning
locative

Further Reading

Larson and Segal's (1995) *Knowledge of Meaning: An Introduction to Semantic Theory* is an excellent introduction to the study of meaning. Our set-theoretic analysis of predication, adjunction, NP number, and NP definiteness is based on Chomsky (1977, pp. 48–51).

Chapter 16

Beyond Pluralization: Inversion and Noun Modification in Kiowa

Having dealt with set types (universal, existential, and generic) in the previous chapter, we are now in a position to examine the **functional category** of noun phrase or **NP number** in greater detail, focusing on Kiowa. Before we pursue this topic further, let us review what we have learned thus far about NP number.

Recall from Chapter 15 that number basically fixes the set size of an NP, with {singular} denoting a set with a single member and {plural} – in English – denoting a set size of two or more members. Given this and given the by now familiar sentence *The striped dishes are on a red table*, speakers of English know that:

- the plural NP *the striped dishes* denotes the set size ≥ 2: there are two or more striped dishes;
- the singular NP *a red table* denotes the set size = 1: there is only one red table.

In Part I of this book, we maintained that 'singular' and 'plural' are innate concepts for all human beings and that these concepts are morphologically expressed in a relatively small number of ways in different languages. Moreover, as discussed in Chapter 7, the **dual** morphology of Yakima and of Western Apache requires us to think beyond the two-way contrast 'singular/plural'. For in these and other languages, morphologically marked dual is the expression of a mental grammar in which 'number' has <u>three</u> values: singular, dual, and plural.

Our investigations of plural noun formation in Part I revealed that some languages nearly always mark their nouns with a morpheme {plural} that has phonological or spoken content at the surface, as in standard English and Spanish. But in other languages, such as Mandarin Chinese and Nicaraguan English, the expression of the concept 'plural' with a phonologically-realized morpheme in the NP is, as we have seen, constrained under a variety of conditions.

In still other languages, as we briefly noted in Chapter 7, there is little or no overt presence of spoken number morphemes in the NP. In Western Apache,[1] for example, "the plural is shown in the verb, not in the noun, except for [nouns denoting prepubescent persons, such as] 'boys', 'girls', 'children', etc." (Perry et al., 1972, p. xi). The following sets of Western Apache sentences (repeated from Chapter 7) illustrate this fact. In (1a–c), whether the noun *gósé* 'dog' is to be interpreted as singular, dual, or plural only shows up at the surface in the morphology of the verb:

(1) a *Gósé higaal.*
        'The dog is walking.'

     b *Gósé hi'ash.*
        'Two dogs are walking.'

     c *Gósé hikah.*
        'Three or more dogs are walking.'

In (2a–c), we see a slight variation on how NP number is shown for one of the "exceptional" nouns. *Ishkiin* 'boy', which is [+singular, −plural], has a [−singular] form *ishikín*, whose second feature [−plural] or [+plural] is realized at the surface as either dual or plural – in the verb morphology, however:

(2) a *Ishkiin higaal.*
        'The boy is walking.'

     b *Ishikín hi'ash.*
        'Two boys are walking.'

     c *Ishikín hikah.*
        'Three or more boys are walking.'

Since an infant is innately equipped to acquire any language, Universal Grammar must specify all the ways that NP number is expressed in the world's languages. By this, we do not mean the particular phonological forms that plural morphemes take in each language, but rather the general properties of pluralization: whether a language has dual NP number or not; whether semantic or grammatical features of nouns are brought into play or not; and so on. We turn now to a brief discussion of the role of features in NP pluralization.

---

[1] We repeat the following from Chapter 7, note 2: "The Western Apache language belongs to the Athapaskan family of languages. Others in the Southwest speaking these languages are Mescalero, Chiracahua and Jicarilla Apaches, and Navajos" (Perry et al., 1972, p. 91). Mithun (1999, p. 358) adds, "Western Apache is spoken in Arizona on the San Carlos and Fort Apache reservations . . . It is considered the most viable of the Apachean languages, with 12,000 speakers of all ages reported in 1982."

Features, Noun Classes, and Plural Formation

As we learned in Part I of this book, a noun taken from the lexicon of a language may belong to a particular class of nouns, which – in turn – may have consequences for the form that noun pluralization assumes. For example, recall that Cherokee nouns fall into at least two classes, distinguished by the binary or two-valued semantic feature [±animate]. The Cherokee morpheme {plural} /di-/ is prefixed to [–animate] nouns but infixed and nasalized as /-ni-/ for [+animate] nouns, as in:

[–animate]: /taluja/ 'basket' : /ditaluja/ 'baskets'
[+animate]: /asgaya/ 'man' : /anisgaya/ 'men'

In Mandarin Chinese, by contrast, the relevant semantic feature for noun pluralization is [±human].

In other languages, though not in English, nouns are categorized by **grammatical gender** as opposed to natural gender. For example, in Spanish, nouns are distinguished by the binary feature [±feminine], with gender as well as pluralization then spreading through an NP:

[–feminine]: *el libro nuevo* 'the new book' : *los libros nuevos* 'the new books'
[+feminine]: *la bañera nueva* 'the new bathtub' : *las bañeras nuevas* 'the new bathtubs'

In Icelandic, there is a three-way distinction for grammatical gender: [±feminine, ±masculine], with [–feminine, –masculine] being the neuter gender:

[+feminine, –masculine]: *borg* 'city, town'
[–feminine, +masculine]: *bátur* 'boat'
[–feminine, –masculine]: *blóm* 'flower'

Note that grammatical gender is clearly distinct from natural gender. In Icelandic, for example, *hross* 'horse', *barn* 'child', and *blóm* 'flower' are all neuter nouns. And both *hundur* 'dog' and *köttur* 'cat' are masculine.

Moreover, in language, there may be – as there is in Icelandic – interaction between grammatical gender and the forms that plural NPs take, in the way that there is interaction between the feature [animate] and NP pluralization in Cherokee. In Icelandic, the plural of *borg* 'city' is *borgir*; the plural of *bátur* 'boat' is *bátar*; and the plural of *blóm* 'flower' is *blóm*.[2]

---

[2]   These are the nominative (subject) forms; the nouns take other forms for other grammatical relationships. Moreover, within each gender class there are subclasses of nouns.

The feature system of number

To summarize the analysis of NP number thus far: For languages with the two-way 'singular/plural' contrast, we express this with one binary feature: [±plural]. For languages with a three-way contrast 'singular/dual/plural', that contrast is captured with the features [±singular] and [±plural]. Using these two features and the two possible values for each, we specify that:

- a singular noun is [+singular, −plural];
- a plural noun is [−singular, +plural], plural ≥ 3 for languages with dual morphology;
- a dual noun is [−singular, −plural].

The fourth possible combination of these two features and their values would result in a contradiction: *[+singular, +plural]; for while it is possible for number to be neither singular nor plural, it is not possible for it to be both singular and plural.

   In the light of this discussion of NP number, let us revisit the tree we presented at the end of Chapter 1, slightly modified here, in which an NP and the morpheme {plural} merge to form a plural NP:

(3)

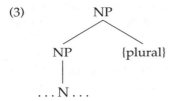

Clearly, the tree in (3) does not fully capture the possibilities in language for the 'singular/plural' and the 'singular/dual/plural' contrast. Thus we modify the tree, representing number with two features and their values:

(4)

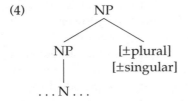

The tree in (4) shows that the concepts 'singular', 'dual', and 'plural' are semantically represented in an NP as a result of the NP and the number features merging.

   We assume that Universal Grammar is biased toward fewer forms rather than toward a greater number of forms. Thus infants will initially assume that just one of the binary number features shown in (4) – [±plural] – is required, the case for Spanish and English, for example. Faced with positive evidence of duality, they will complicate this picture to incorporate the two binary features shown in (4), [±plural] and [±singular]. Infants acquiring Western Apache, for example, know from the positive evidence available to them that both of these features are active in their language. Apache infants will also come to know that [+singular], [–singular, –plural], and [+plural] are not spoken in the NP for nouns like *gósé* 'dog', and that these features and their values are copied onto the verb and realized in the spoken verb morphology – as in the set of sentences in (1) and (2) above, where there are three different forms of the verb *naghaa* 'to walk': *higaal, hi'ash, hikah*.

We turn now to an investigation of Kiowa noun pluralization in which number plays a role in classifying nouns and in NP pluralization.

Problem Set 19: How Do Kiowas Talk About More Than Two Dogs?

Kiowa is the language of the Kiowa people; more specifically: "The Kiowas are a Plains Indian tribe of North America whose language is related to that of the Tanoan pueblos of New Mexico and Arizona. . . . Today they live primarily in southwestern Oklahoma, and especially in Caddo, Kiowa, and Comanche counties. The recently [as of 1984] completed Kiowa Tribal Complex is located in Carnegie, Oklahoma" (Watkins, 1984, p. 1). According to *Ethnologue: Languages of the World* (2005), there were 1,092 speakers in 1990 out of a population of 6,000; "[s]peakers are older adults." Mithun (1999, p. 441), citing Parker-McKensie, writes that there may be no more than "300 adult speakers of varying fluency" – an indication that Kiowa is an endangered language.

Investigating Kiowa Noun Pluralization

As we have seen, nouns can fall into different classes based on a semantic feature or on grammatical gender. Kiowa, offers another feature basis for noun classification and for pluralization: number; for in this language, nouns have **inherent number** in a more articulated way than we have seen thus far.[3]

In many languages, nouns have the inherent number 'singular' in the lexicon, as indicated in any standard dictionary, say, *The American Heritage Dictionary* for English. We express this inherent number as [–plural]. Nouns are then pluralized by inverting [–plural] to [+plural] in languages without duality.

In Kiowa, pluralization is more complicated, for each Kiowa noun belongs to one of four noun classes according to its number properties, as shown below. Note that in the data that follow:

---

[3]   This problem set has its origins in Harbour (2000, 2003). Here the data are somewhat simplified, with nasality and tone diacritics omitted. For earlier analyses, see Merrifield (1959), Watkins (1984), Wonderly et al. (1954). For a thorough reworking of Kiowa number, see Harbour (2003).

- /!/ after a consonant indicates that the consonant is articulated with a glottal stop;
- vowel length is shown by doubling the vowel, as in /aa/ 'tree or pole'.

Class I: In their bare form, nouns in this class are inherently either singular or dual:

/xegun/ 'dog'	means 'one or two dogs';
/togul/ 'young man'	means 'one or two young men';

and so on for other Class I nouns.

Class II: In their bare form, nouns in this class are inherently either dual or plural:

/aa/ 'tree or pole'	means 'two or more trees or poles';
/kutaa/ 'pencil'	means 'two or more pencils';

and so on for other Class II nouns.

Class III: In their bare form, nouns in this class are inherently dual:

/saaneei/ 'blackberry'	means 'two blackberries';
/k!ɔn/ 'tomato'	means 'two tomatoes';

and so on for other Class III nouns.

Class IV: Nouns in this class are unrestricted as to number:

/holda/ 'dress'	may be used to refer to any number of dresses;
/toude/ 'shoe'	may be used to refer to any number of shoes;

and so on for other Class IV nouns.

Noun Number: Employing the Feature System of Analysis

In terms of the feature system for number, Class I nouns are either:

- singular: [+singular, −plural], or
- dual: [−singular, −plural].

We characterize the "essence" of Class I noun number most parsimoniously by reducing it to the feature and value that singular and dual share:

Therefore, Class I nouns are [−plural].

Class III nouns are unambiguously dual; thus we can do no less, and need do no more, than refer to this class with the features that characterize dual, the absence of both singular and plural:

Therefore, Class III nouns are [−singular, −plural].

Since Class IV nouns are unrestricted as to number, they can be:

- singular: [+singular, −plural];
- dual: [−singular, −plural]; or
- plural: [−singular, +plural].

Class IV nouns cannot be characterized in any more parsimonious way than the list just given.

A   What then is the essence of Class II noun number, its most parsimonious characterization

Pluralization and Inversion

Say that a speaker of Kiowa wishes to talk about more than two dogs (Class I), or about one pencil (Class II), or about one tomato or more than two (Class III), or one, two, or more than two shoes – without using specific number words. What is she or he to do?

To meet this need – in part, Kiowa has an **inverse morpheme {INV}**, which has several phonological forms. We take the suffix /-gɔ/ as its default, most common form. The adjective *inverse* has its normal meaning: reversed in order, nature, or effect – with the emphasis in this context on effect. Merging this morpheme with a noun gives us the inverse of a noun's inherent number; that is, {INV} changes the value of the feature, or features, that identify a particular class of nouns:

B	If	Class I	/xegun	-gɔ/	is [+plural]; that is, = 'three or more dogs,'
			dog	{INV}	
	then	Class II	/kutaa	-gɔ/	= how many pencils?
			pencil	{INV}	
	and	Class III	/klɔn	-gɔ/	= how many tomatoes?
			tomato	{INV}	

Explain why you answer as you do.

C   Formulate a hypothesis that explains the effect of {INV} on the inherent number of Kiowa Class I, II, and III nouns.

D   Why is Class IV excluded from being merged with {INV}?

E   Does suffixing {INV} to Class I, II, and III nouns yield just one interpretation of number (that is, singular, dual, or plural) for each class? Why do you answer as you do?

Before you move on in the problem set, be sure to think through and construct reasoned, convincing answers for A–E.

Noun Number and Verb Morphology

It still remains to be seen how, if at all, Kiowa distinguishes:

- between singular and dual with respect to dogs (that is, for Class I nouns);
- between dual and plural with respect to pencils (for Class II nouns);
- between singular and plural with respect to tomatoes (for Class III nouns);
- between singular, dual, and plural with respect to shoes (for Class IV nouns).

First, review the discussion earlier in this chapter about the relationship in Western Apache between verb morphology and noun pluralization. Then, consider the following Kiowa sentences and the translation for each of them:

Class I   /xegun   Ø-dɔɔ/
              dog   singular-be
              'It's a dog.'

              /xegun   ɛ-dɔɔ/
              dog   dual-be
              'It's two dogs.'

              /xegun-gɔ   e-dɔɔ/
              dog-{INV}   {INV}-be
              'They're dogs.'

Class II   /aa-gɔ   e-dɔɔ/
              tree-{INV}   {INV}-be
              'It's a tree.'

              /aa   ɛ-dɔɔ/
              tree   dual-be
              'It's two trees.'

              /aa   Ø-dɔɔ/
              tree   singular-be
              'They're trees.'

Class III   /k!ɔn-gɔ   e-dɔɔ/
              tomato-{INV}   {INV}-be
              'It's a tomato.'

              /k!ɔn   ɛ-dɔɔ/
              tomato   dual-be
              'It's two tomatoes.'

              /k!ɔn-gɔ   e-dɔɔ/
              tomato-{INV}   {INV}-be
              'They're tomatoes.'

Class IV   /toude   Ø-dɔɔ/
              shoe   singular-be
              'It's a shoe.'

              /toude   ɛ-dɔɔ/
              shoe   dual-be
              'It's two shoes' or 'It's a pair of shoes.'

              /toude   gya-dɔɔ/
              shoe   plural-be
              'They're shoes.'

F   Based on these sentences, is there a <u>unique</u> way to express each number (singular, dual, and plural) for each class of Kiowa nouns? As usual, explain why you answer the way you do, discussing specific examples.

G   Clearly, acquiring Kiowa noun pluralization would be daunting for an adult native speaker of English, Mandarin Chinese, or the other languages that we have examined. But what about a baby who is meeting Kiowa as its first language? What specific information must be in Universal Grammar that allows the baby to acquire noun pluralization in Kiowa – or for any language it meets?

To answer this question, construct a typology of noun pluralization based on Kiowa and the languages we investigated in Part I (Armenian, English, Spanish, Nicaraguan English, Mandarin Chinese, and Cherokee). In constructing the typology, consider the typology for question formation in Part II, Chapter 11 as a model; consider also the brief discussion of the morphological parameters whose values must be determined and fixed by the language acquirer in Chapter 7 and the more extended discussion at the beginning of this chapter.

Before you move on to Chapter 17, be sure you think through and construct reasoned, convincing answers to F and G.

Terms

functional category
NP number
dual
grammatical gender
inherent number
inverse morpheme, {INV}

Chapter 17

Argument Structure: The Conceptual System of Language

Thus far in Part IV of this book, we have seen that the meaning of a sentence is more than just the meaning of each of its lexical elements. Meaning is compositional. Our discussion in Chapter 15 of the striped dishes illustrated the fact that the meaning of a sentence is composed of the meaning of its parts and the rules that combine them in syntactic structure, from its predications and its expressions of number (set size) and definiteness (set type). In Chapter 16, our investigation of Kiowa pluralization further revealed the compositionality of meaning, for in that language, words and morphemes merge and converge on singular, dual, and plural NPs (noun phrases) that may numerically mean something very different from the individual lexical elements themselves.

We now set aside Kiowa and the striped dishes in order to examine another aspect of meaning, one that was only slightly illustrated by the striped dishes being on a red table: **argument structure**, that is, the <u>roles</u> that NPs and PPs (prepositional phrases) play in a sentence. For example, at the end of the discussion in Chapter 15 of the sentence:

(1)   *The striped dishes are on a red table.*

we said that *on a red table* is a locative PP; that is, this PP plays a locational role in that sentence. We also pointed out that in the sentence:

(2)   *Emma broke the striped dishes.*

the NP *the striped dishes* takes on a different role than it did in sentence (1).

Let us now examine this part of the conceptual structure of language further.

Thematic Roles vs. Grammatical Functions

We begin by replacing the informal term 'role' with a technical term of linguistics: **thematic role**, or **θ-role** (theta-role). The θ-roles of NPs and PPs are quite distinct from the **grammatical functions** (such as subject, object, and so on) that NPs and PPs have in a sentence. The following sentences – and the NPs they contain – illustrate the difference between θ-roles and grammatical functions:

(3)   *The cat chased the rat.*
(4)   *The rat was chased by the cat.*

In sentence (3), the NP *the cat* functions as the subject of the sentence and the NP *the rat* functions as the object. In contrast, in sentence (4), *the cat* functions as the object of the preposition and *the rat* functions as the subject. These grammatical functions follow from tree geometry, as introduced in Chapter 8 of this book and as shown in the syntactic tree diagrams below.

In (5), the syntactic tree for sentence (3), the subject of the sentence, *the cat*, is the NP immediately dominated by S (sentence), while the object, *the rat*, is immediately dominated by the √P (root phrase):

(5)

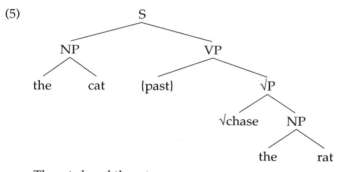

The cat chased the rat.

In (6), the tree for sentence (4), the NP *the rat* is immediately dominated by S; thus, it is the subject of the sentence. The NP *the cat*, however, is immediately dominated by the PP; thus, it is the object of the preposition *by*:

(6)

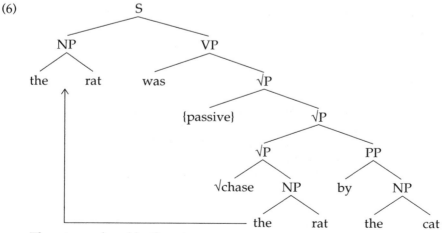

The rat was chased by the cat.

A moment's reflection reveals that the grammatical functions of *the cat* and *the rat* obscure the roles that these NPs play in conveying the meaning of sentences (3) and (4). For although these NPs have different grammatical functions in sentences (3) and (4), both sentences mean the same thing: if sentence (3) is true, then sentence (4) is necessarily true, and vice versa. So there must be something else about these NPs that contributes to the meaning of sentences (3) and (4).

That 'something else' is their θ-roles, which are the same in both sentences: *the cat* is the **agent** that chased *the mouse* and *the rat* is the **patient** or whatever is affected by the chasing.

Importantly, θ-roles remain fixed through syntactic transformations: thus, sentence (4), which has been affected by NP-movement, means the same thing as sentence (3). We can see this structurally by comparing trees (5) and (6). In (6), the NP object of the root √chase, *the rat*, has been raised to become the subject of sentence (4), leaving a copy behind in its underlying object position – its point of interpretation as the patient of √chase.

Argument Structure and Roots

Where do θ-roles come from? One source is roots. In the case of the NPs just discussed, we know that the θ-roles **agent** and **patient** are not inherent to *the cat* and *the rat* respectively, for these NPs could switch thematic roles in other sentences (as in *The rat chased the cat*, for example). Rather, these θ-roles are inherent to the root √chase which merges with the verb-generating morpheme {past} in sentences (3) and (4).

Thus, we say that in sentences (3) and (4) the root √chase surrounds itself with these two θ-roles:

- **agent**: *the cat* is the conscious initiator of the action or event;
- **patient**: *the rat* is what or who is affected by the action or event.

The set of θ-roles associated with a given root is the **argument structure** of that root. An English speaker's **lexicon** or mental dictionary will specify these two θ-roles as part of the entry for √chase. These roles are implied in dictionary definitions of the word *chase* as well, a definition from the *Oxford English Dictionary*, for example: "To pursue with a view to catching." Clearly, the meaning of *chase* requires someone or something (the agent) to be in pursuit of someone or something else (the patient).

Other roots have a different set of θ-roles associated with them. Take the root √give, for example:

(7)   *Emma gave Alex a book.*

In sentence (7), the following θ-roles are associated with √give:

- **agent**: *Emma* is the conscious initiator of the action or event;
- **goal**: *Alex* is the individual toward which the action or event is directed;
- **theme**: *a book* is the object moved from the agent to the goal.

Compare the argument structure of the root √give to that of the root √bake, as in:

(8)   *Emma baked Alex a cake.*

In sentence (8), the following θ-roles are associated with √bake:

- **agent**: *Emma* is the conscious initiator of the action or event;
- **beneficiary**: *Alex* is the individual benefiting from the action or event;
- **patient**: *a cake* is the object affected by the action or event.

Notice that both sentence (7) and sentence (8) can take another surface form, one in which the θ-roles **goal** and **beneficiary** are mediated by the prepositions *to* and *for*, respectively, as in sentences (9) and (10):

(9)   *Emma gave a book to Alex.*
(10)   *Emma baked a cake for Alex.*

Since the prepositions *to* and *for* are inherent to the goal and beneficiary roles, they can be omitted under the appropriate conditions – as they are in sentences (7) and (8).
  Now consider sentence (11), built around the root √put:

(11)   *Emma put the book on the shelf.*

Here we find that a somewhat different set of θ-roles is associated with √put:

- **agent**: *Emma* is the conscious initiator of the action or event;
- **patient**: *the book* is the object affected by the action or event;
- **location**: *on the shelf* is the place at which the action or event is situated.

Note, however, that sentence (11) cannot take a form (analogous to sentences (7) and (8)) in which the preposition *on* is omitted; that is, (12) is not a well-formed English sentence:

(12)   **Emma put the shelf the book.*

This is because, unlike the θ-roles **goal** and **beneficiary**, the θ-role **location** is "fine-tuned" by a large set of different prepositions, as sentences (13–15) illustrate:

(13) *Emma put the book under the shelf.*
(14) *Emma put the book next to the shelf.*
(15) *Emma put the book near the shelf.*

The prepositions *on, under, next to,* and *near* are not deletable under the constraint on **recoverability of deletion** discussed in Chapter 14: that is, the precise meaning of any deleted constituent must be fully recoverable from the sentence that results from deletion. Since the θ-role **location** is fine tuned, we cannot know which preposition has been deleted in sentence (12). Since full recovery of the meaning of *on* is not possible for sentence (12), deletion of *on* is not allowed. Notice, however, that in a sentence like *Emma shelved the book,* the precise nature of a location (*on the shelf*) has been incorporated into the verb *shelved* itself.

Despite appearances thus far, not all roots have a two-role argument structure like that of √*chase* or a three-role argument structure like that of √*give,* √*bake,* and √*put.* For example, √*run* takes just one argument (agent), as in sentence (16):

(16) *Emma ran.*

Three other θ-roles in addition to the six already mentioned (agent, goal, theme, beneficiary, patient, location) are illustrated in sentences (17), (18), and (19), respectively:

- **source**: the place from which the action or event originates: *from prison* (17);
- **instrument**: the secondary cause of the action or event, one requiring or implying an agent: *with a file* (18);
- **experiencer**: the individual perceiving or experiencing the action or event: *Emma* (19).

(17) *Emma escaped from prison.*
(18) *Emma cut the bars with a file.*
(19) *Emma heard the sirens.*

Summing Up

The contribution of argument structure to meaning is that it specifies <u>exactly</u> the role that a constituent is playing in a sentence. As we said earlier, the thematic or θ-role that a constituent plays in a sentence is importantly different from its grammatical function, with which it is often confused. For example, in sentences (17), (18), and (19) above, *Emma* is the subject (a grammatical function), but *Emma* plays the agent role in sentences (17) and (18) and the experiencer role in sentence (19).

As we have seen, θ-roles remain fixed through syntactic transformations. Consider, for example, sentence (20), the passive form of sentence (18):

(20)   *The bars were cut with a file by Emma.*

In sentence (20), as in sentence (18), *Emma* is the agent, *the bars* is the patient, and *a file* is the instrument. These three roles are inherent to the root √cut and are <u>always</u> mentally computed. For example, in sentence (21), in which the agent is left unexpressed, we know that there is an implied agent – be it Emma or someone else:

(21)   *The bars were cut with a file.*

These θ-roles are played out as a consequence of the argument structures associated with particular roots and – as we shall see in Problem Set 20 – prepositions. *Emma* has a particular inherent meaning (as the name of a particular person), but the role of this proper noun in any given sentence is determined by the root it hangs with in syntactic structure.

Problem Set 20: θ-Roles and Prepositions in English

The discussion of argument structure and θ-roles thus far has been organized around roots that have become verbs through merger with verb generators, in particular the morpheme {past}. However, roots of this sort are not the only source of θ-roles.

In fact, we have already seen how certain prepositions in English participate in assigning a θ-role. For example, in sentence (1), where the goal *Alex* is not immediately next to the verb *gave*, that θ-role is mediated by the preposition *to*. And in sentence (2), where the beneficiary *Alex* is not immediately next to the verb *baked*, that θ-role is mediated by the preposition *for*:

(1)   *Emma gave a book to Alex.*
(2)   *Emma baked a cake for Alex.*

The deletion of the preposition in these cases leads to surface forms with odd interpretations. For example, by omitting the preposition *to* in sentence (1), we get sentence (3), which presents us with the strange image of Alex being <u>given to</u> a book:

(3)   *??Emma gave a book Alex.*

Clearly, then, prepositions play an important role in argument structure, and in some cases, prepositions themselves have argument structure; that is, they are the sole assigners of the θ-roles involved. Take the following sentences, for example:

(4)   *Emma sat by the river.*
(5)   *Emma wasn't captured by the FBI.*

(6)   *The FBI was fooled by Emma's clever trick.*
(7)   *Emma opened the door with a key.*

A   For <u>each</u> of the sentences (4–7), what θ-role do the prepositions *by* and *with* assign to their NP objects?
B   There appear to be at least three English words *by* – and certainly more than that as you would learn by consulting a dictionary. But which of the three illustrated in sentences (4–6) appear to be related in meaning? Explain why you answer the way you do.
C   There are also several *with*'s, the one illustrated in (7) being just one example, each of them assigning a different θ-role. For example, in the sentence:

(8)   *A person with red hair came into the room.*

with assigns possession. Although we may not have named these other θ-roles, illustrate at least two more *with*'s in sentences of your own, informally labeling or defining the θ-role each *with* assigns.

Before you move on in this chapter, be sure to think through and construct reasoned, convincing answers for A–C.

What Do Questions Mean, and How?

In the two previous chapters, NP number was dealt with in some detail, and thus far in this chapter, we have focused on the meaning of NPs in the context of the thematic roles assigned to them by roots and prepositions. Having exhausted what we have to say about NPs, let us now return to questions, the focus of Part II of this book, and to what questions mean and how questions come to mean what they do.

The meaning of yes/no questions

To begin our investigation of the meaning of yes/no questions, let us first recall from our earlier discussion of meaning how assertions come to mean what they do. For example, consider the following sentence:

(22)   *The woman gave some books to her daughter.*

The meaning of this sentence is composed of the following:

* a predication: it is predicated of *the woman* that she gave some books to her daughter;
* expressions of number: [+plural] for the NP *some books*; [–plural] (that is, singular) for the NPs *the woman* and *her daughter*;

- expressions of definiteness: [−definite], or indefinite, for *some books*; [+definite] for *the woman* and *her daughter*;
- and the θ-roles assigned by the root √*give*: agent to *the woman*; theme to *some books*; goal to *her daughter*.

Beyond its meaning, sentence (22) – as an assertion – also has a **truth value**: If indeed the woman gave some books to her daughter, then sentence (22) is true; if she did not, then sentence (22) is false.

Questions, on the other hand, do <u>not</u> have truth value (nor do commands). For example, the yes/no question in (23) is neither true nor false, but it has an infinite number of possible answers that could be true or false.

(23)   *Did the woman give some books to her daughter?*

While question (23) has no truth value, it does have a meaning that is composed pretty much the same way as the meaning of an assertion, as in sentence (22). Moreover, questions like (23) are asked with some intention and not always with what would seem to be their obvious intention, but determining a speaker's unstated intention is a matter for a discussion of **Broad Meaning**. (Recall from Chapter 15 that we are focusing narrowly on **Meaning**, the contribution of mental grammar to the meaning of a sentence.) Thus, taken in its most neutral sense, the yes/no question in (23) is a request for information about a statement: Is it a fact or not that the woman gave some books to her daughter? Yes or no? Or don't know? The answer can be "yes" only if every aspect of the statement is known to be true; otherwise, if any aspect of the statement is known to be false, the answer must be "no."

That yes/no questions are asking about a statement in its entirety is exemplified by the near-to-underlying syntactic structure of question (23), shown below, in which the unspoken yes/no question particle (Y/N) merges and imposes a yes/no question mood over S (sentence):

(24)

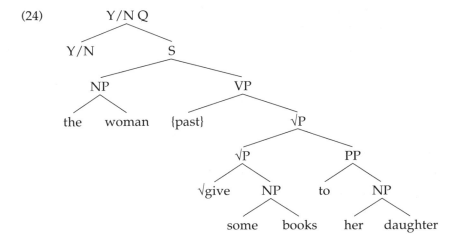

We see once again that meaning is compositional: the meaning of question (23) is a function of the meaning of its parts and of the mergers of these parts that converge on the structure in (24). Speakers of English – and of any language – know unconsciously that this is how yes/no questions come to mean what they do.

The meaning of WH-questions

Unlike yes/no questions, WH-questions cannot be interpreted structurally as a right-or-wrong request for information. The meaning of WH-questions is a request for a different kind of information – the specific information picked out by WH-words. For example, we could ask the following questions:

(25)   *What did the woman give to her daughter?*
(26)   *Who did the the woman give some books to?*

The meaning of questions (25) and (26) depends in large part on the meaning of the WH-words in them. But what <u>do</u> WH-words mean?

Although the meaning of the other constituents in questions (25) and (26) can be composed as they are for assertions, the meaning of WH-words cannot be so composed. WH-words are different, for they are not complete NPs insofar as their meaning is concerned. We label them **variables** since crucial pieces of their meaning remain open to be fixed in an answer. For example, from its entry in the lexicon, we know that the *what* that the woman gave her daughter in question (25) has to be [–human]. Although this particular semantic feature is fixed, the meaning of *what* leaves number (set size) and definiteness (set type) open. And similarly, we know that the *who* of question (26) is [+human], but that it is unspecified in the lexicon for number and definiteness.[1]

Beyond their lexical meaning, WH-words find a significant piece of their meaning in syntactic structure. Consider the near-to-surface structures of questions (25) and (26) shown in (27) and (28), respectively. (Note that we ignore

---

[1]   Although the WH-words *what* and *who* are not specified for semantic number, they are grammatically singular. This can be seen from sentences in which WH-words are grammatical subjects, for example:

(i)   *What stands in the way?*
(ii)   *Who knows the way?*

With plural agreement, these questions would be ill-formed:

(iii)   **What stand in the way?*
(iv)   **Who know the way?*

the appearance of *did* in second position in these WH-questions, since it is irrelevant to the analysis of their meaning.)[2]

(27)

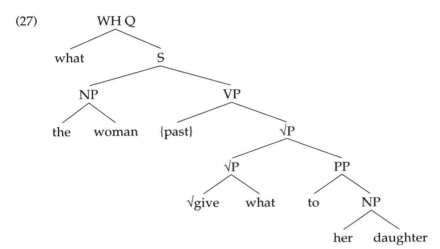

What did the woman give to her daughter?

(28)

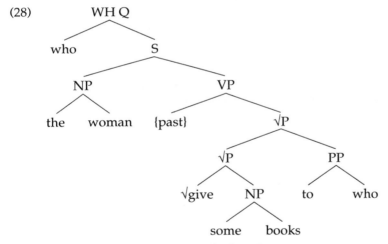

Who did the woman give some books to?

2 *Did* and the other forms of *do* result from raising a {past} or {pres} that has not become attached to a root through √-raising. Since the tense morphemes are then stranded by auxiliary movement, they must be supported in order for tense to reach Phonological Form (PF). In English, *do*-support does the trick, inserting the pro-verb *do*, which then takes on the tense, {past} or {pres}, that it supports.

The fact that {past} and {pres} can move independently (not attached, that is, to a root) lies behind tense being a constituent merged outside the √P (see Chapter 8).

As these trees remind us, in English WH-question formation, after copying the WH-word to the WH-question particle position at the left edge of the structure, a copy of the WH-word is left in its underlying position. The position of the copy is the point of interpretation of the moved WH-word. Thus we say that the WH-word is <u>bound</u> to the structural and thematic position occupied by its copy – which is a source of a piece of its meaning. For example, in (27), *what* is bound to its copy in the 'theme' position within the argument structure of the root √give. Because of this, we know that *what*'s θ-role is 'theme' – it is whatever is moved by the woman to her daughter. In (28), because *who* is bound to its copy in the 'goal' position within the argument structure of √give, we know that *who* has the θ-role 'goal' – it is whoever the woman is moving some books to.

So let us put this all together to arrive at the meaning of questions (25) and (26). Taking what is known from the lexicon and the syntactic structure about the meaning of *what* and *who* in these questions, we replace the variable part of *what* and *who* with the variable x familiar from algebra. We can then represent the **Logical Form (LF)** of questions (25) and (26) as follows:

(29)   *For which x, x a thing or things, the woman gave x to her daughter?*
(30)   *For which x, x a person or persons, the woman gave some books to x?*

This is how WH-questions come to mean what they do to speakers of English – or any language. The logical notation in (29) and (30) for questions (25) and (26) provides a Universal Grammatical way for us to express the meaning of questions for every language – with due allowance for small structural differences among languages that are irrelevant to the basic meaning of questions.

Summing Up

In these three chapters on meaning, we have introduced various aspects of the contribution of mental grammar to meaning, including

- predication, both primary and secondary (the latter being a result of adjunction);
- NP number, or set size;
- in-/definiteness, or set type;
- argument structure, or θ-roles;
- the interpretation of questions and WH-words.

These aspects of meaning are part of Logical Form (LF), the point at which mental grammar interfaces with systems of thought in the construction of the meaning of a sentence or question.

Recall from Chapter 15 that we diagram the relationship among underlying structure, surface structure, **Phonological Form (PF)**, and the LF of a sentence or question as follows:

(31)   Underlying structure

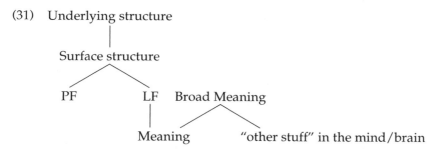

As we have seen, underlying structures are transformed into surface structures (by, for example, movement). PF, derived from surface structure by the rules of phonology, interfaces with the sensorimotor systems, the systems that underlie speaking/signing a language and hearing/seeing it. The output of the interpretation of surface structures by semantic rules is LF, the part of meaning (Meaning) that is internal to mental grammar. LF interfaces "with systems of conceptual structure and language use" (Chomsky, 1995, p. 131).

By focusing as we have on the meaning of a sentence or question that emerges at LF, we have focused on meaning in the narrow sense, what in Chapter 15 we termed Meaning. We contrasted Meaning in the narrow sense with the Broad Meaning of a sentence or question, which, as indicated in the diagram above, derives from Meaning plus "other stuff" in the mind/brain of a speaker: knowledge of context, systems of belief, expectations, and so on. Beyond mental grammar – but still internal to the mind, this "other stuff" allows a speaker to – among other things – interpret the possible connotations of another speaker's sentence or question.

There is much more to Meaning. However, what we have examined here in this book should convey some sense of the diverse grammatical and conceptual factors that make up the Meaning of a sentence, factors that are at work regardless of what "other stuff" lies outside the sentence.

We now turn to a discussion of the acquisition of Meaning (hereafter referred to, again, simply as meaning).

Acquisition of Meaning

How much of what we have called meaning has to be learned, either by an infant developing knowledge of its first language or by an adult (= an adult or a child older than five or six years) developing knowledge of a second language? Probably very little. In order to clarify this statement and elaborate on it, let us go through the various pieces of meaning that we have discussed thus far.

Do we learn the meanings of words and forms of our languages?

This might appear to be a non-question. Of course we do, don't we? Or do we simply learn words and forms – labels for the concepts expressed in language, the meaning of which we somehow already know?

Consider the rate at which an infant acquires vocabulary items: 14,000 words by age six, "nine new words a day, or almost one per waking hour" (Carey, 1978, p. 264). Given the rate at which new words are acquired and the complexity of the concepts involved, it is quite unlikely that the infant is doing anything other than learning the labels in its language for preexisting concepts. This would mean, for example, that the infant already "knows" that there is a concept 'give' and that 'give' has an argument structure in Universal Grammar (UG) that relates its arguments (an agent with a goal and a theme) in a particular way. The infant's task is simply to learn the label that names the concept 'give' in whatever language it faces: the roots √give in English, √dar in Spanish, √ma:k in Tohono O'odham, √gei in Mandarin Chinese, and so on (Fodor, 1975).

On learning a second language, the adult must now learn labels for already "known" concepts. However, not all the concepts of the mind will have a label in an adult's first language. On this view, the universal set of innately given concepts is analogous to the universal set of innately given phonological distinctive features: A particular language chooses only a subset of each of these universal sets – a very large subset in both cases, but a subset nevertheless. In English, for example, [−continuant] consonants contrast between [+voice] and [−voice] sounds: /b/, /d/, and /g/ as opposed to /p/, /t/, and /k/. There is no such contrast in Mandarin Chinese.

To illustrate how languages can differ in the set of concepts that they label, consider the fact that not all languages have labels that allow counting by integers: the whole number concepts 'one', 'two', 'three', and so on to infinity. In its place, many languages have a set of quantity labels for the concepts 'one', 'two', 'few', 'several', and 'many'. But do people who know such languages also "know" the whole number concepts although these remain unlabeled by their language? That is, can they count without labels in their language?

Consider the following thought experiment: Suppose that a person who speaks a language with the quantity labels for 'one', 'two', 'few', 'several', and 'many' owns a herd of sheep that is large enough to be in the quantity category 'many'. Now let's say that each night a thief steals one or more of the sheep. Would the owner of the sheep not notice the thievery until the number of sheep fell into the category defined by the word for 'several'? This seems highly unlikely. From this we infer that the owner can count independently of having labels in her or his language for the integers.

Strong evidence that numerical concepts are present in the minds of speakers of such languages comes from the fact that when the need arises, as when, say, a decision is made to teach mathematics in the language, labels for the integers are formed almost immediately (for discussion of such a case in Aboriginal communities in Australia, see Hale, 1975). There is now much recent research confirming the existence of numerical (as well as geometrical) concepts independent of specific labels for these concepts (see Gelman & Gallistel, 2004; Dehaene et al., 2006; and references there).

Before proceeding, and lest we think that English labels all the concepts that there are, recall Kiowa inversion and Apache duality.

A final point on labels and their meaning: A distinction must be made between two kinds of concepts, which we will call **natural** and **technical**. The discussion thus far has been about natural concepts, but the book you've been reading is strewn with labels for technical concepts – specialized vocabulary items. These are the words you learn in school and college – in a linguistics class, for example. They do not label natural concepts; they label stipulated concepts. For example, the terms *root* and *θ-role* mean exactly what linguists have agreed they should mean – no more, no less. But the word *table* has the wide range of meanings that any reasonable dictionary will try to cover, with this range changing over time. An infant learns the word *table* more or less instantly without reflection and never forgets its meanings; a student learns the term *root* and, unless she or he goes on to be a linguist, forgets its meaning as soon as it is convenient to do so. Much of education is given over to learning technical vocabularies (and forgetting them!); the rest of a person's vocabulary life is about learning the labels for natural concepts and keeping them in mind forever. (For discussion of this issue, see Chomsky, 1980 and 1988, pp. 30–34.)

This distinction is not an easy one to keep clear since the labels for natural concepts are often specialized as technical terms as well. For example, the word *force* labels a number of natural concepts, but it also has a stipulated meaning in physics; that is, this is all and only what it can mean in that branch of science: "**F**, a vector quantity that tends to produce an acceleration of a body in the direction of its application."

Conceptual structure

Conceptual structure must also pre-exist in the infant since one cannot know the meaning of words without at the same time knowing conceptual structure. For example, knowing the meaning of nouns involves, in part, knowing the semantic categories they belong to: [+animate] for *cat*, or [–animate] for *table*; [+count] for *cat* and *table*, or [–count] for *jam* and *milk*; and so on. These semantic features are in the mind of the infant as it goes about learning the labels of its language.

Conceptual structure also includes the full set of θ-roles: agent, theme, patient, goal, beneficiary, source, location, experiencer, and so on. This set is given by UG and is expressed in every language. To know √*put*, for example, requires knowing its argument structure and how this is played out in syntax. A dictionary definition ("to place in a specified location") omits the θ-roles agent and patient, mentioning only location, and says nothing about syntax. Given such a definition, we automatically fill in the fact that an agent is doing the placing and that something is being placed in the location specified, and that all of this happens in certain syntactic structure and order. On learning the label for the concept 'put' in the next language, we would do the same.

Predication, assertions, questions, and commands

Do we learn that there is predication; that language is used to make assertions, ask questions, issue commands, and so on? Since the basic expressive relationship in language is predication – to express something about something else – and since asserting, asking, and ordering (among other aspects of the expression of thought) constitute what we can do with language, it seems highly unlikely that an infant has to learn either this universal expressive relationship or these universal functions of language. From among the ways allowed by UG, the infant must, of course, acquire the particular ways in which predication is done in its language, and the particular ways in which questions, statements, and commands are structured. Equipped with UG, the infant "knows" what to look for in the positive evidence it gets about its language. For example, is there WH-copying or not in the formation of a WH-question in the language? And how do adjuncts – secondary, dependent predications – play out in terms of word order?

And so it is for the adult acquiring a second language. Here too it is the particulars of the next language that have to be learned, not the universals of language. For example, consider adjunction. Sentences (32) and (33) illustrate a language-particular difference for adjunction in English and Mandarin Chinese, respectively; relative clauses follow the nouns they modify in English, while in Mandarin Chinese, they precede them (with the particles *that/de*, respectively, marking the beginning/end of the relative clause):

(32)   *He lost the letter that I gave you.*

(33)   *Ta   wo gei   ni   de   xin   diu-le.*
       she/he I   give you REL letter lost
       'She/he lost the letter that I gave you.'

In addition to new labels for – in this case – already labeled concepts, a new way of adjoining relative clauses has to be learned by an English-speaking person learning Mandarin Chinese, or by a Mandarin Chinese-speaking person learning English. That there are relative clauses; that they depend on the nouns they connect to for their interpretation; and that they are predicated of the nouns with which they are connected: These things do not have to be learned.

Pragmatic knowledge

Pragmatics is the interpretation of meaning in the context of language use, which brings us back to Broad Meaning, which we broke away from many pages ago. Though we have not examined pragmatics, let us assume that there <u>are</u> rules of pragmatics – that is, rules for using language appropriately within a culture. We can then ask – and briefly consider – whether infants must learn pragmatic rules.

The word *culture* in the previous paragraph is obviously important; for the ways in which language use can vary from group to group is largely a matter of culture, of social structure and institutions. For example, from sociolinguistic studies, we know that who gets to initiate talk in a certain cultural setting may be determined by age, by gender, by rank, and so on. And narrative or story-telling forms vary (within limits) from culture to culture within languages as well as between languages, as the study of folk tales and their structure has revealed.

Nevertheless, though pragmatic knowledge about how to behave in a language may differ from culture to culture, the ways in which other cultures use their language, while possibly strange, may also feel familiar. How can this be? And how do we come know the particular pragmatic rules of our own culture?

Let us assume that there is a pragmatic module of mind, call it Y, that constrains experience under the further assumption that the pragmatic knowledge that is specific to a language and its culture is not free to develop in any and all directions. Let us also assume that pragmatic knowledge arises in the infant, as knowledge of language does, through the interaction of Y and experience. We can capture this process in an input–output diagram of the sort used throughout this book:

Experience in a culture → Y → Pragmatic knowledge of that culture

The cognitive module is labeled Y since little is known about it: like pragmatic knowledge itself, Y is largely a promissory note. However, under the assumption that there is a pragmatic module, Y has to exist, for if it did not, the infant would have no way of focusing on what counts as experience relevant to the development of appropriate language use in its culture. This is analogous to the fact that if UG did not exist, the infant would not be able to pick language out from among the various kinds of acoustic noise that it is surrounded by. Just as language development is not slowed down by having to figure out that the door slamming, the telephone ringing, and the dog barking are not instances of people talking, the development of pragmatic knowledge is not hindered by irrelevant experiences.

But what the relevant experiences in culture might be and what specific constraints Y must contain are unknown to us. We must stop here; for these topics belong in another book – one that we do not know how to write.

Terms

argument structure	instrument
thematic role, θ-role (theta-role)	experiencer
grammatical function	truth value
agent	Broad Meaning
patient	Meaning
lexicon	variable
goal	Logical Form, LF
theme	Phonological Form, PF
beneficiary	natural
location	technical
recoverability of deletion	pragmatics
source	

Further Reading

See Larson and Segal (1995) for a thorough discussion of thematic roles, to which we are indebted in our own presentation.

Chomsky (1980), as do Larson and Segal (1995), has a brief, clear discussion of pragmatic knowledge and its relation to mental grammar.

Chapter 18

On Thinking Linguistically:
Looking Back and Looking Ahead

Let us summarize where we have been in this book and where we hope that we have arrived – both in our investigation of knowledge of language and in our examination of first and second language acquisition.

Knowledge of Language

In the chapters and problem sets in Parts I–IV of this book, we have investigated knowledge of language, or mental grammar – that is, knowledge of the grammatical structure of language. Unconsciously, we know the structure of the language or languages we speak and we act on this knowledge in our everyday lives. When we stop to examine this knowledge, as we have done here, we are surprised by what we know – and we are equally if not more surprised by what we do <u>not</u> know about what we know. Surprises of this sort lead us to wonder, and motivate our investigation of knowledge of language. We now come full circle, understanding more clearly that

> Serious inquiry begins when we are willing to be surprised by simple phenomena of nature, such as the fact that an apple falls from a tree, or a phrase means what it does (Chomsky, 1993, p. 25).

Or that nouns are pluralized as they are, or that questions are asked and answered in particular structural ways, or that the meaning of a sentence is constructed in the way that it is – the phenomena we have examined here in some detail.

From this beginning, we have pursued serious, scientific inquiry by doing linguistics. What have our efforts revealed?

To most people, languages <u>appear</u> to differ in all possible ways. But on close analysis, we have found that differences between languages are relatively superficial. All languages have ways of distinguishing the concepts 'singular' and 'more than one' and all languages have ways of distinguishing a question from a statement. By investigating the particular ways that languages accomplish just these tasks, we have come to understand that appearances can be deceiving: languages are more alike than they are different since the number of possible ways that languages make these distinctions is very small.

Yet much is made of linguistic differences, both in our society and others. For example, a deeply held belief in the United States is that the standard variety of English is grammatically and in all ways superior to other varieties (and even to other languages) and that nonstandard varieties are degraded versions of the standard. Our investigations of different Englishes reveal the falsity of this belief. We have come to understand that all languages – and all varieties of a language – are <u>rule-governed</u> and complex in their grammatical structure and depth of expression.

Clearly, we have learned much about knowledge of language, and we have done so through the close examination of a variety of languages. For those languages we know, the data have been readily accessible. For those languages we don't know or have limited knowledge of, we have examined data gathered from speakers of those languages and from other resources, such as grammars and dictionaries. Regardless of our starting point, however, apparent mysteries about the data quickly presented themselves. We have then attempted to turn these apparent mysteries into problems to be solved.

We have found how difficult a task solving these problems can be; for making explicit a speaker's tacit or unconscious knowledge of language (especially our own) requires <u>conscious</u>, critical, scientific inquiry. This work, for example, depends crucially on speakers of a language being able to judge utterances; that is, they must distinguish well-formed pieces of language from those that are ill-formed or at least less well-formed. This is not something that a speaker consciously does in using her or his language. By itself, however, judging utterances is not sufficient. Examining and explaining the patterns that emerge from these data can only be accomplished by honing and developing the methods of scientific inquiry that are available to us all.

Thus, by doing linguistics we have come to understand more clearly not only the nature of knowledge of language, but also the nature of scientific inquiry, observing that:

- formulating a hypothesis to explain a phenomenon involves looking for patterns in the data and possibly extending or generalizing what is already understood about similar phenomena;
- progress is made in evaluating a hypothesis by searching for both confirming and disconfirming evidence (counterexamples);
- a hypothesis may need to be reformulated in order to provide the best possible explanation and coverage of data;
- parsimony, or economy of explanation, is an important measure of progress.

Language Acquisition

In this book, we have also examined acquisition of knowledge of language, noting that swiftly and more or less effortlessly, infants acquire the language or languages of their environment, without their caretakers paying much attention except at the very earliest stages. Thus by the time they reach the end of early childhood, children have attained adult status in this domain of human knowledge and behavior. Although their vocabularies will, of course, continue to grow throughout life, for all essential purposes, structural knowledge of their first language (or first languages, in the case of infants who are simultaneously becoming bilingual) is perfect and complete by four or five years of age.

Knowledge of a first language arises in infants as an automatic – we might even call it a reflexive – interaction between their experience with the language of their environment and the innate predisposition that humans have to acquire language. This innate predisposition, referred to as Universal Grammar (UG), encompasses the principles universal and particular to language. That is, infants are born with tacit knowledge of the structural properties that are possible in all languages. For example, among the universal parameters that we have discussed at length are those that frame the acquisition of question formation: whether the question particle is located at the left or the right edge of the structure, whether the particle attracts elements to itself or not, whether movement is obligatory or not, and so on. Parametric possibilities of this sort are then narrowed to those of the language in the environment through the interaction of UG and linguistic experience. What grows out of this interaction is knowledge of the structure of that particular language, referred to as Particular Grammar (PG):

Experience in a language → UG → PG of that language

First language acquisition can, in fact, only be prevented by severely depriving an infant of the necessary language experience, though even under the most deprived conditions, UG appears to manifest itself in language-like behavior (see Curtiss, 1977; Goldin-Meadow, 2003).

When we turn to explaining second language acquisition by people older than, say, about five or six years of age, the process appears at first glance to be entirely different from that of first language acquisition. When we consider generalizing the model for first language acquisition outlined above to second language acquisition, we might initially reject it out of hand. We may have the intuition that UG has been spent in the acquisition of a first language and is thus no longer available to the second language learner. Or we may have the intuition that there is a critical period for language acquisition that ends when the first language is acquired, that the second language learner is too old to acquire a new language perfectly. Or we may have the intuition that knowledge of the first language stands between UG and the new language in the environment; that is, knowledge of the first language interferes with the language learner's attempts to "become" an infant again, one with a fully available UG.

As the research we have discussed shows, the facts of the matter are a good deal more complicated than any of these simplified interference models allows; for people <u>do</u> acquire languages throughout their lives – generally imperfectly, to be sure, but imperfectly in interesting ways.

Consider this: When we meet people who speak our language, that is, persons who have knowledge of language that is more or less equivalent to ours, we tend to focus on the ways in which their way of speaking differs from ours. This is true whether we are dealing with someone who speaks our language as a second language or with a person who speaks a different variety or dialect of our language. Unfortunately, people's judgment of these differences is often less than charitable.

That aside, the natural tendency to concentrate on 'difference' rather than 'sameness' misses the fact that a great deal of knowledge is shared in such situations, far more than we realize and far more than is not shared. Moreover, if we look more closely both at speakers of a different dialect from ours and at second language learners, we find that the differences generally lie in the more superficial components of the language: in phonology – or more accurately, in pronunciation (productive phonology). For example, in an article on bilingual education and the wisdom of starting second language instruction at an early age, a reporter commented on "the famously thick German accent of former Secretary of State Henry Kissinger, who arrived in America at age fourteen" as opposed to that of "his younger brother [who] developed a standard American accent" (Sailer, 2000). But what the reporter neglected to say and what people fail to notice – because it <u>seems</u> that there is nothing to notice – is that the elder Kissinger speaks flawless English morphologically, syntactically, and semantically and he clearly controls the vocabulary of English. And given the research on such matters, we assume that the elder Kissinger has near-perfect tacit knowledge of English phonology despite his imperfect pronunciation of English; to put it another way, he has imperfect productive use of his knowledge of English phonology.

Thus, understanding second language acquisition requires explaining not only language learners' errors of production (of pronunciation, for example), but also their more or less flawless acquisition of major components of their second language (L2). The explanation for this level of second language acquisition follows from the claim that UG is alive and well in second language acquisition to the extent that it has not been diminished by a person's first language knowledge: PG1. We have captured this subtractive, partial interference model of L2 acquisition (referred to earlier as Model 2) as follows:

Experience with L2 $\rightarrow$ UG – PG1 $\rightarrow$ PG2

In attempting to specify what 'subtraction' means in this model, we have argued that UG and therefore L2 learners value economy and other UG preferences based in markedness. For example, since irregularity is uneconomical – requiring very narrowly defined rules – L2 learners fail to acquire word-stress patterns of English that are irregular (O'Neil, 1998b). And children whose L1 is Spanish do not acquire the [–ATR] vowels of Catalan because they do not activate the phonological feature [ATR] (Pallier et al., 1997), which would have the costly effect of increasing the number of vowels in their PG2 relative to their PG1. And finally, since optional rules are marked and uneconomical, native speakers of French acquire English WH-question formation without interference from the fact that WH-movement in French is optional.

Where economy is not at stake, where there are no UG preferences, there is no PG1 interference, as in the acquisition of English WH-question formation by native speakers of Mandarin Chinese. Thus, insofar as it allows for UG to play a role, this model appears to be compatible with the results from L2 acquisition research. Second language learners are neither imprisoned by their first language, nor are they entirely free of it.

Looking Ahead

The cognitive science of linguistics provides us with some answers to questions about what we know about language, and why and how we know what we know. These answers support a generous view of humankind: we are born equally endowed with the predisposition to acquire language. Moreover, in its focus on universal principles of language, linguistic inquiry provides us with an important model for how to examine diversity: We value and study differences between languages and varieties of a language for what they might reveal about the universals of language. As well, we value and study first and second language acquisition for what those patterns might reveal about the universal course of linguistic growth in infants, children, and adults.

We believe that linguistics should have a prominent place in education. The domain of inquiry is captivating, and the phenomena are accessible to investigation and explanation of some depth – with effort. Through the investigation of language, students of all ages can learn not only about language, but also about the nature of scientific inquiry, and indeed, something about themselves as well.

Moreover, teachers too can be linguistic researchers, learning something about the structure of the languages and language varieties that their students speak or of the second languages that they are learning to speak. They can also come to see that teaching and learning about language can turn their students into critical thinkers. This has certainly been our experience.

We encourage you to think linguistically and to pursue this possibility.

Further Reading

For a rationale and examples of the educational use of linguistics to develop students' understanding of both language and scientific inquiry, see Honda's *Linguistic Inquiry in the Science Classroom: "It is science, but it's not like a science problem in a book"* (1994); for less detail, see Honda and O'Neil (1993), O'Neil and Honda (1996), or O'Neil (1998a). Chapter 2 of Honda (1994), Honda and O'Neil (1993), and related papers can be found at http://web.mit.edu/waoneil/www/k12/.

For a similar inquiry-based approach to the study of Yaqui, see Martínez Fabián (2001).

References

Aaron, Jane E. (2001). *The Little Brown Compact Handbook* (4th ed.). New York: Addison Wesley.

Baker, Mark. (2001). *The Atoms of Language*. New York: Basic Books.

Berko, Jean. (1958). The child's learning of English morphology. *Word, 14*: 150–177.

Blank, Marion, Gessner, Myron, & Esposito, Anita. (1979). Language without communication: A case study. *Journal of Child Language, 6*: 329–352.

Borer, Hagit. (1996). Access to Universal Grammar: The real issues. *Behavioral and Brain Sciences, 19*: 718–720.

Boysson-Bardies, Bénédicte de. (1999). *How Language Comes to Children: From Birth to Two Years*. Cambridge, MA: MIT Press.

Brown, Cynthia. (2000). The interrelation between speech perception and phonological acquisition from infant to adult. In John Archibald (Ed.), *Second Language Acquisition and Linguistic Theory* (pp. 4–63). Malden, MA: Blackwell.

Carey, Susan. (1978). The child as word learner. In Morris Halle, Joan Bresnan, and George A. Miller (Eds.), *Linguistic Theory and Psychological Reality* (pp. 264–293). Cambridge, MA: MIT Press.

Cassidy, Frederic G., & Hall, Joan Houston. (1996). *Dictionary of American Regional English, Volume III*. Cambridge, MA: Harvard University Press.

Cattell, Norman Raymond. (1969). *The New English Grammar*. Cambridge, MA: MIT Press.

Cheng, Lisa L.-S. (1991). On the Typology of WH-Questions. Doctoral dissertation, MIT.

Chomsky, Noam. (1957). *Syntactic Structures*. The Hague: Mouton.

Chomsky, Noam. (1977). Questions of form and interpretation. In *Essays on Form and Interpretation* (pp. 25–59). New York: Elsevier North-Holland.

Chomsky, Noam. (1980). *Rules and Representations*. New York: Columbia University Press.

Chomsky, Noam. (1988). *Language and Problems of Knowledge: The Managua Lectures*. Cambridge, MA: MIT Press.

Chomsky, Noam. (1993). *Language and Thought*. Wakefield, RI/London: Moyer Bell.

Chomsky, Noam. (1995). *The Minimalist Program*. Cambridge, MA: MIT Press.

Chomsky, Noam. (2001). *Beyond Explanatory Adequacy, MIT Occasional Papers in Linguistics, 20*. Cambridge, MA: MITWPL.

Chomsky, Noam. (2004). *The Generative Enterprise Revisited*. Berlin: Mouton de Gruyter.

Clancy, Susan A. (2005). *Abducted: How People Came to Believe They Were Kidnapped by Aliens*. Cambridge, MA: Harvard University Press.

Cole, Peter, Hermon, Gabriella, & Tjung, Yassir. (2002). How irregular is WH in situ in Indonesian? *Studies in Language 29.2.*

Crain, Stephen. (1991). Language acquisition in the absence of experience. *Behavioral and Brain Sciences, 14:* 597–612.

Crain, Stephen, & Lillo-Martin, Diane. (1999). *An Introduction to Linguistic Theory and Language Acquisition.* Malden, MA/Oxford, UK: Blackwell.

Crain, Stephen, & Thornton, Rosalind. (1998). *Investigations in Universal Grammar: A Guide to Experiments on the Acquisition of Syntax and Semantics.* Cambridge, MA: MIT Press.

Cristófaro-Silva, Thais, Gomes, Christina, Guimarães, Daniela, & Huback, Ana Paula. (2005). The acquisition of irregular plurals in Brazilian Portuguese (abstract for a paper presented at the Tenth International Congress for the Study of Child Language). Online: http://www.ctw-congress.de/scripts/abs-view/abstract.php?id=7992&day=16&kid=23.

Curtiss, Susan. (1977). *Genie: A Psycholinguistic Study of a Modern-Day "Wild Child."* New York: Academic Press.

Dehaene, Stanislas, Izard, Véronique, Pica, Pierre, & Spelke, Elizabeth. (2006). Core knowledge of geometry in an Amazonian indigene group. *Science, 311:* 381–384.

Ellidokuzoglu, Hasanbey. (2002). Availability of Innate Linguistic Knowledge in Second Language Acquisition and Its Implications for Language Teaching. Doctoral dissertation, METU, Ankara, Turkey. (Sections on *wanna*-contraction are online: http://maxpages.com/thena/Turkish_Learners.)

Ethnologue: Languages of the World (15th ed.). (2005). Online: http://www.ethnologue.com.

Feeling, Durbin. (1975). *Cherokee-English Dictionary.* Talequah, OK: Cherokee Nation of Oklahoma.

Fodor, Jerry. (1975). *The Language of Thought.* New York: T. Y. Crowell.

Gelman, Rochel, & Gallistel, Charles R. (2004). Language and the origin of numerical concepts. *Science, 306:* 441–443.

Goldin-Meadow, Susan. (2003). *The Resilience of Language: What Gesture Creation in Deaf Children Can Tell Us about How All Children Learn Language.* New York: Psychology Press.

Grondin, Nathalie, & White, Lydia. (1996). Functional categories in child L2 acquisition of French. *Language Acquisition, 5:* 1–34.

Guasti, Maria Teresa. (2002). *Language Acquisition: The Growth of Grammar.* Cambridge, MA: MIT Press.

Gulian, Kevork H. (1977). *Elementary Modern Armenian Grammar.* New York: Frederick Ungar Publishing Co.

Hale, Kenneth L. (1975). Gaps in grammar and cultures. In M. Dale Kinkade, Kenneth L. Hale, & Oswald Werner (Eds.), *Linguistics and Anthropology: In Honor of C. F. Voegelin* (pp. 295–315). Lisse: Peter de Ridder Press.

Halle, Morris. (2003). Phonological features. In William J. Frawley (Ed.), *International Encyclopedia of Linguistics, Volume 4* (pp. 314–320). New York: Oxford University Press.

Halle, Morris, & Clements, G. N. (1983). *Problem Book in Phonology: A Workbook for Introductory Courses in Linguistics and in Modern Phonology.* Cambridge, MA: MIT Press.

Harbour, Daniel. (2000). The Kiowa case for feature insertion. Manuscript, MIT.

Harbour, Daniel. (2003). Elements of Number Theory. Doctoral dissertation, MIT.

Hawkins, Roger. (2001). *Second Language Syntax: A Generative Introduction.* Oxford, UK: Blackwell.

Holm, John. (1978). The Creole English of Nicaragua's Miskito Coast. Doctoral dissertation, University College London.

Holm, John. (1988). *Pidgins and Creoles.* Cambridge, UK: Cambridge University Press.

Honda, Maya. (1994). *Linguistic Inquiry in the Science Classroom: "It is science, but it's not like a science problem in a book," MIT Occasional Papers in Linguistics, 6.* Cambridge MA: MITWPL. (Doctoral dissertation, Harvard Graduate School of Education.)

Honda, Maya, & O'Neil, Wayne. (1987). Nicaraguan English/El inglés nicaragüense. *Wani: Una Revista sobre la Costa Atlántica, 6:* 49–60.

Honda, Maya, & O'Neil, Wayne. (1993). Triggering science-forming capacity through linguistic inquiry. In Kenneth L. Hale and Samuel J. Keyser (Eds.), *The View from Building 20: Essays in Linguistics in Honor of Sylvain Bromberger* (pp. 229–255). Cambridge, MA: MIT Press.

Honda, Maya, & O'Neil, Wayne. (2004). *Handbook 10: Understanding First and Second Language Acquisition (Awakening Our Languages: An ILI Handbook Series).* Santa Fe, NM: The Indigenous Language Institute.

Jusczyk, Peter W. (1997). *The Discovery of Spoken Language.* Cambridge, MA: MIT Press.

Kayne, Richard S. (1994). *The Antisymmetry of Syntax.* Cambridge, MA: MIT Press.

Klein, Elaine. (1993). *Toward Second Language Acquisition: A Study of Null-Prep.* Dordrecht, The Netherlands: Kluwer Academic Publishers.

Larson, Richard, & Segal, Gabriel. (1995). *Knowledge of Meaning: An Introduction to Semantic Theory.* Cambridge, MA: MIT Press.

Li, Charles N., & Thompson, Sandra A. (1981). *Mandarin Chinese: A Functional Reference Grammar.* Berkeley/Los Angeles: University of California Press.

Lipski, John M. (1996). Review of Ellen Bialystok and Kenji Hakuta (1994) *In Other Words. Language, 72:* 160–164.

Marcus, Gary. (1993). Negative evidence in language acquisition. *Cognition, 46:* 53–85.

Martínez Fabián, Constantino. (2001). ¿Cómo dicen los Yaquis "y"? ¿haisa yoemem "into" hia? How do Yaquis say the "y"? *Horizontes: Revista de Encuentro entre Sonora y Arizona, 6, 11:* 13–20.

Merrifield, William R. (1959). Classification of Kiowa nouns. *International Journal of American Linguistics, 25:* 269–271.

Mirizon, S. (1998). Wh-movement in the Acquisition of a Second Language: An Empirical Study of Native Indonesian Speakers at the University of Essex. Masters dissertation, University of Essex, UK.

Mithun, Marianne. (1999). *The Languages of Native North America.* Cambridge, UK: Cambridge University Press.

O'Neil, Wayne. (1993). Nicaraguan English in history. In Charles Jones (Ed.), *Historical Linguistics: Problems and Perspectives* (pp. 279–318). London/New York: Longman.

O'Neil, Wayne. (1998a). Linguistics for everyone. Applied Linguistic Association of Australia and Australian Linguistics Society Plenary. Online at: http://www.cltr.uq.edu.au/als98/oneil.html.

O'Neil, Wayne. (1998b). The Rhythm Rule in English and the growth of L2 knowledge. In Suzanne Flynn, Gita Martohardjono, & Wayne O'Neil (Eds.), *The Generative Study of Second Language Acquisition* (pp. 333–347). Mahwah, NJ: Erlbaum.

O'Neil, Wayne, & Honda, Maya. (1996). Linguistics in education: What can you learn from plural nouns and voicing? *Keio Studies in Theoretical Linguistics, 1*: 125–146.

The Oxford English Dictionary. (1989). Oxford, UK: Oxford University Press. Online: http://dictionary.oed.com/.

Pallier, Christophe, Bosch, Laura, & Sebastián-Gallés, Núria. (1997). A limit on behavioral plasticity in speech perception. *Cognition, 64*: B9–B17.

Perry, Edgar (Jaa Bilataha), Quintero Sr., Canyon Z., Davenport, Catherine D., & Perry, Corrine B. (1972). *Western Apache Dictionary.* Fort Apache, AZ: White Mountain Apache Tribe.

Pinker, Steven. (1994). *The Language Instinct.* New York: W. Morrow and Co.

Pinker, Steven. (1995). Why the child holded the baby rabbits. In Daniel N. Osherson, Lila R. Gleitman, & Mark Liberman (Eds.), *An Invitation to Cognitive Science: Volume 1: Language* (2nd ed., pp. 107–133). Cambridge, MA: MIT Press.

Pinker, Steven. (1999). *Words and Rules: The Ingredients of Language.* New York: Basic Books.

Reed, Alonzo, & Kellogg, Brainerd. (1889). *An Elementary English Grammar, Consisting of One Hundred Practical Lessons, Carefully Graded and Adapted to the Class Room.* New York: Effingham Maynard & Co.

Sailer, Steve. (2000). Analysis: New views on Arizona's bilingual vote. United Press International Press Release, 31 October.

Scherre, Maria Marta Pereira. (2001). Major linguistic patterns in noun phrase agreement in Brazilian Portuguese. In Rosa Bianca Finazzi & Paola Tornaghi (Eds.), *Cinquanta'anni di recerche linguistiche: problemi, resultati e prospettive per il terzo millennio. Atti del IX convegno internazionale di linguisti* (pp. 461–473). Alexandria: Edizioni dell'Orso S.r.l. Online: http://www.ai.mit.edu/projects/dm/bp/scherre-etal01.pdf.

Tucson Citizen. (2001). Census 2000: Tribe's new blood. Online: http://www.tucsoncitizen.com.

Ullman, Michael, Corkin, Suzanne, Coppola, Marie, Hickok, Gregory, Growdon, John H., Koroshetz, Walter J., & Pinker, Steven. (1997). A neural dissociation within language: Evidence that mental dictionary is part of declarative memory, and that grammatical rules are processed by the procedural system. *Journal of Cognitive Neuroscience, 9*: 289–299.

Vaux, Bert. (2003). Syllabification in Armenian, Universal Grammar, and the lexicon. *Linguistic Inquiry, 34*: 91–125.

Walker, Willard. (No date). An experiment in programmed cross-cultural education: The import of the Cherokee Primer for the Cherokee community and the behavioral sciences. Manuscript.

Watkins, Laurel J., with the assistance of Parker McKenzie. (1984). *A Grammar of Kiowa.* Lincoln, NE: The University of Nebraska Press.

Werker, Janet F. (1995). Exploring developmental changes in cross-language speech perception. In Daniel N. Osherson, Lila R. Gleitman, & Mark Liberman (Eds.), *An Invitation to Cognitive Science: Volume 1: Language* (2nd ed., pp. 87–106). Cambridge, MA: MIT Press.

White, Lydia, & Juffs, Alan. (1998). Constraints on WH-movement in two different contexts of nonnative language acquisition: Competence and processing. In Suzanne Flynn, Gita Martohardjono, & Wayne O'Neil (Eds.), *The Generative Study of Second Language Acquisition* (pp. 111–129). Hillsdale, NJ: Erlbaum.

White, Lydia, Spada, Nina, Lightbown, Patsy M., & Ranta, Leila. (1991). Input enhancement and L2 question formation. *Applied Linguistics, 12:* 416–432.

Wonderly, William L., Gibson, Lorna F., & Kirk, Paul L. (1954). Number in Kiowa: Nouns, demonstratives, and adjectives. *International Journal of American Linguistics, 20:* 1–7.

Yamada, Jeni E. (1990). *Laura: A Case for the Modularity of Language.* Cambridge, MA: MIT Press.

Yang, Charles. (2006). *The Infinite Gift: How Children Learn and Unlearn the Languages of the World.* New York: Scribner.

Zepeda, Ofelia. (1983). *A Papago Grammar.* Tucson: The University of Arizona Press.

Index

Numerals in boldface indicate where a term is defined or explained.